FILMM

edited by.
ANTHONY SLIDE

Irene Dunne

First Lady of Hollywood

Wes D. Gehring

Filmmakers Series, No. 104

The Scarecrow Press, Inc.
Lanham, Maryland, and Oxford
2006

SCARECROW PRESS, INC.

Published in the United States of America
by Scarecrow Press, Inc.
A wholly owned subsidiary of
The Rowman & Littlefield Publishing Group, Inc.
4501 Forbes Boulevard, Suite 200, Lanham, Maryland 20706
www.scarecrowpress.com

PO Box 317
Oxford
OX2 9RU, UK

British Library Cataloguing in Publication Information Available

The hardback edition of this book was previously cataloged by the Library
of Congress as follows:

Gehring, Wes D.
    Irene Dunne : First Lady of Hollywood / Wes D. Gehring.
    p. cm.—(Filmmakers series ; no. 104)
      Includes bibliographical references and index.
    ISBN-13: 978-0-8108-5864-0 (alk. paper)
    ISBN-10: 0-8108-5864-9 (alk. paper)
      1. Dunne, Irene, 1904– 2. Actors—United States—Biography. I. Title.
    II. Series

PN2287.D85G44 2003
792'.028'092—dc21   2003008009

Manufactured in the United States of America.

To
Sarah & Emily

The comic charm of Irene Dunne and Cary Grant in director Leo
McCarey's watershed screwball comedy *The Awful Truth* (1937).

WELL DUNNE, IRENE!

The awesome truth about
The Awful Truth girl
Was that she was the
Ultimate screwball heroine,
Dunne up beautifully.

While an Irene film
Situation was often hopeless,
It was seldom serious,
Except for that Dunne—
In leading man.

Her antiheroic male merely
Had a sure grasp of
Confusion, and she kept
Him confused—no
Sooner said than Dunne.

Still, there was a screwball
Sweetness to her, in
Celluloid and sound—
No *She Done him
Wrong* Mae West here . . .

She was Hollywood's
Captain of comedy,
Whose equally perfect retirement
Timing involved not being
Undone by the system.

No elderly scream queen
But rather a legacy
Of laughter for anyone
Who loves films—
That's the unawful truth.

"Good Night, Irene."

—Wes D. Gehring

CONTENTS

PREFACE AND
ACKNOWLEDGMENTS

movie lovers . . . [climb] into a movie as into a time machine or a
bottle of whiskey and set the dial for "never come back."[1]

—novelist Michael Chabon

An inordinately large number of my metaphorical time machine
movies star Irene Dunne. A complete list would necessitate hiring a
husky stenographer. But suffice it to say, I would be especially
happy to join her in the screwball world of *The Awful Truth* (1937), or
My Favorite Wife (1940), and "never come back." Here was a heroine
whose wackiness was a garment she wore only in the most comically desperate of situations—winning most of her points with practical wisdom and drop-dead beauty. Indeed, while her image, both
on screen and off, was forever intertwined with being "The First
Lady of Hollywood," she had a sexiness about her that was probably predicated, in part, by time machine fantasies about her losing
that ladylike status.

In fact, one would not even have to resort to fantasy. Film historian Maria DiBattista reminds us, in her celebration of *Fast-Talking
Dames*, that the normally ever-so-proper Dunne is the "only comic
actress working under the strictures of the Production [censorship]
Code who actually ends two of her comedies [*The Awful Truth* and
My Favorite Wife] under the covers, enticing her chosen mate [Cary
Grant] into her bed under the guise of keeping him at bay."[2] Though
she came to excel in numerous genres, including her beloved melodramas, today's audience still associates the actress most with sexy
screwball comedy.

Regardless, the comic irony of this, or any "Author's Preface," is that while they open a book, prefaces are the last thing written for the texts. That is, though one plunges into the task of writing a book with a preconceived plan, the creative process has a tendency (thankfully) to throw periodically insightful riffs one's way. But this always scrambles the game plan of even the most organized author. Thus, the preface becomes a tidying-up detail, affixing order to all those random epiphanies that occur during the course of creating a book. Plus, it is a last chance to throw in a final scrap of pertinent information that has somehow been neglected.

This process, of course, is greatly assisted by the fact that I am not unlike the central character in Walter Percy's classic 1961 novel, *The Moviegoer*: who and what I am is forever connected with film.[3] My favorite pieces of time are not just memories; they are *movie* memories. For example, an ongoing special image of my younger daughter, Emily, is how she often recycles a central line from a scene in *My Favorite Wife*. The movie situation finds Dunne discovering that her husband (Cary Grant), who innocently thought she was lost at sea, has both remarried and gifted his new wife with her most special piece of jewelry. Dunne's amusing response comically distorts a central word of dialogue, "I used to have one [a jewelry pin] zactly [*sic*] like it . . . Z-A-C-T-L-Y." Emily now uses the term (with equal emphasis, "Z-A-C-T-L-Y"), whenever she needs a comic mantra to work through those instances when life seems to have shortchanged her.

The writing of this biography, however, went beyond being a student of the movies . . . even Dunne movies. The real catalyst was a phone interview with the actress years before I had a book contract. Fresh out of graduate school, I was in Los Angeles doing research on a screwball comedy text. My college mentor, film historian Richard Dyer MacCann, had made arrangements for me to call Dunne. (By then she had all but eschewed the traditional sit-down interview.) Still, on the phone she was funny, disarmingly honest, and steadfastly protective of her favorite director—Leo McCarey. (While I would like to think my conversation skills kept her on the line thirty minutes, the real secret was confessing early that my dissertation had been on McCarey.)

Dunne was at her comically candid best when she discussed the tendency of actresses, herself included, to feel one side of their faces photographed better. But unlike so many of her contemporaries, such as Jean Arthur and Claudette Colbert (who were adamant about only that side being shot), Dunne felt it would be presumptuous for her to make such a request. Her favorite take on the subject, consistent with her longtime auteurist tendencies, involved director Alfred Hitchcock. She related how an actress, who will remain nameless, asked the master of suspense what her best side was. Hitchcock paused, and then said, "You're sitting on it." Besides being a funny, well-told story (further enhanced by two endearing traits synonymous with Dunne's screen persona—that throaty laugh, and a tendency to put pauses in unexpected places), one had to love her cheery, no-nonsense approach to both film and life. Here was that intrinsic "something" author Alan Schwarz credits as a mainspring for drawing one to a particular memorable life in American history—giving us what we need.[4] And after that phone call, I knew it was only a matter of time before I would write her biography.

* * * *

This book would not have been possible without the assistance of a great number of people. University of Southern California (Los Angeles) film archivist Ned Comstock was pivotal (as he has been for several of my past biographies) in the preparation of this book. With USC housing Dunne's private papers, he was a tireless advisor and guide to a wealth of material.

I owe a special debt to several individuals from Dunne's Madison, Indiana hometown. First, I must acknowledge the generosity of Charles Davidson for providing me with complete access to his collection of Dunne correspondence. Other special thank-yous go to Kimberly D. Franklin (Historic Madison, Inc.), Jane Jacobs (publisher, the *Madison Courier*), Ronald Grimes (Jefferson County Historical Society), and Harold W. "Pee Wee" Lakeman (office of the Madison mayor). Plus, the entire staff of the Madison Public Library were enthusiastically helpful.

Several major libraries on either coast were instrumental in my Dunne research. As with all my books, whether biographies or studies of comedy genres, my first stop is the Performing Arts Library (Billy Rose Collection) of the New York Public Library at Lincoln Center. Its countless period clipping files of film artists and individual movies are critical to any serious cinema study. (During Dunne's 1930s and 1940s heyday the most detailed and insightful film criticism was provided by a host of New York–based newspapers.) The Performing Arts Library also has an extensive collection of now extremely rare pioneering film journals. Complementing the Lincoln

Center Library is New York's main branch at Fifth Avenue and Forty-second Street—particularly the microfilm "Tombs" (dead newspaper) department. "Leads" from Lincoln Center can often be further fleshed out at the "Tombs."

On the West Coast the Academy of Motion Picture Arts and Sciences' Margaret Herrick Library (Beverly Hills) is also a must-stop, especially for its clipping files. (These holdings, however, often underline the importance of the New York newspapers—all of which are well represented.) It, too, has an extensive collection of rare early cinema journals.

Naturally, a number of film friends were central to the satisfactory completion of this book. Joe and Maria Pacino provided research assistance and a place to crash when I was in the Los Angeles area. Ball State teaching colleague and film author Conrad Lane furnished frequent advice, as well as a close reading of the manuscript. Janet Warrner supplied valuable editorial help, while Jean Thurman was responsible for the computer preparation of the manuscript. And my new department chair, Nancy Carlson, was both supportive and helped facilitate university financial help. (Along related lines, a generous recent Lilly Grant, for research on a digital project targeting American Film comedy, also complemented this book.)

Ultimately, however, the energy level necessary to sustain a project of this scope begins with the comfort zone provided by my daughters, Sarah and Emily, and my parents. Their love and support make all things possible.

NOTES

1. Michael Chabon, *Wonder Boys* (New York: Picador, 1995), 251.
2. Maria DiBattista, *Fast-Talking Dames* (New Haven, Connecticut: Yale University Press, 2001), 205.
3. Walter Percy, *The Moviegoer* (New York: Vintage Books, 1961).
4. Alan Schwarz, "Stealing Home," *New York Times*, October 13, 2002, Book Review section, 19.

PROLOGUE:
THE KENNEDY CENTER AWARD

Irene Dunne's portion of the televised (December 27, 1985) ceremony was narrated by her long-time friend Jimmy Stewart, who called the actress "an authentic American thoroughbred."

The annual Kennedy Center Awards are the highest honor bestowed upon performing artists in the United States. This two-day celebration of entertainers who have made a major contribution to both the arts and the humanities involves a State Department dinner, a White House reception, and a Kennedy Center profile of their lives and careers. (The latter biographical segment of the ceremony is also broadcast to the nation on national television.)

Irene Dunne's Kennedy Center medal (attached to a rainbow-striped ribbon) was an honor long overdue. During Hollywood's Golden Age of the 1930s and 1940s, Dunne (1898–1990) was one of the film industry's most popular and critically acclaimed actresses. For example, the same year she received her *Awful Truth* (1937) Oscar nomination for Best Actress, Dunne also ranked highly in *Boxoffice* magazine's "most popular star" poll.[1] Moreover, she was arguably the most versatile performer during Hollywood's hey-day—a claim made by no less an actor than Jimmy Stewart on the occasion of Dunne receiving her Kennedy Center honor.

Stewart's case for Dunne's diversity was based in the fact that her five Best Actress Oscar nominations occurred in almost as many *different* genres: the Western *Cimarron* (1931), two screwball comedies: *Theodora Goes Wild* (1936) and *The Awful Truth* (1937), the romantic comedy *Love Affair* (1939), and the populist *I Remember*

1

Mama (1948). And this says nothing of her critical and commercial success as a singing star of such classic musicals as *Roberta* (1935, top billed over Fred Astaire and Ginger Rogers), *Show Boat* (1936), and the neglected *High, Wide, and Handsome* (1937). Moreover, Dunne's early film career was fueled by excellent notices and huge box office returns in the genre of melodrama, especially *Back Street* (1932) and *Magnificent Obsession* (1935).

During the 1930s Dunne's genre versatility also made her a greater box office draw in the all-important European market. At that time the various varieties of American comedy did not play as well in Europe. No less a period filmmaker than Wesley Ruggles, a friend and frequent director of Carole Lombard, observed in a 1938 *New York Times* article that Dunne was a much bigger star in Europe.[2] This was strictly because Lombard was perceived as only an American comedy performer.

Dunne's almost immediate Hollywood success with *Cimarron* put her in the show business fast lane until her early 1950s retirement from film. Fittingly, that first Academy Award–nominated role, as a Congresswoman from Oklahoma, generated the most high-profile rave review of her memorable career. Will Rogers, the Oklahoma humorist who was then America's most beloved and quoted entertainer (though a decidedly anti-women-in-politics male), was moved to declare, "If women like Irene Dunne would run for Congress, I'd vote for them."

Though she excelled in film genres in addition to those already noted, such as romantic fantasy (*A Guy Named Joe*, 1943), or the biography film (*The Mudlark*, a 1950 profile of Queen Victoria), Dunne's list of Oscar-nominated parts reveals one final fact—her forte was comedy. Of these highlighted roles, easily the two most celebrated by today's viewers are the screwball comedies—*Theodora Goes Wild* and *The Awful Truth*. Moreover, this says nothing of her funniest excursion into this genre—*My Favorite Wife* (1940), which was a critical and commercial smash but somehow failed to impress the Motion Picture Academy.

In the 1930s, screwball comedy was famous for two kinds of heroine—the Carole Lombard type, who was bonkers from film frame one, and the more normal Dunne version, who assumed a calculated zaniness midway into the picture. Both varieties abound in the genre, but Lombard and Dunne are the pivotal models, with respective breakout examples appearing the same year (1936): *My Man Godfrey* and *Theodora Goes Wild*.

The Dunne type has worn better over time, as well as offering more possible creative variations. For instance, in the aptly titled *Theodora Goes Wild*, Dunne becomes the most comically uninhibited of sophisticates, whereas in *The Awful Truth* and *My Favorite Wife* she essays an equally uninhibited but decidedly unsophisticated Southern belle in order to comically toy with costar Cary Grant in both films.

Besides this "Dunne Goes Wild" screwball comedy legacy, the actress brought other comedy gifts to the genre. First, she had a whimsical awareness of her normally ladylike persona (both on screen and off); thus, her ability to suddenly shift into a zany mode had an added comic surprise all its own. Second, the casualness with which Dunne was willing to derail her proper image also brought an endearingly self-deprecating charm to her screwball roles, further explaining her ongoing popularity with audiences. Third, Dunne had an aptitude for peppering her comedy characters with inventive nuances that were frequently aped by other actresses. For example, Dunne had a signature throaty laugh which went on just long enough to imply, "You have no control over what I'm about to do." No less a performer than Katharine Hepburn borrowed this trait when she appeared in her first screwball comedy—*Bringing Up Baby* (1938).

The final uniquely Dunne trait that she showcased in screwball comedy was a warmly maternal slant completely alien to the genre's other pivotal period heroines, including Lombard, Hepburn, and Jean Arthur. Indeed, when Dunne wasn't mothering Cary Grant in *The Awful Truth*, *My Favorite Wife*, and the often comic family drama *Penny Serenade* (1941), she was taking care of their children (in the latter two films). Even *Theodora Goes Wild* has a subplot with a baby whose comedy payoff is predicated upon Dunne appearing to be a new mother. Not only was this child-related connection otherwise rare for the genre, but Dunne's softer motherly characterization makes her a more palatable screwball heroine. Whereas the in-your-face eccentricity of Lombard in *My Man Godfrey* or Hepburn in *Bringing Up Baby* can prove grating to some (especially to my college students), Dunne's motherly one-foot-in-reality perspective further enhances her characterizations.

This parental tie would also be central to Dunne's best post–World War II film roles, after she had moved beyond screwball comedy. In *Anna and the King of Siam* (1946) she portrays a British widow who goes to Siam in 1862 with her son to teach the wives and children of King Mongkut. *Life With Father* (1947) has Dunne playing a comically

entertaining balance to William Powell's irascibly funny title character. In *I Remember Mama* (1948), a writer recalls in flashback her wise
and warmly generous immigrant mother. Dunne's winning performance in this title role is a capstone to her lengthy film career.

These matriarchal tendencies would also define Dunne's private
life, from the 1936 adoption of a daughter (with husband Dr. Francis
Griffin), to the actress' lifelong involvement with various charities.
The latter activities were ultimately recognized by President Dwight
D. Eisenhower when he appointed her an alternate delegate to the
United Nations Twelfth General Assembly in August of 1957.

The only downside to the Kennedy Center honor was that the
fragile health of the then eighty-seven-year-old Dunne kept her from
attending the televised portion of the award ceremony, which aired
December 27, 1985. An old back problem flared up after the previous day's State Dinner, and a bad reaction to pain medication put
her in the Georgetown Hospital. Ironically, Dunne's good-natured
acceptance of the problem (she was widely quoted as saying "The
show must go on"[3] without her) and her prior reclusive tendencies
had critics second-guessing her absence from the crowning portion
of the Kennedy Center recognition.

Though she was periodically on record in her last years as wanting
"to be remembered the way I was in the movies," it seems unlikely she
skipped the final segment of the Kennedy Center program out of van-
ity.[4] There are three good reasons for this conclusion. First, besides
being very happy over the recognition, Dunne was especially pleased
with her fellow 1985 award winners. Prior to the festivities she
observed, "There I'll be with my favorite comedian [Bob Hope], my
favorite opera singer [Beverly Sills], and the two fellows who wrote
my favorite show of all [Frederick Loewe and Alan Jay Lerner—
authors of *My Fair Lady*]."[5] (Choreographer Merce Cunningham was
also honored at the 1985 ceremony.)

Second, if Dunne had really been determined not to let her legion
of fans see her as an octogenarian, she would neither have made the
trip to Washington, D.C. in the first place (with her granddaughter
Ann Shinnick in tow), nor posed for the official portrait of the 1985
Kennedy Center recipients. Third, as one of the oldest artists ever
honored by the Center, common sense should suggest that an absence for health problems is not that surprising. But this brings up a
provocative piece of misinformation—Dunne's age was generally
listed as eighty-one in 1985. Like many actresses protecting their ca-

reers, however, she had long ago moved her birthday up several years. If Dunne's actual age of eighty-seven had been generally known at the time of the Kennedy Center honor, there might have been less second-guessing of attendance motives.

Regardless, the Kennedy Center honor was a fitting conclusion to America's rediscovery of an artist long neglected after her many movie accomplishments of the 1930s and 1940s. Paradoxically, part of this later inattention was an outgrowth of Dunne's earlier triumphs. That is, an inordinately large number of the actress' films have been remade. This means through the years her best movies were often kept out of circulation (including television screenings) because of questions of copyright. Dunne profiler Margie Schultz went so far as a tongue-in-cheek suggestion that "Irene must hold a record" for this remake phenomenon.[6] The Dunne titles meriting one or more new versions include: *Cimarron*, *Back Street*, *Roberta*, *Magnificent Obsession*, *Show Boat*, *The Awful Truth*, *Love Affair*, *My Favorite Wife*, *A Guy Named Joe*, and *Anna and the King of Siam*. But the general consensus among film scholars is that the Dunne originals are clearly superior, as are her individual performances. Indeed, movie critic John Hartl considered some of the remakes' actresses in the Irene roles "wooden" by comparison.[7]

One should add Cary Grant's take on why the much-nominated Dunne never took home an Oscar: "She should have won, you know. And she would have, too . . . but she was so good—her timing was so marvelous—that she made comedy look easy. If she'd made it look as difficult as it really is, she'd have won."[8]

In examining a comic musical duet between Dunne and Ralph Bellamy in *The Awful Truth*, film theorist Stanley Cavell compared Dunne's modest but pleased acceptance of her great gift of song to Fred Astaire's equally balanced ego toward his gift of dance. Appropriately, Cavell defined this symmetry as "sophistication."[9] What he neglected to say was that "sophistication" characterized *all* aspects of her creative talent. Dunne was truly an American original.

NOTES

1. "Clark Gable No. 1 in New Film Poll," *New York Times*, January 4, 1937, 21.

2. Douglas W. Churchill, "Latest Scarlet Letter," *New York Times*, December 18, 1938, sec. 9, p. 7.

3. Guy D. Garcia, "People," *Time*, December 23, 1985, 61.

4. James Watters, "Irene Dunne: No Oscar, Just Love," *New York Times*, September 23, 1990, sec. 2, p. 20.

5. Charles Champlin, "Irene Dunne: Always a Lady of the House," *Los Angeles Times*, December 5, 1985.

6. Margie Schultz, *Irene Dunne: A Bio-Bibliography* (Westport, Connecticut: Greenwood Press, 1991), 25.

7. John Hartl, "Belle of the Screwball," *Chicago Tribune*, September 25, 1990, sec. 5, p. 3.

8. "Irene Dunne, Leading Star of '30s and '40s, Dies at 88," *Los Angeles Times*, September 5, 1990, A1, A2.

9. Stanley Cavell, *Pursuits of Happiness: The Hollywood Comedy of Remarriage* (Cambridge, Massachusetts: Harvard University Press, 1981), 246–47.

ONE

The Early Years

Daddy, I want to walk and see the prites [bright lights]. Please
Daddy.[1]

—Irene Dunne as a preschooler

Even as a child Irene Dunne seemed destined for the fast track, the
proverbial "bright lights." Of course, at this point that phrase simply represented the glow of downtown Louisville (Kentucky),
where she was born December 20, 1898. But Dunne was fated for
first Broadway and then Hollywood. High-profile entertainer is a far
cry from the lackadaisical atmosphere she knew in a childhood split
amongst Louisville, St. Louis, and the sleepy Ohio River valley town
of Madison, Indiana.

Irene's father was a tall, handsome, black-mustached Irishman
named Joseph J. Dunn of Louisville. (Irene added the "e" to Dunn as
a young adult.) Joseph was a chief engineer on several riverboats
and later received an appointment as a United States supervising
inspector of steamboats. Irene's mother was Adelaide Henry of
Madison. She was a gifted musician and singer who had studied at
the Cincinnati Conservatory of Music. Adelaide's father, Charles
Henry, was a prominent steamboat builder in Madison.

Charles and Joseph met through their joint interest in steamboats.
And when the elder Henry introduced his daughter to the young
Irishman, it was said to be love at first sight for both parties. Joseph
was soon courting her on a regular basis—no small task, since it
meant a fifty-mile trek (one-way) by horse and buggy from Louisville
to Madison. Despite the future distractions of Hollywood, Irene

would later credit her happy thirty-seven-year marriage to Dr. Francis Griffin to her parents' romantic union. This marriage was further idealized by her father's tragic death (from a kidney disorder) when the future actress was only eleven. Though Joseph died young, he left an indelible mark on his daughter. Rare was the article and/or interview during her later film career which did not credit him with leaving some life lesson for her to follow. The most poignantly moving example of this occurred in a 1944 *Photoplay* essay. Dunne prefaced her remarks by observing, "Undoubtedly, the most important thing I've ever learned is something my father taught me." On his deathbed he told her:

> Happiness is never an accident. It's the prize we get when we choose wisely from life's great stores. So don't reach out wildly for this and that and the other thing. You'll end up empty-handed if you do. Make up your mind what you want. Go after it. And be prepared to pay well for it.[2]

Joseph was in poor health for over a year before his death. Thus, his wise pronouncements to a young, impressionable daughter had an added impact, sort of a children's version of *Tuesdays With Morrie*, the later best-selling chronicle of life's lessons from a retired professor to a devoted former student.

Joseph "schooled" Irene in such additional populist topics as going after "the rooted things," from the importance of home and family, to the significance of satisfying work. But the most pivotal patriarchal advice to Irene always came back to the heart of the aforementioned quote. For instance, an *American Magazine* article, which appeared shortly after the *Photoplay* piece, had Dunne shortening her father's memorial advice to, "he told me something that I've never forgotten. He said, 'Irene, make up your mind what you want, and go after it. But be prepared to pay well for it.'"[3] Not surprisingly, this had become Dunne's philosophy of life, too.

Coupled to this creed and quote, moreover, was the actress' tendency to define herself as a stubborn Irishman—a trait which she also associated with her beloved dad. Without playing the Freudian card too strongly, her eventual marriage to a much older, nonentertainment professional (medical doctor) was no doubt tied in part to the lingering influence of her father. Even Dunne's later celebrated skills as a singer, normally credited to her mother's considerable music tutelage, was something for which Irene gave equal credit to her dad. In his youth he was a popular song-and-dance man in a minstrel outfit. And one of Dunne's earliest memories was her parents singing a duet at the family piano. Regardless, Irene showcased her father's signature spunk, or stubbornness, from birth. She was supposed to die of pneumonia. Her doctor gave up hope. But the attending nurse made the baby her personal mission, mixing medicine and prayer—lots of prayer. It was fitting; the Dunns were a religious Catholic family. And the church would be a centerpiece of Irene's adult life. (Her later charity work resulted in Dunne's 1949 reception of the Laetare Medal—the highest possible honor for a Catholic layperson.)

Also coupled with Dunne's birth was a passing remark by an adoring aunt, which proved prophetic—"Oh, what a little lady!" Throughout her lengthy later film career, she was known as the "First Lady of Hollywood."[4] This elevated status had been earned through her poised, gracious manner on screen and off. Period profiles had titles like "Lady Irene," "Dignified," and "The Lady Speaks Her Mind."[5] No less a mainstream critic than James Watters, entertainment editor of *Life* magazine, observed at the time of her death: "Offscreen her ladylike personality was as real as Norma Shearer's was phony."[6] (Shearer was an acting contemporary of Dunne sometimes also referred to as a "Hollywood Lady.")

What made Dunne's "lady" moniker so appealing was the actress' willingness to affectionately spoof her image from time to time in her film comedies, such as her tendency to play the screwball in the latter portions of *Theodora Goes Wild* (1936), *The Awful Truth* (1937), and *My Favorite Wife* (1940). One of the most memorable examples of this occurs near the close of director Leo McCarey's *The Awful Truth*. The actress' memory of the scene, where she does a "burlesque bit," also showcases McCarey's preference for improvised material:

> I tried to embarrass Cary Grant's would-be in-laws [by being his screwball sister]. The idea was to play against my own image, which was very ladylike, you know. Leo said, "Do a [stripper] bump." I tried but told him I never could do that. "Great," he said. "Use that line when we shoot." And that's how we shot it.[7]

Dunne's propensity to parody her screen persona both humanizes these characters and gifts the audience with the most fundamental approach to laughter—comic surprise. Moreover, that her comedy roles were closely modeled on the real Dunne (a phenomenon

especially common to screwball comedy) further underlines the importance of closely examining the early years to better understand
the later films. The elements were all there—the proper lady of a
mother and the free-spirited father. Indeed, when the actress dis-
cusses *Theodora* in a 1980 interview, she observed, "I know lots of
friends of mine like it better than almost anything I ever made. Because they say, that's the real *you*."[8]

Not surprisingly, given Dunne's great admiration for her father,
she attributed her inspired comedy skills to Joseph Dunn's "keen
sense of humor."[9] This was no modest accreditation, given that one
of the actress' greatest accomplishments was that master farceur
"Cary Grant always said that I had the best timing of anybody he
ever worked with."[10] Regardless, while the actress' in-film character
normally controlled this "Dunne Goes Wild" trait, her comedies often had well-publicized scenes where her coiffeured ladylike persona was comically scrambled, too. The most high-profile examples
would include the *My Favorite Wife* scene where she is bumped into
a pool (just after declaring how self-sufficient she is), as well as the
Together Again (1944) nightclub raid where she is mistaken for a
stripper. Both of these segments generated a great deal of print media attention, with even the normally staid *New York Times* being
moved to declare of the nightclub scene, "Miss Dunne will exhibit
her nether limbs (and undergarments) for the first time cinematically."[11]

If one were to liken any of Dunne's later movies to her childhood, however, *Show Boat* (1936) would immediately be addressed.
With both her maternal grandfather and father being involved in
riverboat careers, the subject was always front and center in
Dunne's youth. Once again, her father's influence was paramount,
given that he was a fascinating storyteller about life on the Ohio
and Mississippi Rivers. He seemed to know every boat and bayou.
Irene later remembered that crowds gathered whenever he started
to spin a tale. In fact, Mr. Dunn's storytelling skills about riverboat
life were so mesmerizing that the actress felt she had "inherited her
acting ability from him, and . . . [felt certain] that if he had lived
[longer] he would have been very pleased that she went on the
stage, and later into the movies."[12] Appropriately, young Irene's
most cherished memory as a child was a trip down the Mississippi
from St. Louis to New Orleans with her parents: "We had the cap-

tain's suite and because of my father's position [U.S. supervising inspector of steamboats] everything imaginable was done to make us feel important. I was so excited. I loved the boat and the lazy river."[13] (Fittingly, her father's father had also been the friend of another riverboat storyteller . . . Mark Twain!)

As a child of the Ohio River valley, of course, just watching the floating parade go by could be memorable. But the most exciting experiences were the passing showboats. Irene felt a special connection, or attachment, to these gliding entertainment palaces. Fittingly, the actress reminisced about just this subject while on a New York press junket for *Show Boat*: "We used to sit on the hilltops and wait for them to come 'round the bend in the river with the calliope playing the popular tunes."[14] Dunne might have been justified in believing that the showboat phenomenon was a special talisman for her. Besides her childhood enchantment with the subject eventually leading to a starring role in the film *Show Boat*, her 1929 star turn in a stage production of *Show Boat* landed Dunne her first Hollywood contract.

Like a lazy river, Irene's youth was often an idyllic adventure. The only sad note was the late 1909 death of her father. With his passing, Dunne's mother Adelaide moved her young family (eleven-year-old Irene and nine-year-old Charles) back to her small hometown of Madison. Living near her parents (Charles was named for Adelaide's father), Irene's mother wanted to guarantee a safe and secure setting for her children. History suggests the relocation very much accomplished this task. A Madison neighbor of the family later recalled, "She was a fine, happy little girl, usually dressed charmingly, and always friendly and happy."[15] Unlike Dunne's later screwball comedy contemporary Carole Lombard, whose childhood move to Hollywood helped fuel a free-spirited lifestyle, Dunne's later straitlaced adulthood was strictly grounded in the conservative traditional values of small-town Madison.[16]

Irene, or "Dunnie," as her new friends were soon calling her, blossomed in this nurturing environment. She graduated from the eighth grade in 1913. More significantly, this was the same year Dunnie had her first acting experience. Appropriately for someone best known in later years for her screwball and romantic comedies, this first stage outing was in a school production of Shakespeare's *A Midsummer Night's Dream*. Her character of Mustardseed, a fairy attendant to Titania, was known for her delicately comic and agile nature—a description which would have been equally at home in later reviews of Dunne's comedies. In 1936 the actress remembered:

> As I look back over the years nothing in my whole life surpasses the thrill of that first taste of footlights . . . . With the glorious ego and confidence of childhood, I actually thought the whole play—in fact the whole world—revolved about me. Never-the-less, the inconsequential role of Mustardseed was important to my future. It gave me an early sense of the theatre and a lasting love for it.[17]

Adelaide complemented her daughter's budding interest in drama by giving her voice and singing lessons at home. Irene's parents had always wanted her to be a professional singer. But the one-time acting aspirations of Dunne's mother probably made this profession more of a possible option for Irene, too.

The future actress sometimes chafed, however, under her mother's constant lessons. When Dunne later had a daughter of her own, she attempted to give the child more fun time. In contrast, the young Irene had once felt, "Whenever I wanted to play with the neighborhood children I had to practice [music]. There were lessons, lessons, lessons, always lessons."[18] Still, the musical benefits started to pay off quite early. There was a scholarship for a special music course at the Oliver Willard Pierce Academy of Fine Arts in Indianapolis. Plus, Irene's unique voice earned her the then-substantial amount of ten dollars per week to sing in Madison's First Baptist Church choir each Sunday . . . following family attendance at St. Michael's Catholic Church.

It was not, however, all music practice and church choir obligations. When Irene was sixteen, Adelaide sent her daughter to stay with rich society friends in Memphis, Tennessee. It was early 1915 and Dunne, surrounded by wealth and romance, had her society "coming out" in high style. Irene was schooled in the decidedly antifeminist Southern creed, "'tis better to be dead than not pursued by some male."[19] The future actress became a master coquette overnight—Romance Acting 101. To Dunne's credit, while several proposals were forthcoming, her adopted Hoosier practicality kept her from making any matrimonial mistakes. She returned to Madison both wiser and single, though Irene briefly retained a Southern accent she later forever described as so thick "you could cut it with a knife." But she entertainingly remembered that "to be sixteen and pretty was to be a big dog in a small town."

What makes her Southern sojourn so fascinating for today's fan is that the actress seems to have directly drawn upon it for her celebrated excursions into screwball eccentricity. Late in both *The Awful Truth* and *My Favorite Wife* Dunne assumes a new zany characterization to keep Cary Grant from romantically straying. In each case her creation is a terrible flirt with the thickest of Southern accents. Dunne was obviously recycling her teenage Tennessee tutorial in below-the-Mason-Dixon-line coquettishness. Working with improvisational artists like McCarey (who produced *My Favorite Wife*) gave Irene a greater opportunity to draw upon personal experience.

Interestingly enough, the fact that the young Dunnie was a hardworking student (both in private music lessons and public school) was also a factor in her later movie improvisations. That is, to be better prepared for those scenes where a filmmaker like McCarey might say, "Just ad-lib," Dunne got into the habit of assigning herself character homework. The actress later revealed that "Even in more finished screenplays [versus McCarey's habit of creating as you shoot], there were details of a scene not specifically explained in dialogue or action descriptions. I would go off and write the scene out myself, thinking through precisely how my character should respond."[20] Since Irene's roles often represented a variation of herself, the actress could write reams of commentary. And just as she was a driven young student (following her father's axiom of "Go after it"), the later actress was obsessed with perfection—"I'd write and write and write. . . . If anybody had read it over, they would have wondered about my sanity, because I would just ramble on, just to have thoughts of my own."[21]

Besides her Southern adventure, Dunne had another most memorable experience at the age of sixteen—attending an opera performance, with the great Geraldine Farrar in the title role of *Madame Butterfly*. So significant was this evening for the teenage Irene that she later remembered—"It was as if I'd been asleep all my life and . . . Farrar and the beauty of her singing had awakened me."[22] Mustardseed had found music—young Dunne was now in touch with what would become the twin passions of her life—singing and acting.

The future film star graduated from Madison High School in 1916. Dunne then returned to St. Louis, where her family had last lived when her father was alive, in order to attend the city's Webster College. (St. Louis also held warm memories for Irene by way of her music classes at the city's Loretto Convent.) By 1918 she had earned a Webster College teaching certificate. Her goal was to supervise both music and art programs somewhere in the public school system of Indiana. After passing her state certification tests in Indianapolis (where she had once taken a music class at the Oliver Willard Pierce Academy of Fine Arts), she sent out her teaching applications. An appointment was forthcoming from a school in Gary, Indiana. With assistance from her mother on putting together an appropriate wardrobe for a young instructor, she left home for the Chicago area in late August of 1918. But fate would throw her a curve.

With Gary so near Chicago, Irene had made time to visit some cousins in the then-fashionable "Windy City" suburb of Irving Park. While there her cousin Wallis Bennett noticed a *Chicago Tribune* article about open tryouts for music scholarships at the Chicago Musical College, now part of the city's Roosevelt University. Even then it was a celebrated center for music, and it had been founded by Dr. Florenz Ziegfeld, father of the famous New York stage producer Flo Ziegfeld. Curious as to just how good a singer she was, as well as suddenly being more enamored of performing than teaching, Dunne decided "in a flash" she had to win a scholarship.[23] Her resolve was greatly assisted by the confidence of Bennett, who "decided then and there that Irene should win."[24]

Ironically, while her college education had been a direct rebuttal to the aforementioned "Southern Creed" of catching a man and settling down, Irene determined that *anything* was fair in order to win this audition. Thus, besides singing and looking her best, she later confessed, "And if there were any elderly gentlemen on the board of judges, I was going to smile prettily at them. My Memphis training to the fore!"[25] But upon arriving at the audition site her resolve began to melt. She later entertainingly described in Thurberesque terms, "I would have run away had not my knees refused to function."[26]

Paradoxically, instead of a flirtatious Dunne smile making the difference, it was a supportive wink from the orchestra maestro, Edouardo Sacerdote, which altered Irene's life. She was struggling at the beginning of her audition number when she gave him an anguished glance. But the maestro looked at her and winked. To Dunne, "That wink said, 'You're doing beautifully! Never mind these other people—you and I are just running through a song you know backwards!' It said, 'Come on child; sing.'"[27] That wink of kindness changed Irene's life; she won a scholarship to the Chicago Musical College and began aiming for a career in the performing arts. Moreover, for the first time since her fatherly-influenced child-hood, she had learned another important life lesson: always make it a practice to show a little kindness.

Luckily, the Gary school board showed Dunne some kindness and let her out of the teaching assignment. And the Irving Park cousins she had only planned to briefly visit ended up being roommates, after a fashion, as Irene commuted from this suburban home to the Chicago Musical College. It was still the Midwest, but as far as Dunne was concerned, it was her metaphorical *Field of Dreams*—a private heaven. After a second scholarship year (1919–1920) at the Chicago Musical College was completed, she moved to New York, determined to make it at the Metropolitan Opera. But this time her audition did not go well. Her scorecard read, in part, "too young, too inexperienced, and too slight."[28]

Not to be denied, Dunne made a prophetic decision and audi-tioned for a *musical comedy*—the road company of *Irene*. The popular arts, such as musical comedy, were where she belonged. However, while later puff pieces during Dunne's film career credited the youngster with winning the lead role in the aptly named *Irene*, she had merely made the chorus.[29] Still, it did not matter. With her mother in tow as a chaperone, an excited young Dunne spent sev-eral months on tour living the life of a performer. Her Madison youth seemed ever so distant. Broadway was now her goal.

The "Great White Way" notwithstanding, intermittently during the next several years Dunne would return to the Chicago Musical Col-lege for further study. By the time of her 1926 graduation with high honors, she had achieved a certain degree of stage success, both in New York and in additional national theatrical tours. Her Broadway debut occurred in the musical comedy *The Clinging Vine* in December 10, 1922. She played a paint factory secretary named Tessie, and her modest part was limited to four minutes in the first act. But Dunne re-alized early the importance of self-promotion. She wrote a tongue-in-cheek note to *The Clinging Vine* author Zelda Sears. The novice thanked the playwright for a part small enough to allow a newcomer time to pursue further theatrical study.

Irene's sense of humor was appreciated by Sears and her Broadway colleagues, as well as eventually being picked up by the New York newspapers.[30] It was the age of the Algonquin Round Table, when New York humorists like Robert Benchley, Dorothy Parker, Ring Lard-ner, Alexander Woollcott, an occasional Marx Brother (Groucho or

Harpo), and others regularly met at the Algonquin Hotel to trade barbs over lunch. Naturally, the then-legion of New York newspapers were peppered with their witticisms, such as Parker's possible tombstone epitaphs, including "This is on me," "Excuse my dust," and "If you can read this, you are standing too close." Dunne, who was only five years younger than Parker, was merely following a comedy lead she saw showcased daily at newsstands across the city.

The ambitious Irene was also the understudy to the lead in *The Clinging Vine*. While on tour in early 1924, Dunne was able to get her break when star Peggy Wood was sidelined with laryngitis. A fellow cast member (J. Donald Heebner) from this tour later remembered Dunne as the most "good-natured" person, despite the difficulties of playing countless one-nighters. But what especially impressed him was the young actress' quiet confidence. Because "The show was a bit highbrow for these audiences," box office was not at capacity. This made Irene work twice as hard, but she also used to softly say, "Someday they'll wish they had come out to see me."[31] Still, she was so well received critically that later that same year she replaced the ailing musical lead (Gloria Dawn) in the Broadway production of *Lollipop*.

Dunne's life was not, however, all about acting. In a 1924 letter to a would-be suitor, Fritz Ernst, she wrote about seeing the then recently completed Democratic presidential convention, "I attended two sessions but they were not the exciting ones, and toward the last day my enthusiasm was not so great."[32] The waning interest was an outgrowth of a convention that took *103 ballots* before the former ambassador to Great Britain, John W. Davis, was nominated! But what had initially fascinated both Dunne and the nation was a nine-day deadlock over the nomination.

Through ninety-five ballots the Democrats were split between New York governor Alfred E. Smith and former Secretary of the Treasury William G. McAdoo. Adopted New Yorker Dunne was especially taken with fellow Catholic Smith, who was also in favor of ending Prohibition. I only belabor this convention component of Dunne's background because it better explains her later brief post-film involvement in politics, from speaking at the 1956 Republican presidential convention, to being an alternate delegate to the Twelfth United Nations General Assembly (1957–1958).

The following year she opened (October 26, 1925) on Broadway in the small-town romance *The City Chap*. Most significantly for Dunne, the production's music was by the great Jerome Kern, with the actress singing "Walking Home With Josie." In later years she would become a pivotal interpreter of the composer's music on film. (Irene was also pleased that *The City Chap* featured another performer from Indiana—Terre Haute's Richard "Skeets" Gallagher, who would find later success as a Hollywood character actor of the 1930s and 1940s.) Her opening was a success, with the *New York Times'* review entitled "'The City Chap' Full of Dances and Fun." More specifically, "The idle rich were handsomely represented in town and country in Irene Dunn, John Rutherford, and a personable chorus."[33] (Though earlier New York productions had spelled her name Dunn*e*, "The City Chap" reverted back to the original family spelling, sans the "e." But in all future professional activities it would be Dunn*e*.)

The following year (1926) was a period of overachievement by Irene. In March she replaced yet another leading lady in the romantic Broadway production *Sweetheart Time*. In the summer she signed on with the St. Louis Municipal Opera Company. Besides representing a homecoming of sorts, the engagement allowed her to briefly return to her initial professional goal of opera star. The Company also stretched her performing skills, requiring that she "essay" a varied assortment of parts. But the year's performing high point was joining a Metropolitan Opera group of singers to perform in Atlanta. Fittingly, for an actress who would later so easily take to screen comedy, the Metropolitan's repertoire for the Atlanta engagement included a great deal of Gilbert and Sullivan.

As if in reward for the talented versatility of 1926, Dunne was now becoming a high-profile Broadway regular. In 1927 she had a prominent part in the musical comedy *Yours Truly*, only to replace the romantic lead early in the production's run. As Mary Stillwell, she was a youth of wealth who mixed social work with nightclub singing—neither of which pleased her millionaire family. But with Jazz Age simplicity, all was comically resolved by the final curtain. The production was critically praised as "One of the best and biggest of the boy and girl shows."[34]

The next year (1928) Dunne had a pivotal part in the musical comedy *She's My Baby*, with songs by Richard Rodgers and Lorenz Hart—a celebrated duo whose music would figure prominently in Irene's future professional career. For *She's My Baby* Irene sang "You're What I Need" and "If I Were You." The *New York Herald Tribune* called the former song "a tricky ballad delivered effectively by Miss Irene Dunne and Mr. Jack Whiting."[35]

The apogee of the actress' Broadway career would occur in September 1928. The Great White Way's then-favorite substitute star was finally granted the honor of originating a musical comedy lead on Broadway. Dunne, as the title character of *Luckee Girl*, must win her lover back from another romantic entanglement. The *New York Times* praised the musical as "A Tuneful Comedy," while the *New York Post* said of the actress, "Dunne is way out ahead of most leading ladies; charming voice, unusually lovely face and a bright, guileless clarity which was not without dignity, too."[36] As the *Post*'s high praise suggests, the production produced the best reviews of Dunne's career up to this point. But as much as the role literally made Dunne feel like a *Luckee Girl*, there were two other period parts which soon usurped this and any other roles she would ever attempt. One part forever redefined Irene's private life, while the other made her screen career possible. The late 1920s would be a major period of transition for the young actress.

NOTES

1. Caroline S. Hoyt, "Irene Dunne's True Life Story" (Part 1), *Modern Screen*, December 1938, 28.
2. Roberta Ormiston, "To Make You Happier," *Photoplay*, April 1944, 107.
3. Jerome Beatty, "Lady Irene," *American Magazine*, November 1944, 117.
4. "Irene Dunne," *Current Biography 1945*, ed. Anne Rothe, New York: H. W. Wilson Company, 1945, 160.
5. Beatty, "Lady Irene"; Irene Dunne, "Dignified," *American Magazine*, August 1942, 84–85; J. Holland, "The Lady Speaks Her Mind," *Silver Screen*, May 1946, 35.
6. James Watters, "Irene Dunne: No Oscar, Just Love," *New York Times*, September 23, 1990, sec. 2, p. 20.
7. Jack McDonough, "Screening a Star: A Rare Interview with Irene Dunne," *Chicago Tribune*, May 12, 1985, sec. 13, p. 8.
8. James Harvey, "Irene Dunne Interviewed by James Harvey," *Film Comment*, January–February 1980, 30.
9. John Hartl, "Belle of the Screwball," *Chicago Tribune*, September 25, 1990, sec. 5, p. 3.
10. Harvey, 31.
11. Fred Stanley, "Hollywood Round-Up," *New York Times*, August 20, 1944, sec. 2, p. 3.
12. Elizabeth Wilson, "Men She'll Remember," *Silver Screen*, April 1941, 72.
13. Hoyt, 31.

14. John T. McManus, "Magnolia of the Movies," *New York Times*, May 17, 1936, sec. 9, p. 3.

15. Jim Wallen, "Life of Irene Dunne Is Related by Writer" (Part 2), *Madison Courier*, July 26, 1951, 4.

16. See my forthcoming *Carole Lombard: The Hoosier Tornado*, Indianapolis: Indiana Historical Society, Fall 2003.

17. Beulah Livingstone, "The Story of Irene Dunne," *Table Talk*, September 21, 1936, 14.

18. Elizabeth Wilson, "The First True Story of Irene Dunne's Baby!" *Screenland*, June 1937, 21.

19. Hoyt, 83.

20. McDonough, 9.

21. Harvey, 29.

22. Adele Whitely Fletcher, "If You Had One Hour," *Movie Mirror*, November 1936, 113.

23. Dunne, "Dignified," 85.

24. Wilson, "Men She'll Remember," 72.

25. Hoyt, 84.

26. Dunne, 85.

27. Ibid.

28. Rothe, 161.

29. Margie Schultz, *Irene Dunne: A Bio-Bibliography*, Westport, Connecticut: Greenwood Press, 1991, 4.

30. See the Irene Dunne clipping file, Billy Rose Theatre Collection, Performing Arts Library, New York Public Library at Lincoln Center.

31. J. Donald Heebner, "The Big Wig Mystery—With Irene Dunne," *Photoplay*, September 1937, 121.

32. Irene Dunne to Fritz Ernst, July 10, 1924, from the "Charles Davidson Collection of Irene Dunne Letters," a private collector.

33. "'The City Chap' Full of Dances and Fun," *New York Times*, October 27, 1925, 21.

34. Review of *Yours Truly*, *New York Herald Tribune*, January 26, 1927.

35. Review of *She's My Baby*, *New York Herald Tribune*, January 3, 1928.

36. "'Luckee Girl' Proves a Tuneful Comedy," *New York Times*, September 17, 1928, 28; Review of *Luckee Girl*, *New York Post*, September 19, 1928.

Two

Marriage and the Magnolia Role . . . Plus an Epic Western

> I really didn't think marriage and the stage were compatible but we
> love each other and we were both determined to make the marriage
> work.[1]
>
> —Dr. Francis ("Frank") Griffin

Irene Dunne met her future husband, Dr. Frank Griffin, at a 1924
party at New York's Biltmore Hotel. For the doctor it was the
proverbial love at first sight. A later *Photoplay* article had Griffin
even buying her a diamond the next day.[2] The downside to this romantic tale was that the young actress, though taken with the handsome, wealthy dentist, took years to both accept the ring and ultimately say, "I do" (July 16, 1928, though sometimes listed as 1927).
Besides Irene's both practical and serious-minded nature, there was
another stumbling block to an early marriage. The attentive Griffin,
who was twelve years Dunne's senior, felt she should retire from
the stage once they married.

The actress had worked too hard to give it all up. Not surprisingly,
Irene later confessed they argued about this point constantly
throughout their courtship.[3] Plus, in the early years, Dunne was
often on the road touring or back at the Chicago Musical College.
But all was not negative. They both loved New York, all aspects of
music, a sophisticated yet casual lifestyle, traditional values, conservative politics, and a romantic mindset. Indeed, Griffin demonstrated a flair for the latter when he averted a possible tragedy for
the couple on an early date. While they were taking a hansom cab to
a costume party, a passing fire truck spooked their driver's horse.

Suddenly, Griffin was your favorite cowboy, stopping a potential runaway horse by fielding an errant bridle.[4]

The closest thing to a serious relationship prior to Frank was with a Chicago businessman, Fritz Ernst, formerly also of Madison, Indiana. Nearly twenty years Dunne's senior, he was a wealthy, well-traveled sophisticate who maintained a long-term friendship (largely through correspondence) with the actress from 1919 until his 1959 death. But through the recent surfacing of a cache of letters from Dunne to Ernst (in the hands of Madison private collector Charles Davidson), it is now known that Fritz proposed marriage in the spring of 1921.

The actress' mother was opposed to the relationship, and Dunne allowed her to write Fritz a letter along those lines in May of 1921. On the eighteenth of that month she also wrote him—"I was positively beside myself for over a week (when I did not write you and which now I realize was most unfair) . . . I have made this decision Fritz and all I can do is hope for the best." The actress' 1921 reasons for turning down Fritz were based in putting career first and just not being prepared for marriage at that time. Their friendship endured, however, until his death. (He never married.)[5]

The beauty of Dunne's later-developing (1924) relationship with Frank Griffin, which is certainly the secret of any marital success, was that both Irene and Frank were flexible about issues which might have divided other couples. For example, Dunne eventually came around to a variation of Griffin's initial suggestion to retire, if not when they married, at least sometime in the immediate future. But conversely, Frank decided if it meant that much to Irene, she should continue with her acting career.

The Dunne part which would change their lives and make her career was the Magnolia role in Flo Ziegfeld's highly successful 1929–30 road company production of *Show Boat*. However, before addressing this watershed part, a long-neglected aspect of Irene's continuing career merits comment. Prior to her pivotal part in *Show Boat*, the actress' best reviews by far had come in the 1928 Broadway production of *Luckee Girl* (see previous chapter). Significantly, this play opened two months to the day *after* she had married Griffin. While the career importance to Dunne of her association with *Show Boat*, which for the first time brought her to the attention of Hollywood, should not be lessened, the timing of her involvement in *Luckee Girl* (not to mention her critical acclaim) suggests the couple had made a commitment to her continued acting well before she played Magnolia. (This fact is missed in period literature awash with Dunne's success in *Show Boat*.)

The only disappointment attached to *Luckee Lady* was that despite the critical praise heaped upon Dunne, the play itself was only the most modest of commercial hits, running just under three months. It was at this time that the actress felt some professional doubt and considered retiring from the stage. There was an inclination to please Griffin's original preference for her to leave the glare of the footlights. One should also note, moreover, that the older Frank, who bore a striking resemblance to Irene's beloved father, was like Joseph Dunn in another key way—his decisions tended to rule the household. The actress once observed, "My father was definitely the head of the family. My mother looked to him for decisions. We, my brother Charles and I, knew there was no appeal from his authority."[6] And as independent as Irene grew up to be after her dad died young, she was still attracted to the fatherly Griffin's take-charge tendencies.

As Irene seemed to be drifting towards retirement in early 1929, fate introduced a wild card into the equation—the Griffins went to a new Broadway production, *Show Boat*. Dunne was bowled over by Norma Terris' Magnolia. But what made the character for Irene were her songs: "Make Believe," "Why Do I Love You?," and "Can't Help Lovin' Dat Man." Dunne went so far as to buy the sheet music and started singing it at home. Her ongoing fantasy was to play Magnolia. What next occurs was either an opportune coincidence (Irene's perspective), or a classic example of the actress applying her father's "go for it" axiom. That is, Dunne just happened to run into Flo Ziegfeld near his office when she was allegedly visiting a friend in rehearsal for an unnamed production. As a tongue-in-cheek *American Magazine* noted in 1944, "Neither you nor I nor Dr. Griffin would ever suspect that she deliberately went to Florenz Ziegfeld . . . and suggested that she'd like to play Magnolia in the road company."[7]

Regardless, Dunne was not unknown to Ziegfeld. Besides her recent Broadway successes, years before she had met the younger Ziegfeld with a praising letter of introduction from his father, the founder of the Chicago Musical College and an early mentor to the actress. Though nothing had worked out then, this time around Ziegfeld was especially taken with the auburn-haired beauty and asked her to try out for the road company production of *Show Boat*. When she ran this opportunity by her husband, he was not overjoyed but in the spirit of fairness said, "That's fine. Of course you must try for it. If you don't, you'll always regret it."[8]

Naturally, Dunne won the part and scored an unprecedented forty-week triumph on tour through most of the major cities east of the Mississippi. The *Chicago Tribune* said of the performance: "It is much as when I saw the diversion in New York . . . [but] I prefer Dunne [in the lead]."[9] The *St. Louis Daily Globe-Democrat* credited Irene with creating "the real character of Magnolia . . . Her voice charms, and [she is] charming and personable . . . [and] can also sing."[10] The critic for the *Detroit Times* observed, "Irene Dunne as Magnolia is quite as lovely as [the Broadway original] Norma Terris and an even finer vocalist."[11] And the *Cleveland Plain Dealer* reviewer also preferred Irene: "Dunne, who plays Magnolia, is I think, better then Norma Terris."[12] As an impressive topper to this nonstop, standing-room-only success story, she ultimately recorded her *Show Boat* songs. Once again, Dunne proved to be a huge critical and commercial success; the acclaimed actress was now a recording artist, too. The ultimate compliment for the actress came from the *Show Boat* author herself. Irene observed, "When later I went to Chicago, where it [the musical] had such a successful run, Edna Ferber told me I was the ideal Magnolia."[13]

Her surprising *Show Boat* triumph produced yet another marital powwow between Frank and Irene. *Luckee Lady* had almost been her swan song. Then *Show Boat* was to be her theatrical finale. But now both Broadway and Hollywood were clamoring for more. Besides the headiness of finally reaching major star status, these show business envoys, particularly the movie scouts, were offering lucrative contracts. All this was very tempting, especially since it was a time when the "Great Depression" had already thrown countless Americans out of work. Irene and Frank opted to try something new, and the actress signed with RKO studio. (Her husband would negotiate the contract.)

This initial contract (April 10, 1930) gave her $1,000 a week in 1930, which escalated to $1,500 a week in 1931, and $2,000 in 1932 (each for a guaranteed fifty-two weeks).[14] Not only was this a sweet salary at the onset of the depression, but cinema beginner Dunne also had a preferential billing clause—"your name will appear in type larger than any other female player, and as large as the featured male player."[15]

RKO wanted to star Dunne in a musical about the Marine Corps initially titled *Present Arms* but later released as *Leathernecking* (1930). Since the film capital's late 1920s conversion to sound, musicals—often advertised as "100% all-singing and all-dancing"—had been the rage with the public. Indeed, the period fascination with this genre was so great that musicals were even taking home critical awards, too.

For example, the Academy Award–winning Best Picture for 1928–1929 was the less-than-memorable musical *The Broadway Melody* (1929).

Sadly for Dunne, by the time RKO had produced *Leathernecking*, the musical fad had passed. Anticipating this development, the studio had dropped several songs during production and added more broad comedy. Even the lure of the final twenty minutes being shot in Technicolor was not enough to offset the public's period saturation with the genre. Moreover, the general critical consensus was that newcomer Irene was not showcased to the best of her abilities. *Variety* complained, "What, for example, is the idea of casting a charming romantic actress like Irene Dunne opposite a comedian like Eddie Foy, Jr.?"[16] (Reviews such as these probably contributed to the actress' later mid-1930s reluctance to accept a screwball comedy assignment.)

There was an added irony for Dunne in having just missed this first Hollywood heyday for the musical. She and Frank had decided upon a major sacrifice to make her movie musical career happen— they would maintain a bicoastal marriage. He had remained in New York and continued his dental practice; she and her mother had relocated to Hollywood for those parts of the year in which she was in film production. Though unconventional, it was not unprecedented. For instance, one of Dunne's favorite Algonquin humorists, the aforementioned Robert Benchley, maintained a bicoastal marriage from the late 1920s until his death in 1945.[17] Benchley spent part of each year as drama critic for *The New Yorker*, and the rest of the time in Hollywood making films. Even after he phased out his New York literary ties (by the early 1940s), there was a need to claim "Gotham City" as at least a part-time home.

East Coast artists of the time, particularly writers, often saw Hollywood as provincial and unappreciative of their talent. But this hostility was further complicated by their inability to resist the high salaries the film capital was able to pay. Thus, New York movie talents like Benchley felt they had sold out their gift for the most culturally shallow of mediums. Dunne's husband was undoubtedly staying in New York to maintain his own identity via his dental practice. But the Griffins both loved the city and closely followed the lives and entertaining times of artists like Benchley; these facts also probably influenced the couple's decision to keep one of them anchored in New York. Indeed, years later Irene remembered her husband telling a West Coast acquaintance in 1931, "Of course, we don't want to settle [in Hollywood]. We are from the East. My wife has just made a couple of films. . . . We belong to the East."[18]

An additional knock against Hollywood, or entertainers in general, was a heightened degree of promiscuity. At the time, Griffin confessed, "I didn't like the moral tone of show business."[19] Dunne indirectly seconded this notion when she later (1935) observed, "Only single men and women really belong in the whirl of Hollywood. But if I regard this merely as a place for business, and save my . . . personal life for New York, I can just manage to make it [her marriage] work out."[20]

Pride in Dunne's *Show Boat* hosannas had helped fuel Frank's encouragement of his wife's potential screen career. But his growing sensitivity to the performing needs of the talented Irene were also tested by a then-unwritten Hollywood law for new on-screen talent: "Marriage hurts. If you must marry don't tell the world about it."[21] This caught the Griffins completely by surprise, since they had encountered nothing like this during Irene's years on Broadway. However, RKO seemingly wanted it both ways, since Dunne was asked to sign a standard studio morality clause in 1931:

> The artist agrees to conduct herself with due regard to public conventions and morals, and agrees that she will not do or commit any act or thing that will . . . tend to shock, insult, or offend the community.[22]

Secure in their marriage, the couple swallowed hard and went along with the secret marriage tradition, confident that if Dunne found screen success it would be impossible to keep their relationship quiet. This is precisely what happened when Irene's second film, *Cimarron* (1931), went on to win an Academy Award for Best Picture. But how Irene won the coveted romantic lead is an even more entertaining story.

After the critical and commercial failure of *Leathernecking*, Dunne was at loose ends. What should RKO do with its new musical star, now that the genre was passé? As was her habit, Irene took the initiative. She began to campaign strongly for the romantic lead, Sabra Cravat, in the studio's forthcoming epic Western *Cimarron*. Four reasons drove her push to win the role. First, the tanking of *Leathernecking* had been frustrating. Dunne was not used to failure. As her journalist friend Adela Rogers St. Johns later observed, the actress had "an admirable sort of ruthlessness, which manifests itself, for all her wit and humor, all her graciousness, in a tempered self-control."[23] Second, the Griffins had initially decided to base Irene's chances for Hollywood success on her first *two* movies. Whether they would have terminated Dunne's film career after a second failure would remain to be seen. But the actress was taking no chances—*Cimarron* had *sure thing* written all over it. Third, Irene was afraid the studio might drop her, especially since the executives continued to only associate her with the musical—the genre then dead in the water. That was why, though numerous RKO actresses had been tested for *Cimarron*'s Sabra Cravat, Dunne had yet to be considered. Fourth, with *Cimarron* being RKO's biggest and most expensive picture up until that time, it was perfectly logical for any and all of the studio's actresses to covet the role.

There might also have been a touch of superstition at work, too. That is, when Dunne had first gone to New York, her much admired Algonquin humorists had included novelist Edna Ferber. Years later, the stage play which had brought her to the attention of Hollywood, *Show Boat*, had been based upon the Ferber novel. And now *Cimarron*, drawn from another Ferber novel, had the potential to launch Irene's film career.

But for all Dunne's determination to get the part, it took the help of several supportive people, starting with *Cimarron*'s leading man, Richard Dix. RKO had purchased the best-selling Ferber property for Dix—the studio's resident male star, and had planned to team him with Fay Bainter as Sabra Cravat. However, when the actress had a falling out with producer William LeBaron, this high-profile part was suddenly available. Dix, who had a history of helping Hollywood newcomers, immediately went to bat for Dunne. He asked LeBaron to encourage director Wesley Ruggles and other studio executives to give Irene the part.[24] Dix's persuasiveness was assisted by both his major star status and his praise of Irene's stage work, with which he was familiar.

Obviously, Dix's support helped the Dunne *Cimarron* campaign along, but despite her Broadway accomplishments, she was still basically an unproven *screen* actress. Among other things, there were RKO concerns that Irene would not be able to play a much older woman—*Cimarron*'s story covers forty-plus years, 1889–1930. Now, rare is the performer who does not like tackling this challenge. Indeed, the chance to hide beneath such things as heavy makeup and wigs is often perceived by an actor as making the job easier—submerging himself or herself into the part. This was certainly true of Dunne, who often gravitated to these roles, from her character of

Magnolia in *Show Boat* (Ferber enjoyed following characters through time), to her entertaining take on Queen Victoria in *The Mudlark* (1950, Irene's last significant film).

Though knowing this was something she could do, Dunne did not take any chances. The actress asked RKO makeup master Ern Westmore to come into the studio on a weekend and age her forty years. He needed little convincing, telling Irene, "If they're too stupid to give you a test, we'll sell 'em the idea with pictures."[25] They were then joined on the lot by RKO photographer Ernest Bracken, who caught the makeover on film. The actress remembered, "Ernie put the set of pictures on LeBaron's desk with a note that read, 'This is Irene Dunne, the girl who should play the lead in *Cimarron*.'"[26] The pictures impressed LeBaron enough to order an immediate screen test. So far so good, but it seemed like every RKO actress had either been tested or was maneuvering to do so. Dunne still felt like it was "pick a number" time—a modest variation on all the actresses who tested later in the 1930s for the role of *Gone With The Wind*'s Scarlett.

Frank was very supportive of Irene's quest to get the *Cimarron* part. Besides their marathon coast-to-coast phone conversations (which regularly averaged seven hundred dollars a month[27]), he frequently took what was then a grueling thirteen-hour cross-country flight to powwow with her over major movie decisions, such as obtaining the role of Sabra. Thus, he had come West to help her prepare for the *Cimarron* test. On the Sunday before the big day, "from breakfast until dinner time . . . he was her audience. This way and that she tried the lines, until, by that intangible magic which a good actress creates, she finally captured the character of Sabra."[28]

Dunne was so secure with the character by the following day—an outgrowth of her nonstop obsession with whatever part she was playing—she even vetoed an article of clothing from wardrobe:

> "Sabra wouldn't wear that hat," she announced with that gentle firmness of hers which too many people do not plumb. "There is a sewing woman in the workroom who has just such a hat as Sabra would wear—so—on top of her head. I will borrow it from her."[29]

The test in question, with the borrowed close-fitting toque hat, was of the senior Sabra (now a Congresswoman) at the film's 1930 close. Consequently, it makes sense that a presumably older RKO seamstress in 1931 would trigger a fashion connection with character-conscious Dunne. But this was just one of *two* tests Irene made as

Sabra. The second was as the young wife of *Cimarron's* pioneering cowboy Yancey Cravat (Richard Dix).[30] For both added effectiveness and a show of support, Dix made the latter test with Dunne.

Dunne's perseverance paid off. After winning the role an ecstatic Irene wrote to old friend Fritz Ernst, "I am so so happy to have a real opportunity [to act]—you must read [the novel] 'Cimarron' so you know what I am doing."[31] Her letter to Ernst also included a *Los Angeles Examiner* newspaper clipping which revealed an added boost to her getting the part—"she was able to look 18 and talk in the voice of an old lady of 70. Many of the other players who had tests made could look young and old but they could not imitate the quavering voice of an old lady."[32]

Not only did Dunne win the coveted part—her performance as Sabra garnered the actress her first Academy Award nomination as Best Actress. But her role was clearly in support of Dix's more flamboyantly free-spirited figure, for which he too was Oscar-nominated, as Best Actor. Dix's Western pioneer (who also doubles as a newspaper editor, lawyer, poet, and lay minister) represents an early example of what film scholar Michael T. Marsden has called the "Savior in the Saddle" phenomenon.[33] This uniquely American character is a blend of Puritan Christianity and vigilante justice. Now probably most associated with Alan Ladd's acclaimed title character in *Shane* (1953, where the loner gunfighter helps the farmers), *Cimarron* was a provocative early example of this Western storyline.

Dix's most telling scene along these lines occurs during his sermon in a saloon—the only place large enough in this pioneer town (Osage, Oklahoma) to hold a church service. In midsermon Dix's man of God finds it necessary to draw his gun and drill the resident villain. This matter-of-fact killing (like swatting a fly) produces no psychological angst, so central to the later "adult Westerns" of the 1950s. Consequently, despite the "Savior in the Saddle" billing, this character has decidedly Old Testament tendencies.

This violence notwithstanding, Yancey cares for all oppressed people. His democratic advocacy includes physically protecting Jewish peddler Sol Levy (George E. Stone), becoming the public defender for the slandered saloon girl Dixie Lee (Estelle Taylor), and most importantly, ongoingly needing to champion the rights of all Native Americans. The "rehabilitation of the Indian" in American popular culture has often been linked to Delmer Daves' revisionist *Broken Arrow* (1950).[34] Though this was definitely a watershed work, *Cimarron* had scored many of the same liberal points years before. Indeed, the use of Dix as *Cimarron*'s Native American conscience was an inspired casting choice, given the actor's earlier much praised performance as a Navajo in the celebrated silent epic *The Vanishing American* (1925, from a Zane Grey novel).

Though this sensitivity to the plight of the American Indian is the now dated Cimarron's greatest attribute, how does the subject relate to Irene Dunne's role? Well, Sabra's embracing of her husband's enlightened views throughout the course of the movie, espcially as they relate to Native Americans, is precisely what gives the part its heartfelt populism. In fact, because Dunne's character is initially slow to embrace all of Yancey's liberal causes, Sabra is made all the more poignantly real. Who has not sometimes been slow to embrace progressive change?

Sabra's position with regard to her Native American daughter-in-law, Ruby Big Elk (Dolores Brown), is a case in point. She had initially not wanted her son Cim (Donald Dillway) to marry this chief's daughter. Yet by Sabra's speech near the film's close as a Congresswoman, she was proud to have "a full-blooded Osage Indian" as a member of her family. Moreover, she had Ruby Big Elk, who was introduced in full Indian regalia, share a Native American axiom during the aforementioned talk—"May you long travel the path of life in days that are calm and peaceful."

Though Sabra's pivotal political speech is significant for several reasons, including its groundbreaking feminism ("The holding of a public office by a woman is a natural step."), one most remembers the advocacy for Native Americans. Indeed, it helps explain the unexpected praise famous period humorist Will Rogers gave Dunne's *Cimarron* performance. As noted earlier, the normally anti-women-in-politics entertainer declared, "If women like Irene Dunne would run for Congress, I'd vote for them." While Rogers was no doubt moved by both Irene's performance and the movie's focus on his beloved home state of Oklahoma, her championing of American Indians probably most affected him.

The humorist was fiercely proud to be both part Cherokee and to have been born in a pre-state Oklahoma known as the "Indian Territory." Moreover, Rogers—arguably the period's most popular all-around entertainer—often used his ongoing endorsement of all things Native American in his humor. His widow later addressed this trait in her biography of Rogers:

Will's pride in the fact he was part Indian inspired a story that has been repeated as often as anything he ever said. He was appearing on one of his lecture tours in Boston's hallowed Symphony Hall . . . [when he] solemnly announced to the distinguished audience that he was honored by the presence of so many descendants of the pioneer Americans, and admitted that his forefathers had not come over on the *Mayflower*—"But," he said, "they met the boat."[35]

Rogers' superlatives for Dunne and *Cimarron* were just the most high-profile comments on a much praised picture. Probably the most entertaining take on the film was from *Variety*, the entertainment industry's bible: "This is a spectacular Western . . . [with] action, sentiment, sympathy, thrills and comedy—and 100% clean. Radio Pictures (RKO) has a corker in *Cimarron*."[36] Calling Dunne an "indomitable Sabra," *New York Times* critic Mordaunt Hall added, "From the first to the last scene one is often stirred by this chronicle."[37] Besides the Oscar nominations for Dunne and Dix, as well as director Wesley Ruggles and cinematographer Edward Cronjager, *Cimarron* took home Academy Awards for Best Picture, Writing (adaptation), and Interior Decoration. Irene's movie career was suddenly on the fast track.

NOTES

1. Joe Hyams, "Irene Dunne's Husband: 'Be a Trailer,'" *New York Herald Tribune*, March 20, 1958, 12.

2. Sara Hamilton, "This Is Really Irene Dunne," *Photoplay*, April 1936, 92.

3. Margie Schultz, *Irene Dunne: A Bio-Bibliography*, Westport, Connecticut: Greenwood Press, 1991, 6.

4. John F. Devine, "Irene Goes Wild," *Modern Movies*, April 1937, 34–35, 73–75.

5. Irene Dunne to Fritz Ernst, May 18, 1921, from the "Charles Davidson Collection of Irene Dunne Letters," a private collector.

6. Caroline S. Hoyt, "Irene Dunne's True Life Story," *Modern Screen*, December 1938, 31.

7. Jerome Beatty, "Lady Irene," *American Magazine*, November 1944, 118.

8. Ibid.

9. Review of *Show Boat*, *Chicago Tribune*, October 2, 1929.

10. Review of *Show Boat*, *St. Louis Daily Globe-Democrat*, January 21, 1930.

11. Review of *Show Boat*, *Detroit Times*, February 4, 1930.

12. Review of *Show Boat*, *Cleveland Plain Dealer*, February 11, 1930.

13. Leon Surmelian, "It's the Irish in Her," *Motion Picture Story Magazine*, July 1936, 68.

14. Irene Dunne RKO contract, April 10, 1930, in the "Irene Dunne Collection," Box 1, RKO folder, Cinema and Television Library, University of Southern California, Los Angeles.

15. Ibid.

16. Review of *Leathernecking, Variety*, September 17, 1930.

17. See my *"Mr. B" or Comforting Thoughts about the Bison: A Critical Biography of Robert Benchley* (Westport, Connecticut: Greenwood Press, 1992).

18. Jane Ardmore, "Irene Dunne: She'll Always Be Hollywood's Perfect Lady," *Photoplay*, December 1975, 86.

19. Hyams, 12.

20. Dorothy Calhoun, "Irene Dunne Leads Two Lives," *Motion Picture Story Magazine*, September 1935, 39.

21. Ruth Biery, "Irene's *Secret* Marriage," *Photoplay*, April 1931, 35.

22. Irene Dunne RKO contract—clause five, December 16, 1931, in the "Irene Dunne Collection," Box 1, RKO folder, Cinema and Television Library, University of Southern California, Los Angeles.

23. Adela Rogers St. Johns, "Thank You, Irene Dunne," *Photoplay*, September 1944, 99.

24. Schultz, 7.

25. Elizabeth Wilson, "Men She'll Remember," *Silver Screen*, April 1941, 74.

26. Ibid.

27. Biery, 135.

28. Elsa Maxwell, "A Very Special Woman," *Photoplay*, January 1948, 78.

29. Ibid.

30. Ardmore, 86.

31. Irene Dunne to Fritz Ernst, August 19, 1930, from the "Charles Davidson Collection of Irene Dunne Letters," a private collector.

32. Louella O. Parsons, "Irene Dunn [sic] Chosen to Play Heroine in 'Cimarron,'" *Los Angeles Examiner*, August 19, 1930, sec. 1, p. 9.

33. Michael T. Marsden, "Savior in the Saddle: The Sagebrush Testament," in *Focus On The Western*, ed. Jack Nachbar (Englewood Cliffs, New Jersey: Prentice-Hall, Inc., 1974), 93–100.

34. George N. Fenin and William K. Everson, *The Western: From Silents to the Seventies* (New York: Penguin Books, 1977), 18.

35. Betty Rogers, *Will Rogers* (Garden City, New York: Garden City Publishing Co., Inc., 1941), 33.

36. Review of *Cimarron, Variety*, January 28, 1931.

37. Mordaunt Hall, *Cimarron* review, *New York Times*, January 27, 1931, 20.

THREE

A Film Career and a Bicoastal Marriage—Plus the Legacy of *Cimarron*

I've seen [*Cimarron*] three times and get the same thrill everytime
. . . [the film] starts Irene Dunne off as one of our greatest screen
artists.[1]

—*Photoplay* (1931)

Cimarron established Dunne as a major Hollywood player and set
four precedents for her film career. First, despite the move by Yancey
(Richard Dix) and Irene's Sabra to the roughest of pioneer towns (Osage, Oklahoma), Dunne's character is always the proper lady—forever after a hallmark of her screen persona. Second, Sabra is a strong
mother figure to two children in *Cimarron*. Being a sympathetic parent eventually became a defining trait of both Dunne the performer
and Irene the private person. Third, Sabra's marriage to the dynamic
Yancey was often a melodramatic affair. His pioneer wanderlust tendencies often had him leaving Sabra and the children for *years*. Fittingly, several of Dunne's subsequent films would fall under the
genre heading of melodrama, including such celebrated outings as
Back Street (1932) and *Magnificent Obsession* (1935). Fourth, for a then-
veteran stage actress, Dunne's *Cimarron* performance showcases an
inspired degree of restraint. There is an intuitive understanding by
the actress that the camera will catch the most modest of movements.
(Frequently the stage-trained performer exaggerates his or her
actions to play to the distant portion of a theater.)

Ironically, one way in which *Cimarron* has *not* aged well is in just
such overreactions by cast members *other* than Dunne, including Dix's
then much praised performance as Yancey. But the stumbling block

for Dix was not stage background but rather his long tenure as a silent film star. Of course, many silent performers were the picture of minimalist restraint, such as the incomparable Buster Keaton, famous as the great "Stone Face." The mere blink of Buster's eyes revealed volumes about his character. Yet, silent cinema's lack of the spoken word encouraged some actors to be more demonstrative. Dix was one such silent actor. Consequently, while there is still much that is wonderful about Dix's heroic square-jawed performance, I must agree with contemporary film critic Leonard Maltin's label of Dix's acting as "overripe."[2] In fact, after a 1975 screening, Dunne herself felt *Cimarron* was now "awfully hammy."[3] But she was too thoughtfully diplomatic to name names. Consistent with this revisionist reading, it should be remembered that Dix fell to "B" roles early in the sound era, never again enjoying the "A" status he had known as a silent star.

In the context of the time, however, *Cimarron* was a great critical and commercial success. As the critic for the *New York Daily News* stated, "We can't describe the grandeur and the punch and the appeal of 'Cimarron.' This is one picture you cannot afford to miss. It is 1931's first great contribution to the screen. We loved every minute of it."[4] Even two years after this Western's release, the movie was still being used as a barometer for greatness. For instance, period reviewers often compared Buster Keaton's epic comic chase in the early sound feature, *What! No Beer?* (1933), to the celebrated land rush scenes in *Cimarron*.[5]

More significantly, Dunne consciously used the Western as a measuring stick for much of what would follow in her career. *Cimarron* also taught the actress a lesson in Hollywood economics. Despite the substantial box office of the picture, it did not earn a profit during its initial release, given the huge (for the time) production cost of approximately $1,500,000. Possibly this factor, as much as anything else, contributed to the stunting of a modest "cycle of epic Western[s]" in the early 1930s.[6] That is, *Cimarron*'s commercial disappointment, coupled with the box office failure of *The Big Trail* and *Billy The Kid* (both 1930), seemed to sour Hollywood's early sound-era interest in the Western.

The critical responses to Dunne's immediate screen roles after *Cimarron* were constantly measured against that movie's memorable reputation, too. Thus, in her first post-*Cimarron* outing, the sophisticated comedy *Bachelor Apartment* (1931), a disappointed *Variety* observed, "Seems Radio [RKO] muffed in setting Irene Dunne for a thing like this after her 'Cimarron' favor. It's like sending a brilliant [baseball] prospect backward."[7] The third picture after *Cimarron* was the romantic comedy *Consolation Marriage* (1931, costarring Pat O'Brien), with the *New York Times* stating, "Miss Dunne's performance is capable, almost as good as her portrayal in 'Cimarron.'"[8] And *Consolation Marriage* was followed by *Symphony of Six Million* (1932), a melodrama *Variety* hailed as RKO's "first twice-daily Broadway [road show engagement] bid since 'Cimarron.'"[9] (Sandwiched between *Bachelor Apartment* and *Consolation Marriage* was a melodramatic loan-out to MGM entitled *The Great Lover*. While the movie gave Dunne her first chance to sing on screen, period critics treated it as minor league fare compared to *Cimarron*.)

Besides becoming an early gauge for Dunne's film career, *Cimarron* greatly impacted her private life, as well. Most importantly, she no longer needed to keep her marriage a secret, which RKO had unofficially encouraged her to do. (This was a standard studio request in the 1930s.) Her sudden *Cimarron* stardom had reporters scrambling for any and all biographical information, with *Photoplay* magazine being the first publication to query the actress about her "*secret* marriage."[10] The epic Western's success also eliminated any more discussions with Irene's husband, Dr. Frank Griffin, about an early screen retirement. In fact, he had become her biggest film fan. Though their bicoastal marriage would continue for several more years as he maintained his New York City dental practice, he was increasingly proud of her acting skills.

This was most poignantly brought home to Dunne after the New York opening of *Cimarron*, to which her husband had taken a party of twelve! Immediately after the triumphant screening he went into a room, alone, and called her. Irene later shared, "When he's excited he doesn't get boisterous or loud. His voice gets deep and throaty. It was so deep that night I could scarcely understand what he was saying."[11]

According to the actress, *Cimarron*'s success even shifted her husband's position on moving to California. Shortly after the Western won the Best Picture Academy Award (November 10, 1931) Frank was in Los Angeles visiting his wife. Out for a drive with Irene and a real estate agent, Dr. Griffin was especially taken with a property in what was then the secluded Holmby Hills area of the city. Though still in denial about ever leaving his beloved New York, he told Dunne and the realtor, "If I ever did consider [moving here], this is a section I would like because it is so high and you can see all over the city."[12] Not surprisingly, they soon owned the lot, though both the building of their dream house and Frank's move West would wait until 1936. While Irene's husband was not a man to be rushed into anything, *Cimarron* made it a foregone conclusion that the Griffins would eventually live under one southern California roof. The promise of Irene's film career was probably best summed up by the epic Western's director, Wesley Ruggles: "She can sing, play comedy or drama. She's bound to have one of the most enviable careers in Hollywood—if she gets a good agent."[13]

Dunne would seem to have taken Ruggles' advice to heart, with regard to an agent, because her post-*Cimarron* salary was soon at $2,500 a week—a phenomenal amount for depression-era America. *Plus*, in 1933 a new contract almost doubled her per-picture minimum (to $45,000), *and* Irene was the beneficiary of a pioneering percentage deal—15% of her picture's grosses![14] Though Irene was always extremely proud of Frank's ability to adjust to her career, the financial windfall associated with Hollywood employment no doubt eased the transition. But in fairness to Griffin, he was, as Dunne later suggested, "way ahead of his time in his thinking, on everything."[15] For instance, Irene's fellow Hollywood Hoosier and future screwball comedy compatriot Carole Lombard was married the same year (1931) that *Cimarron* was released. But despite having a gifted and well-educated husband from within film society itself, William Powell, their marriage soon faltered, largely because he would have preferred a stay-at-home wife. Though the Griffins' early bicoastal marriage was unconventional, the couple were devoted to each other. As Dunne so passionately observed after *Photoplay* outed her union with Frank—"Oh, it's grand to be married and grand to be able to talk about it."[16]

Of course, the downside to their separations, besides the loneliness and astronomical phone bills, was the periodic rumors that the actress was involved with another man. Dunne confessed in 1935, "If I live a rather lonely, old-maidish sort of existence here [in Hollywood], I do it deliberately, by my own choice. It's the only way I can protect something awfully worthwhile—I mean my marriage."[17] To further lessen any sense of impropriety, she minimized her social activities and intensified an already workaholic nature. If Irene did go out she attempted to be in the company of a married couple. Still, in the mid-1930s the actress said "she couldn't begin to enumerate the people who have [warned both her and her husband], 'There is no use courting temptation' [by living apart]."[18]

Besides, however, frequently having her mother on hand as a Hollywood companion, her screen contract stipulated extra time between pictures for periodic visits back to Frank in New York, when he could not make the marathon thirteen-hour flight to Los Angeles. Of course, as Dunne later observed, "It was much more fun when we could go together, back and forth on the Super Chief [train]. That was the elegant way; the train would [even] pick up mountain trout at Denver."[19]

Despite the need for travel in their unconventional marriage, one of the couple's shared passions was visiting new places, or cherished old ones, such as Irene's favorite city—Paris. Since their European honeymoon in 1928, Irene and Frank had squeezed in as much travel abroad as possible. Culture was always high on their joint priority list. He had been born to it, with a privileged New England upbringing which included a then-future president (Calvin Coolidge) as a neighbor. Dunne had been trained to appreciate the arts—first by attentive parents and then by a college education which qualified her to teach music and art. While Irene opted for performing over instruction, she never lost her fascination for culture of all kinds.

This helps explain why visitors found her California home (both before and after Frank moved west) so decidedly unlike that of most movie stars. There were neither decorating schemes heavy on autographed photos, nor industry trade publications like *Variety* and the *Hollywood Reporter* scattered about. She both enjoyed and excelled at making movies, but it was not her whole life. Indeed, film had not even been her first or second career choice. (Though Dunne failed to become a Metropolitan Opera star, she had, of course, managed to achieve success as a Broadway actress.)

Irene had, moreover, reached Hollywood at a more advanced age (thirty-two) than many performers, though her studio age was twenty-six. For instance, fellow Hoosier Lombard had been making movies since she was a teenager. Thus, Dunne had established a non-film-oriented life for some time before becoming a movie star. In addition, her *Cimarron* Academy Award nomination for only her second film was instant validation. Consequently, she was not as driven to succeed as a less established performer scrambling for recognition.[20]

When Irene and Frank were not exploring cultural Europe they were taking their periodic "surprise junket" stateside. This involved throwing their golf clubs in the trunk and driving off wherever the road took them. Though this usually only involved a getaway weekend, one such unplanned adventure stretched into seven weeks—"They simply were having so much fun that they just kept on driving."[21] Interestingly enough, as much as the Griffins enjoyed travel, both here and abroad, Dunne sometimes had an additional motive for these trips. And the reason is surprisingly inconsistent with the normally straitlaced image of the actress. She sometimes used travel to keep the Hollywood powers that be at bay.

Her most famous bit of attempted manipulation occurred when RKO loaned her to Columbia studio to do her first screwball comedy— a genre Dunne thought was beyond her. Describing her part in this projected property, *Theodora Goes Wild* (1936), as a "zany woman who writes a book that scandalizes . . . [a small] town," the actress was desperate to shake the role: "I tried every way to get out of doing it. My husband and I even sailed off to Europe. But when I came back, the studio was right there to meet me, script in hand."[22] Columbia's persistence was lucky for Irene, because the characterization would result in another Best Actress nomination for her. (Both the part and the film will be addressed further later in the text.)

Still, travel was often an effective movie dodge for Dunne. In fact, sometimes mere distance was the secret. That is, when her husband lived in New York, she frequently prolonged her visits by either pretending not to receive studio telegrams, or claiming they were somehow delayed in delivery. The only downside to Frank's eventual move west was the actress' inability to continue this modest scam. Of course, Irene's tendency to occasionally play these games was greatly enhanced by a public and private persona attached to being a lady.

Interestingly enough, much later (1985) the actress revealed that this ladylike persona never took into account her *hardball* tendencies prior to production—"Oh, I was an absolute angel on the set. . . . I did all my negotiating *before* a picture began, and, once all that was out of the way, I behaved like an absolute professional . . . [during] the shooting."[23] In contrast, period acting contemporaries like Bette Davis and James Cagney were much less successful with confrontational walkouts from their studio. But in fairness to this Warner Brothers duo, even their then-combined salaries were well below what RKO was paying Dunne.

Though Irene's parent studio was more generous than most with regard to salaries, RKO was still struggling with just how to use the now high-profile star of *Cimarron*. But even though her immediate followup films after the epic Western received only mixed critical response, reviewers consistently praised the actress. For instance, of *Bachelor*

Apartment, Variety said, "Irene Dunne is best and offers the only real attempt at acting."[24] And the *New York Herald Tribune's* general pan of *Consolation Marriage* still found time to call Dunne "coolly likable," with yet another reference to her *Cimarron* legacy, while *Variety* credited her with having "persuasive grace" in *The Great Lover.*[25]

Though Dunne would consider *Cimarron* her greatest film for much of her screen career, Irene's loan-out starring role in Universal's adaptation of Fannie Hurst's best selling novel *Back Street* (1932) gave the actress another high-profile title for her filmography. While the reviews for this weepy melodrama were mixed, the picture proved a huge commercial success with women viewers. The movie chronicles the sad story of a kept woman (Dunne) pining away her life in a "back street" apartment waiting for fleeting moments with a married lover (John Boles). Her character's pathetic plight is made all the more ironic, given that a missed meeting early in the picture probably kept her from being the wife, instead of the mistress.

As with earlier Dunne films showcasing less-than-universally-stellar reviews, the actress still seemed to garner individual kudos. For example, the *New York World-Telegram's* critique stated "Although it [*Back Street*] smacks a little of popular fiction, it does have its moments of genuine pathos and tragedy, due largely to the playing of Irene Dunne in the principal role."[26] The *New York Herald Tribune's* mixed review also only found praise for the actress. Indeed, the reviewer felt her performance actually exceeded her celebrated *Cimarron* role: "Miss Dunne's portrayal struck me as being among other things more honest and effective than her much admired characterization in 'Cimarron.'"[27]

Of course, like most great commercial successes, *Back Street* was not without its critical champions. *Variety* was the film's most enthusiastic supporter. Besides calling Dunne's characterization "superb," the publication said of the movie, "A winner. It's a tear-jerker, without being artificially sentimental, impressing in the main as a human document faithfully translated into celluloid and sound, which rings true from start to finish."[28] This humanist critical slant gets at the heart of Irene's gift to acting. As the *Variety* review went on to say of the actress, "She is the personification of a real person, an excellent casting assignment."[29] And as noted earlier, with regard to Richard Dix's more demonstrative acting style in *Cimarron*, a hallmark of Dunne's screen persona from the very beginning was its moving minimalism.

Another measure of *Back Street*'s success was that Dunne's follow-up picture, RKO's thriller *Thirteen Women* (1932), had actually been shot earlier. But her home studio held up its release both to capitalize on the industry buzz that Universal had a hit with *Back Street*, and to take advantage of all the publicity generated by this Hurst adaptation.

As a final footnote to *Back Street*, and to 1930s melodrama in general, Irene's heroines in the genre maintain a basic decency, however unseemly the situation. As a later reviewer noted of Dunne's melodramatic title character in *Ann Vickers* (1933), "she stays outside the matrimonial fence but remains a perfect lady."[30] Indeed, Dunne's title heroine in yet another melodrama, *The Secret of Madame Blanche* (1933), is taken from a stage play called *The Lady*. The actress was not only effective at imbuing the traditional "other woman" of a *Back Street* scenario with sympathy, she was equally capable of bringing pathos to situations which would play as bathos for most other performers. Moreover, Dunne managed to give a realistic emotional range to a character (the stereotypical melodramatic heroine) that is sometimes criticized for being a one-note creation. Thus, even in one of Irene's weaker outings in the genre, 1934's *If I Were Free*, the *New York Times* observed, "Considering the limited possibilities of her role, Miss Dunne does remarkably well."[31]

Ultimately, the actress' most acclaimed melodrama (also known at the time as "weepies" and "woman's pictures") was *Magnificent Obsession* (1935). An adaptation of Lloyd C. Douglas' long-time best-selling novel, Dunne was attracted to the work for both professional and personal reasons. First, the property was a higher-quality example of what the actress was becoming best known for. In fact, even two years prior to *Magnificent Obsession* one critic had said of her melodramatic outing in *Ann Vickers*, the movie "may be classified as the type of thing Irene Dunne does for Radio [RKO]."[32]

Second, besides *Magnificent Obsession* being set in the Hoosier actress' own adopted state, in the northern Indiana lake country, the novel has a strong religious foundation which appealed to Dunne's devoted Catholicism. Though novelist Douglas had failed in an early attempt to be a minister, he had successfully imparted a sense of self-sacrificing godliness to this story. The title is a reference to a philosophy of life which is driven by anonymous acts of charity.

The film finds Dunne's character, Helen Hudson, married to a much older, world-renowned doctor, whose death at the beginning of the story might have been averted had a certain piece of medical equipment been available. Sadly, said apparatus had been in use to revive a drunken millionaire playboy, Bobby Merrick (Robert Taylor, in a career-making performance). Ironically, he will then fall in love with the widowed Mrs. Hudson, only to cause her further grief by being the catalyst for an accident which blinds her. And this is only the beginning of the movie's melodramatic quotient! Taylor's character will both win Hudson's love *and* become a famous surgeon who, predictably, gives Dunne's Helen back her sight. (Always the consummate artist, Irene would work closely with a blind consultant, Mrs. Ruby Fruth, on how to walk and carry herself as a sightless person, as well as learn to read Braille.[33])

Taylor's unlikely transformation (as Merrick) is made possible by the spirit of Helen Hudson's late husband, whose giving philosophy also attempted to help people "make contact with the source of infinite power." Though the genre of melodrama often demands a certain suspension of disbelief, which frequently finds critics at cross-purposes with these weepies, most reviewers embraced Dunne's *Magnificent Obsession.* The *New York Post* noted, "Illogical as it may seem, the picture makes out a sound case for the theory that it is possible to be both good and happy."[34] *Variety's* critic went even further. He both praised the picture, and saluted it along public service lines— "*Magnificent* is magnificent. . . . Besides its general creditability to the industry, U [Universal] has a box-office entity of no small caliber. It should capitalize on it handily."[35] As had been the case with earlier Dunne melodramatic triumphs, the movie's success was clearly anchored in the actress' performance. *New York Daily News* critic Kate Cameron was the most articulate along these lines:

> Irene Dunne plays the perfect heroine of the book, Helen Hudson, with a feeling of sincerity that few actresses can command for this type of role. She has always had that faculty of making any person she represents on the screen assume an authority that gives the fictional character life and vitality.[36]

This "vitality" factor is especially apparent when the movie is compared to its wooden 1954 remake, starring Jane Wyman and Rock Hudson.

Dunne's vitality component was democratically important behind the scenes, too. Her stand-in, Kathryn Stanley, later revealed that the actress went out of her way to mentor Robert Taylor into a star turn. On loan-out from MGM and not yet a *name*, Irene constantly encouraged Taylor, rehearsed lines with him, offered suggestions, and assured him, "You're going to be a big star after this picture."[37] This generosity was an outgrowth of a basic populist practicality that the actress had coalesced into an axiom Kathryn Stanley had heard on numerous occasions, "It is the picture as a whole, and not really the star, which determines box-office results."[38] Maybe this was Dunne's heartland common sense kicking in, since her friend and fellow Hollywood Hoosier Carole Lombard practiced the same "What's good for the picture. . . ." philosophy.[39] With the handiwork of Dunne ever present (on screen and off), is it any wonder that the *Hollywood Reporter* critic said the movie "comes as near as can be to earn the title of 'the perfect picture.'"?[40]

For the mid-1930s Dunne, with a husband still residing in the East and a West Coast career in full swing, a euphemism for the actress' "magnificent obsession" would be "melodramatic workaholic." That is, between the 1932 and 1935 releases of her signature outings in the genre, *Back Street* and *Magnificent Obsession*, Irene made eleven pictures, seven of which were melodramas! During this period she had a film opening every three to four months. Fittingly, a common component of her period interviews was the bald statement that filming necessitated being in "Bed by ten, [and] up by six-thirty."[41] As she shared in another 1930s article, "Fortunately, I work very hard and manage to become tired enough not to miss going out often."[42] A bicoastal marriage seemed to serve as an excellent career catalyst; à la, absence makes for accepting more distracting film assignments. (She cut back on movie roles after Dr. Griffin joined her in Hollywood.)

Besides the preponderance of melodramas in the aforementioned eleven feature films, which will be further addressed in the following chapter, the total count also included two musicals, a murder mystery, and a quasi Western set partly in Australia—*Stingaree* (1934). But for a chapter that began with the legacy of *Cimarron*, *Stingaree* brings Dunne's film career full circle. The movie reunited the actress and her *Cimarron* costar, Richard Dix. *Stingaree*, which the often staid *New York Times* was moved to describe as "a pleasant narrative of a highly improbable fable," chronicles a love affair between an opera singer and a nineteenth-century Australian Robin Hood figure.[43]

Ironically, whereas Dix had been the star at the time of their first teaming, Dunne had clearly usurped him when *Stingaree* was released. This difference in status was also reflected in their screen time, with Dunne having more solo scenes—often showcasing her character's singing career in Europe. Period reviewers sometimes criticized Dix's tendency to overact (the cause of his declining credibility), such as in the *New York Post*'s take on *Stingaree*—"It is a preposterous tale, with Mr. Dix doing his best to prevent it from being even faintly credible."[44] But in this one unique case, his reteaming with Dunne, such criticism was rare. More typical was the *New York Herald Tribune*'s perspective: "It is an elegant horse opera. . . . Its mood of improbable romance is its chief charm. [The film is] Rich in background, pleasantly acted, and graced with some delightful songs."[45] *Tribune* critic Howard Barnes was more than a little pleased just to have the duo back together again—"It is fortunate in having Richard Dix and Irene Dunne for hero and heroine. The former co-stars of 'Cimarron' . . . pitch their performances in a mildly rococo vein that is eminently suited to the material."[46]

As was now becoming the norm for the actress, she stole the lion's share of the critical hosannas. Her creative theft was made all the easier by way of having some musical numbers to perform. Consequently, Dunne's *Stingaree* kudos often centered on singing, such as in the *New York Daily News*' observation that "The story of the opera singer gives Irene Dunne the greatest opportunity she has had in the movies of displaying her exquisitely lovely voice, and she makes splendid use of this opportunity."[47]

Other factors in the film's favor were its outstanding action director, William Wellman, and a talented supporting cast, which included Mary Boland and Andy Devine. The latter actor, who would later surface in several classic Westerns, including director John Ford's *Stagecoach* (1939), *Two Road Together* (1961), and *The Man Who Shot Liberty Valance* (1962), was Dix's entertaining bandit sidekick. *Variety* said of Devine's *Stingaree* performance, "He is given one good bit, and the rest of the time breaks in by force of his personality."[48] The same publication also suggested that Dunne's added screen time (over the duo of Dix and Divine) was not due just to her greater star status but also was a reflection of the Western's decline in popularity since *Cimarron*: "Radio [RKO] probably realized that the horse operas have done much to rub the bloom of youth from hard riding."[49] Regardless, as this and the following chapters suggest, while the popularity of a given genre might vary through time, Dunne's box office staying power was consistently strong for years.

NOTES

1. *Cimarron* review, *Photoplay*, April 1931.

2. *Cimarron* entry in *Leonard Maltin's Movie & Video Guide: 2003*, ed. Leonard Maltin (New York: Signet Book, 2002), 248.

3. "Irene Dunne at Filmex Tribute Rates 'Affair,' 'Mama' Her Best," *Daily Variety*, March 25, 1975.

4. Irene Thirer, "'Cimarron' In Globe Premiere," *New York Daily News*, January 27, 1931, 32.

5. For example, see "The Beer Parade," *New York Post*, February 4, 1933, 5.

6. George N. Fenin and William K. Everson, *The Western: From Silents to the Seventies* (New York: Penguin Books, 1977), 178.

7. Review of *Bachelor Apartment*, *Variety*, May 20, 1931.

8. Mordaunt Hall, review of *Consolation Marriage*, *New York Times*, October 30, 1931, 26.

9. Review of *Symphony of Six Million*, *Variety*, April 19, 1932.

10. Ruth Biery, "Irene's *Secret* Marriage," *Photoplay*, April 1931, 35, 135.

11. Ibid., 135.

12. Jane Ardmore, "Irene Dunne: She'll Always Be Hollywood's Perfect Lady," *Photoplay*, December 1975, 86.

13. Mason Wiley and Damien Bono, *Inside Oscar* (New York: Ballantine Books, 1993), 30.

14. Irene Dunne RKO contract (September 1933), in the "Irene Dunne Collection," Box 1, RKO folder, Cinema and Television Library, University of Southern California, Los Angeles.

15. Ardmore, 86.

16. Biery, 135.

17. Dorothy Calhoun, "Irene Dunne Leads Two Lives," *Motion Picture Story Magazine*, September 1935, 39.

18. William F. French, "Untold Stories of Love That Have Lasted," *Motion Picture Story Magazine*, January 1935, 59.

19. Ardmore, 86.

20. Contemporary Carole Lombard toiled long (nine years) and hard (up to six feature films a year) before receiving her first Academy Award nomination.

21. "Topics for Gossip," *Silver Screen*, July 1941, 21, 69.

22. John McDonough, "Screening a Star: A Rare Interview with Irene Dunne," *Chicago Tribune*, May 12, 1985, sec. 13, p. 8.

23. George Shea, "Irene Dunne," *Northwest Orient*, December 1985, 30.

24. Review of *Bachelor Apartment*, *Variety*, May 20, 1931.

25. Richard Watts, Jr., "'Consolation Marriage'—Mayfair," *New York Herald Tribune*, October 30, 1931, 16; Review of *The Great Lover*, *Variety*, August 25, 1931.

26. William Boehnel, "Irene Dunne Effective in Film 'Back Street,'" *New York World-Telegram*, August 29, 1932, 10.

27. Richard Watts, Jr., "'Back Street'—Mayfair," *New York Herald Tribune*, August 29, 1932, 6.

28. Review of *Back Street*, *Variety*, August 30, 1932.

29. Ibid.

30. Review of *Ann Vickers*, *Variety*, October 10, 1933.

31. Mordaunt Hall, Review of *If I Were Free*, *New York Times*, January 5, 1934, 25.

32. Review of *Ann Vickers*, *Variety*.

33. "Actress Prepares to Portray Blind Role," *Times*, November 31, 1935.

34. Thornton Delehanty, "'Magnificent Obsession' On the Music Hall Screen," *New York Post*, December 31, 1935, 9.

35. Review of *Magnificent Obsession*, *Variety*, January 8, 1936.

36. Kate Cameron, "Irene Dunne Gives Real Life to Film," *New York Daily News*, December 31, 1935, 24.

37. Kathryn Stanley (as told to Sonie Lee), "Irene Dunne as I Know Her," *Movies*, August 1941, 54.

38. Ibid.

39. See my *Carole Lombard: "The Hoosier Tornado"* (Indianapolis: Indiana Historical Society, 2003).

40. "U's 'Magnificent Obsession' Sure-Fire Box-Office Picture," *Hollywood Reporter*, December 31, 1935, 3.

41. For instance, see: Helen Fay Ludlam, "Nucleus," *Silver Screen*, July 1935, 20.

42. Calhoun, 73.

43. Review of *Stingaree*, *New York Times*, May 18, 1934, 27.

44. Thornton Delehanty, "Irene Dunne and Richard Dix in 'Stingaree,'" *New York Post*, May 18, 1934, 13.

45. Howard Barnes, "'Stingaree'—Music Hall," *New York Herald Tribune*, May 18, 1934, 17.

46. Ibid.

47. Kate Cameron, "Delightful Romance Reunites Dunne, Dix," *New York Daily News*, May 18, 1934, 62.

48. Review of *Stingaree*, *Variety*, May 22, 1934.

49. Ibid.

FOUR

Queen of the Melodrama, and a Return to the Musical

[T]he status I have achieved has been achieved through tears. And so, for my career, ¹ cry!

—Irene Dunne (1937)[1]

Irene Dunne's comments above on melodrama were taken from a 1937 interview in which she argued that "heavy drama" made for more memorable memories among the public than any other genre, including Dunne's beloved musical. She based this view on numerous experiences with fans, several of which she related. The most provocative example involved a research trip to Paris, when she visited the French Academy of Medicine for background material on Madame Curie. One of Irene's contacts was a professor "renowned for his achievement in medical research. He peered at me over his glasses and said: 'You are the actress who cries so beautifully. I remember you in *Back Street* [1932].'"[2] (On its initial run in Paris, *Back Street* had played at one theater for a year.)

Though this 1937 Dunne interview came before all of the actress' great screen comedies except for *Theodora Goes Wild* (1936), this bias for melodrama was a perspective which still resonated with Irene years *after* her career was over. For example, in a rare 1985 interview Dunne discussed her lengthy early 1930s melodrama period of playing the "long-suffering heroine." Though she confessed to wanting "to get out of that [rut] . . . I never thought of doing straight comedy. It wasn't as satisfying to the serious actress in me as a tear jerker like 'Magnificent Obsession,' a [melodramatic] part I could get my teeth

47

into."[3] This is a very significant admission for 1985—given that by this time the actress' greatest films were routinely considered to be those which *followed* her melodrama phase, such as the screwball comedy trilogy—*Theodora Goes Wild*, *The Awful Truth* (1937), and *My Favorite Wife* (1940).

Dunne's thoughts on comedy will be addressed at length later in the text, but it bears noting here that she felt that the various genres associated with laughter (including screwball and romantic comedy) came too easily for her. Though rightly proud of her celebrated sense of comic timing, the greater demands (for her) of a serious genre somehow seemed more satisfying. Of course, this might merely be an outgrowth of such an intense immersion in melodrama so early in her screen career.

As noted in the previous chapter, seven of the eleven films Dunne made between her signature weepies, *Back Street* and *Magnificent Obsession* (1935), fall into the melodrama camp. *No Other Women* (1933) chronicles a messy courtroom divorce. *The Secret of Madame Blanche* (1933) documents a mother's supreme sacrifice in a story involving suicide and murder. *The Silver Cord* (1933) finds Dunne's career woman trying to cope with an overbearing mother-in-law. *Ann Vickers* (1933), from the Sinclair Lewis novel, follows the trials and tribulations of Irene's title character—a pioneering feminist, social worker, and prison reformer. *If I Were Free* (1933) is about suicidal lovers attempting to break away from their respective failing marriages. *This Man Is Mine* (1934) has Dunne fighting to keep her husband (Ralph Bellamy) from a stereotypical "other woman." (This is the first of the actress' three film appearances with Bellamy.) *The Age of Innocence* (1934), from Edith Wharton's Pulitzer Prize–winning novel, profiles a thwarted 1870s romance between an engaged attorney and a divorcée.

Though none of these women's picture outings are in a league with Universal's *Back Street* and *Magnificent Obsession*, the majority of them were both critically well-received and made money. (RKO produced all the films except for MGM's *The Secret of Madame Blanche*.) A measure of Dunne's growing prominence in the genre can be drawn from the fact that four of these melodramas (*The Silver Cord*, *Ann Vickers*, *This Man Is Mine*, and *The Age of Innocence*) opened at New York City's cavernously prestigious Radio City Music Hall.

No Other Woman is the weakest picture in this Dunne melodrama package. But as has already been demonstrated often, Irene still walks away with rave reviews. For instance, *Variety* said she "interprets her role during most of the running time in a manner which commands sympathy."[4] The actress' next tearjerker release, *The Secret of Madame Blanche*, was more ambitiously entertaining for both the public and Irene. Plus, by making her character an 1890s showgirl, she is given an opportunity to sing. Interestingly enough, this limited use of music also fit Dunne's real-life philosophy for dramatic entertainment; the actress "is not as interested in musical plays as she is in plays with music—dramatic stories, which give an opportunity to sing a song or two but that is all."[5] For Dunne, too much music hurt the "dramatic tempo."

The *Madame Blanche* film also provided Irene with the chance to play a character over time, something she always enjoyed doing. In this case, one first sees her as a young torch singer whose husband will soon commit suicide, thanks to a stern, cruel father (Lionel Atwill). This same callous character then had the courts take the couple's child from Dunne's cabaret singer, claiming she was an unfit mother. Flash forward to a chance encounter with her now-grown son, and an opportunity to protect him from a murder charge, and one has an inspired formula for soap opera.

The critics were universal in praising the actress, with the *New York Herald Tribune* best capturing her melodrama legacy in their kudos: "Miss Irene Dunne, the most long-suffering of cinema heroines, is as sacrificial as ever . . . [and] plays the . . . part with reticence and feeling."[6] *Variety* added, "Miss Dunne, moving through most of a normal lifetime . . . is at all times excellent. She is as much the picture as any part of it."[7] A more succinct *New York Daily News* said the actress was "decidedly commendable," while the *New York Times* was most impressed with the sympathetic consistency she brought to her character over time: "Miss Dunne is ingratiating both as a young woman and as the mother of twenty years later."[8]

Ironically, Dunne followed this role with *The Silver Cord*, in which she is the victim of a mother—her screen husband's controllingly obnoxious parent (Laura Hope Crews). As one period critic stated, "The problem of the mother who tries to bind her sons to her by shutting other women out of their lives is a fundamental one."[9] But that being said, there was also a topical factor going on with *The Silver Cord*. The 1930s Depression forced many young couples to be more dependent upon their parents and/or their in-laws. The subject was timely enough to even provoke a *Photoplay* interview with the actress entitled, "'Don't Live With Your Mother-in-law' says Irene Dunne."

Despite the article's title, the actress was enough of a romantic to suggest that compromises could be arranged with in-laws of "depression wives." That is, a brief "all-living-in-together arrangement . . . [is] preferable to putting off the marriage for years. I think people should marry young and plan their lives together. It's so much more thrilling and practical, too."[10] A more provocative addition to the interview, however, would have been a comment from Dunne's husband on the subject, because Irene's mother lived with her for a time in Hollywood. Consequently, whenever the New York–based Dr. Griffin visited his wife in California, he was confronted with a mother-in-law situation. Presumably, this would not have been a problem, given that he had great rapport with Dunne's whole family. In fact, the aforementioned *Photoplay* piece noted that the actress' grown brother lived with her husband at Griffin's New York men's club. (The couple also maintained a separate New York apartment for those occasions when Irene could escape Hollywood for a holiday with him.)

Be that as it may, *The Silver Cord* was a critical and commercial success. (Acclaimed period baseball star Lou Gehrig even took his own clinging mother to the picture, just prior to his own marriage.) No small part of the picture's popularity, as well as that of Dunne's other period melodramas, was how handsomely they were staged. Recognition of this phenomenon was part of *Variety*'s critique of *The Silver Cord*: "[The] film is in every way adequate on the production side with well built and convincing sets, good lighting and photography and direction which adds much to the value of the adaptation of the story."[11]

Dunne's performance, moreover, struck its own sort of "cord" with viewers. *New York Daily News* critic Kate Cameron reported, "Her determination to leave the husband she loves rather than submit to the galling yoke about to be placed about her and [husband] David by the latter's mother draws a sympathetic response from the audience."[12] Still, the top-billed actress was somewhat upstaged in the movie by the set-chewing performance of Laura Hope Crews as the domineering mother—a figure the *New York Post* described as "altogether poisonous," with the *Chicago Tribune* even suggesting, "You could kill her."[13] An added factor in Crews' movie-stealing favor was she had already played her part to acclaim on stage, where the role had been allowed to be even more dominant.

Back in her adopted home state of Indiana shortly after the release of *The Silver Cord*, the actress confessed to the *Indianapolis Star* that, "She would have preferred not to have been starred in her latest picture, 'The Silver Cord' . . . since the stellar role really is in the hands of Laura Hope Crew, the veteran character actress."[14] But in true Dunne fashion she spoke highly of her costars especially Frances Dee, the other daughter-in-law victimized by Crew's character. And consistent with this thoughtfulness, Irene went out of her way during this brief 1933 Hoosier visit to meet with Dee's father, a local Indianapolis businessman. The *Star* article also revealed both a heartland take on her melodramatic persona, and the fact that Dunne was chafing at her nonstop casting in this genre: "She has suffered untold mental tortures as the downtrodden woman, wife or mistress, and she is eager to be lively and gay—and her own age again."[15]

Be that as it may, the actress' next outing was in yet another melodrama—*Ann Vickers*. But as if in concession to Irene, this was one weepy in which she was the uncontested lead. In this ambitious adaptation of the Lewis novel, her title character is asked to handle more tasks than a traditional host of women's picture heroines. Once again, her character has a messy personal life which she soldiers through nobly, from abandonment by one lover (resulting in a child out of wedlock), to her later involvement with a married judge (Walter Huston). While this would be more than enough material for most melodramas, it was just part of the *Ann Vickers* storyline.

The fickle lover and the subsequent death of their child turn her character, for a time, against all men. Purposely losing herself in the challenging work of prison social worker, she turns reformer with a best-selling book exposing the brutal conditions in this penal institution. Huston's charismatic judge brings her back to the society of man but not without the aforementioned controversy of adultery. One should hasten to add that such controversial 1933 material was still acceptable before Hollywood reluctantly embraced a more stringent censorship policy in 1934. By this time Dunne was a melodrama machine and her reviews reflected the status of this actor as an icon of the genre. The *New York Daily News* waxed most poetic about the actress, stating her "interpretation of Ann is a beautiful performance. She makes the positive honesty and the capability of Ann shine through her purpose to life and she also makes one feel the underlying vigor of the girl."[16] *Variety* called it a "fine performance," while the *New York Herald Tribune* posited that Dunne "suggests the Ann

Vickers of the novel as well as any actress in Hollywood possibly could."[17]

Next up on Dunne's melodrama marathon was *If I Were Free* (1933), with both she and love interest Clive Brook stuck in dead-end marriages. Both parties reject suicide after a chance meeting in Paris. But their difficulties in disentangling themselves from problematic unions then eat up much of the screen time. Critics credited the thin storyline with working by way of the "capable manner in which they [Dunne and Brook] . . . hold it together. Less skilled performers would have made 'If I Were Free' much less acceptable screen fare."[18]

What made doing yet another melodrama palatable, beyond her ongoing professionalism, was that Dunne was soon to get a brief melodrama reprieve. Though her next picture was also a weepy, *This Man Is Mine* (1934), there is a scene with Bellamy near the close that anticipates the broad comedy of their later teamings in *The Awful Truth* (1937) and *Lady in a Jam* (1942). The *This Man Is Mine* moment in question has Dunne crowning him with a painting—payback for his roving eye—prior to their reconciliation. More central to this melodrama respite, however, was the fact that *This Man Is Mine* was quickly followed by her reteaming with *Cimarron* costar Richard Dix in *Stingaree* (1934). This critical and commercial success mixed a swashbuckling Australian Robin Hood with Dunne's opera star.

While this would hardly break the actress' ties to the melodrama, Irene's musical numbers in *Stingaree* paralleled the mid-1930s revival of the Hollywood musical. And RKO had a vested interest in the comeback of the genre. Besides never having fully utilized musical star Irene Dunne, RKO had just stumbled upon what would soon be the most celebrated duo in the history of the genre—Fred Astaire and Ginger Rogers. Fortuitously but briefly teamed in *Flying Down to Rio* (1933), acclaimed producer Pandro S. Berman soon realized the studio had something special in this couple. He went on to produce the rest of their critical and commercial 1930s hits together, including *Roberta* (1935, with Dunne being top billed).

In a 1975 interview, Berman shared with me two personal goals he had for the RKO musical. First, as essentially the architect of the Astaire and Rogers movie, he attempted to mold them in the zany tradition of the then-emerging screwball comedy.[19] This affectionate spoof of romantic comedy, now forever associated with such pivotal period films as *It Happened One Night*, *Twentieth Century*, and *The*

Thin Man (all 1934), gave the women more of a power position than had previously been the norm in comically romantic battles of the sexes. Why this is important, with relationship to Dunne, is that prior to her screwball *Theodora Goes Wild*, no one (including the actress) gave Irene much credit for knowing anything about this genre. (This will be further addressed in the next chapter.)

Berman was very taken with Dunne's talents, having produced two of her early RKO pictures, *Symphony of Six Million* (1932) and *Ann Vickers*. The former movie was especially memorable for him, since it was the initial film he produced for the studio, after being first RKO's chief film editor, and then a special assistant to key producers William Le Baron (an early RKO mentor for Irene) and David O. Selznick. Given this background, Berman's second goal, which did *not* seem to parallel those of the RKO hierarchy, was to utilize Dunne's musical gifts whenever possible. (Parent studios can often get in a creative rut. Or, in this case, a melodramatic rut.) Consequently, following the musically-oriented *Stingaree*, three of the actress' next five films were musicals—Warner Brothers' *Sweet Adeline* (1935), Berman's *Roberta*, and Universal's big-budget production of *Show Boat* (1936). The exceptions were RKO's own large-scale adaptation of Wharton's melodramatic novel, *The Age of Innocence*, and Universal's now classic weepy, *Magnificent Obsession*.

While the latter picture was a critical and commercial hit (see previous chapter), *Innocence* proved a harder sell with both critics and the public. Though not without its champions, such as a *New York Daily News* review entitled "'Age of Innocence' Charmingly Filmed," *Variety* seemingly spoke for more of the critical establishment: a "cream puff of the Mid-Victorian era . . . artistically made but dull. Its box office potentialities are questionable."[20] But the Teflon Dunne, as was her habit, still managed to draw critical kudos. The *New York Herald* called her "splendid and helpful in the part," while the *New York Times* found her "effective," yet not enough to save a flawed film.[21] If *Innocence* had, however, a saving grace for the countless fans of melodrama, it was the reuniting of favored figures of the genre. For instance, Irene's love interest in the picture was played by John Boles, her costar from the celebrated *Back Street*. Plus, *Innocence* also featured Dunne's nemesis from *The Silver Cord*, Laura Hope Crews, in another variation of her frightening mother persona.

Quite possibly, the less-than-stellar performance of *Innocence* with critics helped fuel the push to place Dunne back in the genre which initially brought her to the movies—the musical. This breakthrough, with *Sweet Adeline*, was not lost on period reviewers. For example, the *New York Herald Tribune* opened its rave critique by noting, "Miss Irene Dunne, who originally was summoned to Hollywood because she was a singer, is at last given an opportunity to sing on the screen."[22] The *New York Times*, after praising the production's Jerome Kern and Oscar Hammerstein music, credited Dunne with "adjusting her cool and pleasant soprano" to such memorable romantic songs as "Here I Am," "Don't Ever Leave Me," "Why Was I Born?," "It Was Not So Long Ago," and "We Were So Very Young."[23] *Variety* placed *Sweet Adeline* in "the big-time musical class," while the *New York Post* was so impressed with Dunne's performance the critic even attributed what now seem to be unrealistic superlatives to her appearance: she "is, pictorially, the kind of heroine you would expect in a romantic comedy of the 1890s."[24]

Given the mid-1930s time period in which *Sweet Adeline* was made, today Dunne's role as a 1890s torch singer is more likely to conjure up images of Mae West, who put her signature on both the period and the part in movies like *She Done Him Wrong* (1933) and *Belle of the Nineties* (1934). Not surprisingly, some of Irene's *Sweet Adeline* reviews actually mentioned Mae West.[25] But in yet another tribute to Dunne's performing versatility, she does *not* suffer by such comparisons.

Sweet Adeline was then followed by an even bigger musical comedy success—Berman's *Roberta*, teaming Dunne with Astaire and Rogers. The picture generated the kind of reviews one might have attributed to the performer's parents, with the *New York World Telegram*'s William Boehnel probably best capturing the period's colloquially fun take on the production: *Roberta* is "the last word in musical comedy entertainment—one of those 'drop everything: you've got to see it at once' films that pop up now and then."[26] The more businesslike *Variety* simply stated the basics—"Fast, smart, good looking and tuneful. It rates as box office on entertainment alone but there are Fred Astaire, Irene Dunne, and Ginger Rogers on top of the title to make it that much easier."[27]

As is often the case with films embraced as instant classics, period critics occasionally felt the need to document viewers' responses. Thus, the *New York Daily News*' Kate Cameron reported, "Irene Dunne's singing of 'Lovely to Look At' . . . drew spontaneous applause from the audience and she looked as lovely as the new Kern song sounded."[28] Though the reviews were unanimously good for all the principals, the top-billed Dunne had to face the fact that Astaire and Rogers generated the lion's share of the movie's critical coverage. The 1935 release date for *Roberta* was Astaire and Rogers' box office breakout—the first of three successive years in which they placed in the industry's annual Top Ten box office poll.[29] Dunne, like many other period favorites (such as Carole Lombard, or Jean Arthur), was never quite able to crack that elusive top ten. Interestingly enough, *Roberta* also had an Indiana story connection—a former football player (Randolph Scott) comes to Paris with his friend's Hoosier jazz band, only to inherit his devoted aunt's dress company. (Early on, the band also plays an entertaining rendition of "Back Home Again In Indiana.") Of course, in the best Hollywood "lala land" tradition, the real Hoosier (Dunne) plays *Princess* Stephanie, who also doubles as Scott's love interest and a master fashion designer. But then as the saying goes, "comedy [musical or otherwise] never claimed to be brain surgery."

A provocative final footnote to the film is how its smash release (March 1935) paralleled the opening of director Leo McCarey's equally successful *Ruggles of Red Gap*, a comic Western which mixes elements of populism and screwball comedy. McCarey would, of course, soon become both a close Dunne friend and her most influential director/producer. *Roberta* and *Ruggles* were such simultaneous hits that references to each of the movies frequently appeared in the same reviews. Irene was later on record as stating this was the beginning of her taking note of McCarey.[30] Though no specific critiques were cited, the *New York Daily News'* *Roberta* coverage would be a prime candidate for this catalyst:

> While the male population of New York is traipsing over to the Paramount Theatre to howl itself hoarse over the acting of Charles Laughton in "Ruggles of Red Gap," the women of the town are forming a long queue outside of the Music Hall waiting for their chance to get in to see . . . "Roberta."[31]

But the *Daily News* did not have a corner on this joint recognition. For example, the *New York Times'* *Roberta* review mentioned, in passing, "Now that Charles Laughton and 'Ruggles of Red Gap' have set the 1935 standard for screen comedy . . . [*Roberta* has] established a model for lavishness, grace and humor in the musical film."[32] One must also remember that Irene was an auteurist [putting the director first] years before that philosophy was generally recognized. And the key clause for the actress in her film contracts involved having approval of the director.

For all *Roberta*'s critical acclaim, Dunne's greatest musical comedy recognition would come with her next outing in the genre, the 1936 adaptation of *Show Boat*. This memorable movie will be addressed at length in the next chapter, which also keys upon what a notable (personally and professionally) year 1936 would be for the actress. But before closing this examination of Irene's largely melodrama-directed career up until the mid-1930s, a brief window into her private world is provided, in large part, by a 1933 trip to her Hoosier hometown of Madison.

This was her first visit back in seven years and followed several weeks with her husband in New York City, where he still maintained his dental practice. As was her habit, she always tried to get away for an East Coast marital rendezvous after the completion of a movie, just as he would come west at least twice a year. Besides missing what she called her "home folks," in making the Madison stop she had been fueled by a desire to see an aunt, Mrs. Charles Peters, and to catch up with several old high school friends.[33] One of these school chums, Mrs. J. F. Butts, then hosted a reception where the actress said "I love Madison . . . I believe that my career in pictures has meant more to me . . . because I came from this . . . [small] town. If I had been born and reared in New York, it wouldn't have meant so much."[34]

Long before Thomas Wolfe's famous novel, *You Can't Go Home Again* (1940), Dunne was showing the plus side of just such visits. They also allowed her to proverbially "let her hair down." Whereas her restrained 1930s manner with major mainstream publications sometimes had her being tagged "Icy Irene," or the "Sphinx of Hollywood," she seemed poignantly direct with Hoosier print journalists from Indianapolis and Madison.[35] For instance, Dunne shared more frustration about the difficulties of a bicoastal marriage than was the norm from past national articles: "she frankly admits that parting for her still is sweet sorrow and that the long periods of separation . . . are irksome to her."[36]

In another article from this 1933 Hoosier visit the local reporter "read" the actress as very much missing her husband; "as she talked, her eyes strayed to a portrait of him on her [hotel] desk."[37] Eventually, the piece revealed this was a new photo of Dr. Griffin, which Dunne had persisted in keeping out during her New York visit, to the point of it not being packed for her return to Hollywood—"And I had to bring it whether I just put the picture in a small suit box and dashed to the [train] station, box and picture safely under my arm."[38] This sample of sentimental affection is consistent with her later admission about her husband that "I had never been so attracted to anyone, myself, at a first meeting."[39]

Irene's 1933 Indiana stopover also revealed her to be anxious to return to musical comedy, "which suits me very nicely, for I do really like the musical. . . . That is really what I expected to do [in film] but many of my pictures have been heavy drama, like 'Cimarron' and 'Back Street.'"[40] Still, despite Dunne's frequent separations from her husband and a film climate which did not always allow the actress to embrace her genre of choice (the musical), reading these 1933 travel pieces on this Hollywood Hoosier does paint a rather idyllic life, especially in the midst of the Great Depression. For instance, one such article documented Irene's extended New York holiday with her husband, adding, "She plans to leave Madison tomorrow and will go to the World's Fair in Chicago for a few days before returning to Hollywood and work on her new picture."[41] Coupled with an annual six-figure salary well in excess of what Babe Ruth (America's then most celebrated athlete) was making, this former small-town girl was truly living the good life. And in 1936 things would get even better!

NOTES

1. Sonia Lee, "Discovering the Glamour in Irene Dunne," *Motion Picture Story Magazine*, March 1937, 78.

2. Ibid.

3. John McDonough, "Screening a Star: A Rare Interview with Irene Dunne," *Chicago Tribune*, May 12, 1985, sec. 13, p. 8.

4. Review of *No Other Woman*, *Variety*, January 31, 1933.

5. Helen Fay Ludlam, "Nucleus," *Silver Screen*, July 1933, 62.

6. Richard Watts, Jr., "'The Secret of Mme Blanche'—Capitol," *New York Herald Tribune*, February 4, 1933, 6.

7. Review of *The Secret of Madame Blanche*, *Variety*, February 7, 1933.

8. Irene Thirer, "'Madame Blanche' a Tear Jerker at the Capitol," New York Daily News, February 4, 1933, 22; Mordaunt Hall, review of *The Secret of Madame Blanche*, *New York Times*, February 4, 1933, 11.

9. Kate Cameron, "'The Silver Cord' Faithfully Filmed," *New York Daily News*, May 5, 1933, 58.

10. Virginia Maxwell, "'Don't Live with Your Mother-in-law' says Irene Dunne," *Photoplay*, September 1933, 100.

11. Review of *The Silver Cord*, *Variety*, May 9, 1933.

12. Kate Cameron, "'The Silver Cord' Faithfully Filmed."

13. "New Films on Broadway," *New York Post*, May 5, 1933, 12; Mae Tinee, "Tyranny of a Mother's Love Shown in Films, "*Chicago Tribune*, June 11, 1933, sec. 10, p. 1.

14. Corbin Patrick, "Irene Dunne Comes to Indianapolis," *Indianapolis Star*, June 6, 1933, 5.

15. Ibid.

16. Kate Cameron, "Irene Dunne Shines As Lewis's Heroine," *New York Daily News*, September 29, 1933, 48.

17. Review of *Ann Vickers*, *Variety*, October 10, 1933; Richard Watts, Jr., "'Ann Vickers'—Radio City Music Hall," *New York Herald Tribune*, September 29, 1933, 14.

18. Review of *If I Were Free*, *Variety* (January 9, 1934).

19. Pandro S. Berman, interview by the author, Hillcrest Country Club, Beverly Hills, California (June 1975), author's files.

20. Kate Cameron, "'Age of Innocence' Charmingly Filmed," *New York Daily News*, October 19, 1934, 60; Review of *Age of Innocence*, *Variety*, October 23, 1934.

21. Richard Watts, Jr., "'The Age of Innocence'—Radio City Music Hall," *New York Herald Tribune*, October 19, 1934, 16; Review of *The Age of Innocence*, *New York Times*, October 19, 1934, 27.

22. Richard Watts, Jr., "'Sweet Adeline'—Paramount," *New York Herald Tribune*, January 7, 1935, 8.

23. Review of *Sweet Adeline*, *New York Times*, January 7, 1935, 13.

24. Review of *Sweet Adeline*, *Variety*, January 8, 1935; Thornton Delehanty, Review of *Sweet Adeline*, *New York Post*, January 7, 1935.

25. For example, see the previous review from the *New York Post*.

26. William Boehnel, "'Roberta' Is a 'Must' if You Like Astaire," *New York World Telegram*, March 8, 1935, 31.

27. Review of *Roberta*, *Variety*, March 13, 1935.

28. Kate Cameron, "'Roberta' Scores a Second Hit as Film," *New York Daily News*, March 8, 1935, 56.

29. Cobbett Steinberg, *Real Facts: The Movie Book of Records* (New York: Vintage Books, 1978), 404.

30. Irene Dunne, telephone interview by the author, Los Angeles (June 1975), author's files.

31. Cameron, "'Roberta' Scores a Second Hit as Film."

32. Andre Sennwald, Review of *Roberta*, *New York Times*, March 8, 1935, 25.

33. "Irene Dunne to Appear on Local Stage Tonight," *Madison Courier*, June 6, 1933, 1.

34. Ibid.

35. George Shea, "Irene Dunne," *Northwest Orient*, December 1985, 30. There is a 1941 film of Dunne and fellow Hollywood Hoosier Will Hays made for an Indianapolis banquet that UCLA has preserved.

36. Patrick, 5.

37. "Madison, Ind., Her Birthplace [sic], Still Is Home for Irene Dunne," *Indianapolis News*, June 5, 1933, sec. 2, p. 1.

38. Ibid.

39. William French, "Untold Stories of Loves That Have Lasted," *Motion Picture Story Magazine*, January 1935, 84.

40. "Irene Dunne to Appear on Local Stage Tonight," 3.

41. Ibid.

FIVE

The Most Memorable of Years—Dunne's 1936

She [Dunne] who used to be so prompt is now rarely on time. The studios are thinking of writing Missy [adopted daughter Mary Frances] a letter. . . . "She's decidedly my best audience."[1]

—Irene Dunne

Of the many unique Dunne events of 1936, nothing would compare to the adoption of the actress' only child. Found through a New York City adoption agency, "[Mary Frances] arrived in Hollywood just in time to help her parents celebrate their first Christmas in their new home in Holmby Hills, a Beverly Hills suburb."[2] Yes, coupled with the addition of a baby girl, the year's additional double whammy of joy was that the actress' husband was giving up his New York medical practice to permanently move west to join Irene in their new Hollywood home.

After a long-distance marriage which stretched back to 1930, five factors figured in Dr. Griffin's move. First, once the couple acted on the baby, it was a foregone conclusion that Frank would want to be around on a permanent basis. Second, the doctor turned fifty in 1936 and his eyesight was not what it once had been. The timing was right to leave his New York practice. Third, with each passing year Dunne was becoming a bigger star, and it was increasingly difficult for her husband to manage the actress' growing portfolio from New York, especially with his talent for buying Los Angeles real estate. Fourth, Irene was tired of the press' ongoing theory that the couple was on the brink of divorce. For instance, when she returned to Hollywood from New York and her periodic visits with Dr. Griffin, the actress was regularly asked if there would be a Reno (Nevada) divorce.[3]

Fifth and finally, after over half a decade apart, the couple simply missed each other. Years later, after Dunne was widowed (1965), she sometimes said her only regret in life was in not getting Frank to California earlier. Their obvious devotion to each other was in marked contrast to other high-profile performers then in long-distance marriages. For example, her 1930s Hollywood contemporary Marlene Dietrich had a husband, Paramount studio executive Rudolph Seiber, who lived in Paris. While Dietrich described the arrangement as a "perfect" working marriage, it was really what was once called a "victorian divorce"—where both partners essentially lived separate lives with significant others.[4]

If the greatest joy of 1936 was bringing a baby into their new California home, the year's one note of sadness was the loss of Dunne's mother (December 17, 1936) to two cerebral hemorrhages. The first occurred after a Christmas shopping trip, just as she returned to her daughter's home. Dunne and her husband immediately called their neighbor, Dr. Joel Pressman (husband of actress Claudette Colbert), who administered emergency treatment. A second doctor was soon summoned but Adelaide slipped into a coma, dying of a second stroke early the next morning. Though only sixty-five, she had been weakened by a fall the previous year. Still, Adelaide's death came as a shock to the family. Irene was especially shaken, given that her mother had been the actress' almost constant companion, including the years Dr. Griffin lived in New York. Happily, she had lived long enough to meet her new granddaughter. Not surprisingly, this made Missy all the more precious to Dunne, as if the baby was some sort of heavenly replacement for her mother. (With both of the actress' parents passing prematurely, at this point Dunne assumed she would probably die young, too. Ironically, she would live past ninety.) Adelaide's death was also an added catalyst for the actress to make Mary Frances' upbringing less rigorous than her own had been, with regard to voice and piano lessons. Of course, as the old saying goes, "the fruit doesn't fall far from the tree"—Dunne's Christmas gift to her *baby* daughter that first year was a piano! (That is, Adelaide's greatest gift, besides mentor her daughter, was as a pianist, while the actress' most prized possession was the concert grand piano showcased in her new oversized living room.)

With comic irony, Dunne would later claim the only drawback to her husband coming West was that it deprived the actress of her own private Hollywood/New York double life. But a 1935 *Motion*

Picture Story Magazine article better fleshes out her take on bicoastal variety: "When I tire of being Irene Dunne of Hollywood, I can become a totally different [New York] person with different ideas, behavior, occupations, and even appearance. It isn't everybody who can take a vacation from herself!"[5]

Though it was not quite on a par with a baby, or a husband in the same time zone, the actress was elated to finally have a permanent Beverly Hills home. The interior décor of this nine-room white brick Mediterranean-style house (with a red tile roof) was defined by grille work, archways, Oriental rugs, heavy wooden furniture, and velvet drapes. As one visitor described the setting—it "seemed the background for a smoldering-eyed Latin, instead of the cool, slim, poised loveliness of Irene Dunne."[6]

What became a standard setting for her interviews, a sunroom done in yellow and white, seemed a better fit for an auburn-haired gardener who also just happened to be a movie star. Dunne loved the flowering grounds, from which one could see the Pacific Ocean in the distance. There was a terrace, patios, gardens, fountains, and tropical flowers making "brilliant splashes of color against white walls."[7] But just as she was not the standard star, there was not a swimming pool or a tennis court in sight. On-grounds exercise was limited to practicing her golf shots (Irene's scores were in the 80s) and walking their police dog—"Colonel." This special sanctuary, which Dunne had helped design, was everything she had dreamed of. It would be home for the rest of her life—well over fifty years.

The actress' personal joys in 1936 were matched by her professional accomplishments—both *Show Boat* and *Theodora Goes Wild* were huge critical and commercial successes. But *Show Boat* was a less-than-pleasant production experience for Irene. For Dunne this was one of the great ironies of her acting career. That is, *Show Boat* was a sacred property for her. Irene's acclaim in an earlier road show stage production of *Show Boat* had made her theatrical career and resulted in a ticket to Hollywood. Consequently, this was a property in which she very much wanted to reprise her central role of Magnolia.

The resulting tension, however, during the production of the 1936 *Show Boat* was a result of Universal assigning English director James Whale to megaphone the film. This was the most controversial of choices, given that Whale (both then and now) is associated with such classic horror movies as *Frankenstein* (1931), *The Old Dark House* (1932) *The Invisible Man* (1933), and *The Bride of Frankenstein* (1935).

Hurt by criticism over his selection, and sensing similar feelings among a veteran cast (many of whom had appeared in *Show Boat* stage productions), Whale foolishly vented his frustration on these actors. In a pre-shoot speech Whale said, "You all have played this before, and you all have your ideas of how it should be played. I want you to forget whatever ideas you have, because I will interpret, through you, my conception of each role."[8] Naturally, there was instant resentment. Dunne later observed,

> James Whale wasn't the right director. He was more interested in at-mosphere and lighting and he knew so little about that [Southern riverboat] life. I could have put my foot down about it [her contract gave her director approval] but there would have been no reason to do so because we had so many of the original [*Show Boat* stage cast] peo-ple that you could only expect the best. I knew the whole thing back-wards.[9]

Whale as director was not the only source of *Show Boat* frustration and stress. Dunne, who had signed a three-picture deal with Uni-versal in 1935, was late becoming available for *Show Boat*. Produc-tion delays on *Magnificent Obsession*, the first of her Universal films, kept her from the *Show Boat* shoot until December 1935. Plus, the studio was in financial straits, with founder Carl Laemmle (and his son, Carl Laemmle Jr.) on the verge of being forced out. And finally, this was one of the, if not *the*, most ambitious productions Universal had ever taken on. *Show Boat* was a major drain on both the studio's ready cash and available manpower.

Dunne's instinct to trust in the innate talent of the cast and not replace Whale was a wise decision. The name *Show Boat* veterans included Charles Winninger as Cap'n Andy, Paul Robeson as Joe, Helen Morgan as Julie, and Allan Jones as Ravenal. Other now prominent performers were Donald Cook, Hattie McDaniel, and Eddie Anderson. But what Whale detractors did not anticipate was the director's determination to both make up for his ill-timed open-ing comments and demonstrate his versatility by creating a memo-rable movie which was *not* a horror film.

Dunne's desire to refilm *Show Boat* went beyond her belief in the in-herent professionalism of the cast. First, the property was something she had dreamed about appearing in as a movie since she had starred in the stage production. Second, the actress had periodically been promised just such an opportunity ever since she had come to Hollywood. The last abortive attempt to make the movie occurred in 1933, when Dunne had been set to star for Universal opposite period singing sensation Russ Columbo, with the gifted romantic director Frank Borzage scheduled to direct. In fact, part of Irene's frustration with Whale was probably an outgrowth of her disappointment at not being able to work with Borzage, whom she both admired and felt was more suited for *Show Boat*. Third, without trying to be crass, the film represented a major payday for the actress—$100,000. No matter how artistically driven one is, and Dunne certainly qualified along these lines, this was an amazing Depression-era salary. (The standard farm laborer at this time could expect to receive a dollar a day.)

Though not widely known at the time, the English Whale was a major student of American history, particularly the mid-nineteenth-century Mississippi riverboat perspective showcased in *Show Boat*. Coupling this knowledge with his drive to establish himself outside of the horror genre ultimately proved to be a positive influence on this second screen adaptation of *Show Boat*. (The initial 1929 attempt had been marred by occurring during Hollywood's awkward transition to sound.) Whale's efforts, in part, were greatly assisted by the collaborative nature of his interaction with the great Paul Robeson. Both the director and the actor became major fans of each other. And while Robeson's rendition of "Ol' Man River" remained the single most electrifying scene in the 1936 *Show Boat* (just as it had been in any stage production with which he had been involved), Whale's staging of this song was considered the most cinematic segment of the movie.

These Whale pluses notwithstanding, there remained a decided chill in Dunne's behavior toward the director. Deciding to trust in her *Show Boat* background, Whale avoided any further conflicts with the actress. Despite his abrasive opening remarks, he tended to defer to top-billed Irene's interpretation of Magnolia. For instance, at the movie's close Whale acquiesced to Dunne's decision to minimize the aging process for her character, beyond the obligatory graying of her hair. Of course, another Whale "reading" might simply be that the director was so overwhelmed with his first million-dollar-plus production that he was only too happy to let many of the various performers fall back on their past *Show Boat* stage experiences.

The prolonged shoot concluded March 11, 1936, two weeks over schedule, which made the production approximately $400,000 over budget. Part of the overrun was a result of three weeks of rain in February. But at a time when many directors, such as John Ford and

Leo McCarey "edited in the camera" (shot little excessive footage), Whale had exposed over fifty hours of film. And when April callbacks were required, Dunne and other cast members were convinced Whale had fumbled his directing assignment. But while the shoot and reshoot was an ongoingly stressful situation, the end product was a metaphorical home run.

The critics were downright reverential towards the picture, with the *New York Times* proclaiming "We have reason to be grateful to Hollywood this morning, for it has restored to us Edna Ferber's Mississippi River classic, 'Show Boat.'"[10] The *New York World-Telegram*'s equally magnanimous review also found time to salute Dunne's first screen classic, 1931's *Cimarron*: "Universal has done right by our great American classic—'Show Boat' . . . a grand pageant of song, sentiment, and loamy nationalism—the finest piece of filmic folklore since 'Cimarron.'"[11] *Variety* correctly predicted the movie's ultimately huge box office success: "'Show Boat' . . . is a smash film-musical. A cinch for big grosses, from the deluxers [theaters] down."[12] The *New York Sun* seconded this notion, with the opening of its review documenting viewer joy: "Yesterday, before a properly appreciative audience, 'Show Boat' returned to the town that loved it so well." And the *Sun* critique credited Whale's take on the story as even superior to the Broadway play—"his is the third version of Edna Ferber's popular story [preceded by the stage play and the flawed 1929 screen adaptation]; right at the moment it seems by far the best."[13]

Of course, the previously maligned Whale was probably more taken with the following *Sun* comment: "They have made no mistakes this time. James Whale, although an English director, has caught the spirit, the musical comedy spirit . . . of the Mississippi water front."[14] And trade publication *Daily Variety* even mixed its affectionate praise with a touch of comedy: "Result looks as if Whale had been born on the Mississippi."[15]

Whale's critical raves were only matched by the kudos for Dunne. Positives for Irene's performance were often coupled with her *Show Boat* stage pedigree. For instance, the *New York Daily News*, calling her voice "sweet and clear," went on to say, "Dunne is the lovely Magnolia . . . entirely at home in the role which she played all up and down these United States in the No. 1 road company of the Ziegfeld production."[16] In later years the only revisionist knock against Dunne's Magnolia was that the then thirty-seven-year-old actress was too old to play a teenager during the movie's early scenes. But there were no such reservations by period critics. For example, *Variety* observed, "Irene Dunne maintains the illusion of her Magnolia throughout— from her own secluded girlhood; into sudden stardom on the Cotton Blossom [riverboat]; and later, as a more mature artist."[17]

For the student of Dunne's later comedies, the real *Show Boat* eye- opener would be the humorous touches she brings to her Magnolia performance. These amusing nuances include her comic shuffle while singing "Birds Gotta Fly," the mischievous laugh later so syn- onymous with her screwball roles, and ultimately Irene's entertain- ing dance while singing the comic song "Been Galavantin' Around." Unfortunately, the latter routine is now very politically incorrect; Dunne does the number in blackface. But if one can get past this red flag, which a historian has to do, the actress' seemingly sudden emer- gence as a screwball comedy star later that year (with 1936's *Theodora Goes Wild*) is hardly the surprise some period critics made it out to be.

By the time Irene began production on *Theodora Goes Wild*, more- over, she could hardly have had any lingering reservations about playing comedy. One has only to read several of the *Show Boat* re- views found in the actress' own scrapbooks (now housed at the University of Southern California's Cinema and Television Library) to believe she felt ready to take on a totally funny film.[18] For exam- ple, her scrapbook *Screen Play* review said, Dunne "turns out to be quite something as a comedienne,"while a carefully pasted *Screen Book Magazine* critique entertainingly observed, "her comedy antics came as a delightful surprise, the goofy dance drawing gales of laughter."[19] Other similar scrapbook notices included both *Screen- land*'s plug, "wait until you see Miss Dunne, the dignified [actress] going into a low-down shuffle!," and the *Hollywood Reporter*'s rave, "Besides the blackface routine, she breaks into a shuffle that is a howl."[20]

Of course, one could call *Show Boat* an amalgam of several genres. Not only did Dunne excel at song and dance and comedy, the prop- erty had a healthy dose of melodrama, especially in relationship to Irene's character. As if back in the land of weepies, her Magnolia has yet another love interest leave her high and dry with a child, only to have him turn up at the end of a long involved story, à la the conclu- sion to *Cimarron*. Plus, in Dunne's eyes, *Show Boat* even offered her a bit of Shakespeare's *Romeo and Juliet!* The actress had always wanted to play the balcony scene, which she felt her first meeting of *Show Boat*'s Ravernal (Allan Jones) approximated—where she leans over

the top deck of the ship and throws a rose to her river Romeo "Then,"
she later laughed:

> [I]nstead of the classic lines of the Bard, Allan Jones and I burst into a
> Jerry Kern song! But it is a beautiful love scene, and Allan and I put our
> hearts (and lungs) into it with as much earnestness as if we had really
> been doing a Shakespearean play.[21]

Show Boat also continued another Dunne professional accomplishment;
it opened at America's then number one movie showcase—New York's
Radio City Music Hall. (During Hollywood's golden age of the 1930s
and early 1940s more Dunne features premiered there than those of any
other actress.) On this occasion Irene was also on hand the night of the
opening. But in a *New York Times* interview/article shortly after this
gala, the actress was quick to point out the appearance was merely a
lucky coincidence. That is, she had already been in New York to visit
her husband. That was what really brought her east.

This *Times* piece, entertainingly entitled "Magnolia of the
Movies," covered an assortment of topics, from connections between
her childhood and the subject of *Show Boat*, to various theatrical
superstitions that still bothered the actress. For instance, "she firmly
believes that if a touring company passes a cemetery on the left on
the way to an engagement, the show is certain to have an early closing."[22] (*Show Boat* opened so strong one might have thought there
were no unlucky cemeteries to pass anywhere in New York, regardless of which side of the street you were on.) The most refreshing
aspect of the interview, however, was when Dunne corrected several
Universal press kit errors for *Times* author John T. McManus,
including the claim that her father was a lawyer and the misinformation that she had been raised to follow him into the courtroom.
Of all her contemporaries, Irene was easily the most driven to be
honestly direct about her life.

In the flamboyant 1930s the more typical norm was to be entertaining copy, instead of boringly truthful. For instance, in 1930 Lombard made a film, *Fast and Loose* (1930), in which her screen credit
permanently changed from Carol to Carole. Numerous explanations
have been given for the spelling change, including the studio's story
that it was an outgrowth of the starlet's interest in numerology (derived from her mother). Lombard later, off the record, refuted this:
"That's a lot of bunk. But since they're paying me so well, I don't
care how they spell my name."[23] The truth, of course, was a great

deal less fanciful—there was simply a spelling error made on the poster material by Paramount's marketing department! But this way the press kit boys had an entertainingly offbeat story for the public.

Well, this was the kind of thing (fabrications) for which Dunne had little time, other than the standard tendency of actresses to fudge on their age. This honesty sometimes hurt her image among magazine authors. As Irene observed in 1935, "You know what interviewers always say about me—*'a nice sensible woman but such bad copy.'"*[24] Through the years this has also been interpreted to mean her personal life was much too normal, as well. Still, as with the aforementioned *New York Times* piece on Dunne and *Show Boat*, her set-the-record-straight persona could also be perceived as refreshingly unique in an era largely populated with beloved hucksterish types, such as Carole Lombard, or baseball's Dizzy Dean.

Having established this straight-arrow Irene trait, so significant for a greater understanding of the actress, one must briefly backpedal on the phenomenon with regard to one incident involving *Show Boat* and her 1936 follow-up film, *Theodora Goes Wild*. That is, earlier in the text, it was noted that Dunne was so fearful of playing screwball comedy in *Theodora* that she and her husband fled to Europe to avoid the assignment. Needless to say, this is a dramatically excellent statement about a kind of performance anxiety. But the story now seems like a rare example of the actress actually tweaking her material for better copy.

That is, after *Show Boat*'s May premiere in New York, she sailed to England for the film's June 10 London opening. Was this PR trip the aforementioned European getaway to avoid a new comedy genre? In Dunne's defense, maybe she lingered overseas hoping Columbia would assign someone else to *Theodora*. But since this comedy started shooting in late summer, Dunne's *Show Boat* junket is undoubtedly the same trip referred to earlier. Regardless, the fact that Irene would embellish this story should simply underline the actress' initial fears of screwball comedy.

In the context of that eccentric genre (screwball comedy) this particular European sojourn had a schizophrenic air to it. For instance, stateside coverage of Dunne's trip had the actress explaining the voyage as research for her anticipated future role as Madame Curie.[25] But upon her landing in Britain, the London papers stated the obvious— "She took this trip just to be at the first night of her 'Show Boat' picture last night."[26] Indeed, one dockside banner greeting Irene and the other *Queen Mary* passengers (which included *Show Boat* director James Whale) even punningly observed, "Welcome to the Two 'Show Boats.'"[27] However, later reporting back home treated the whole trip as simply more of a vacation for the actress—"I love sea voyages. You get such a lovely sense of peace and rest."[28]

Regardless, the film opened to great critical acclaim and long lines at the London box office. Not surprisingly, this gala event was treated as a special tribute to British director Whale. Following the movie's premiere there was a star-studded dinner in his honor at London's Dorchester Hotel, marking the apogee of his career. Though less than a fan of Whale, Dunne was gracious enough to attend the invitation-only gathering, diplomatically observing of the director, "He received great acclaim."[29] Besides Dunne, other special guests included actors Paul Robeson, Jack Buchanan, and Sir Cedric Hardwicke. Plus, there were special congratulations from both the new chairman of Universal Pictures, J. Cheever Cowdin, and the company's new president, Robert H. Cochrane—each via transatlantic hookup from New York.

Paradoxically, despite a generally strong critical and commercial British response to *Show Boat*, the prestigious *London Times* struggled to even give the picture a mixed review. And as if playing into the Whale-Dunne differences, the director was not even mentioned in the critique, and the only thing the *Times* consistently found winning was the performance of Dunne: "Without . . . [her] most tactful accomplishment the process of adaptation would be much harder than it is. There is a subdued and ironical wit . . . and her mock innocence is exactly what the film requires."[30] The *Times* even seconded the actress' concern over Whale's staging of the film-closing reunion of the aging couple (Dunne and Allan Jones): "Unfortunately it [the movie] wanders into stagey and preposterous tragedy towards the end, just when it has recovered from the genuine tragedy of the beginning."[31] (Irene's rebellion against said scene, as suggested earlier, was to minimize her character's aging process.)

Dunne's next picture, her career-changing *Theodora Goes Wild*, was in many ways a throwback to her Madison (Indiana) childhood. In the film Irene's title character lives with older relatives in a conservative small town, where her part-time job is singing in church. All these things were true of the young Dunne, including staying for a time with her Madison grandparents. But Theodora is also secretly the author of a popular, provocatively sexy novel centering upon the most worldly of heroines. While her book is a bestseller in urban settings like New York, it is an ongoing scandal in small-town America. Though Theodora is safe because of a pseudonym, this conservative hometown has her second-guessing being a controversial author.

A visit from Theodora's cover artist (Melvyn Douglas), however, changes all that. They fall in love, but Douglas' character has his own personal baggage, and he quietly lams out of Theodora's small town one night. Then, as in all screwball comedies, the heroine goes in pursuit of the antiheroic male. This, of course, is where the title comes from; to get her man she *Goes Wild*. This screwball transition is both inspiringly entertaining and a model for two future Dunne classics in the genre—*The Awful Truth* (1937) and *My Favorite Wife* (1940).

The actress who once was afraid she could not play a screwball heroine proved to be a master of the form. But she did it in a distinctly Dunne *thinking woman* manner. Unlike the genre's stereotypical leading lady, who exhibits bonkers behavior continuously, à la Carole Lombard in *My Man Godfrey* (1936), or Katharine Hepburn in her later watershed foray into screwball comedy, *Bringing Up Baby* (1938), Dunne's screwball heroine chooses when she "goes wild."

The dominating nature of the genre's female lead is further enhanced by sometimes giving these films an Adam-and-Eve quality, which is certainly apparent in *Theodora*. The pen name of Dunne's character is Caroline Adams, and her bestseller has the title *The Sinner*. Her hometown is straight out of Lysistrata, with female domination underscored by a name that suggests a woman's garden— Lynnfield. Theodora will go on to best the visiting man (Douglas) in several Garden-of-Eden encounters, from picking berries to catching fish. Even when Douglas eventually flees, his note explains he has gone "to tend other gardens." His eventual *fall*, however, has been foreshadowed by the painting he was working on when they first met—*Eve and the Serpent*.

Fittingly for a woman (Dunne) originally from a small town, screwball comedy tends to celebrate the rural and/or American village setting (though not country characters). While the zany antics tend to transpire in the city, the genre's heartland segments are most often casually romantic. For example, in *Theodora*, there is a leisurely pace to the fishing and berry picking of Dunne and Douglas. In fact, the segment's biggest laugh depends upon it. The two are returning from an early morning fishing trip on foot and unhurried, content in each other's company. They are so blissfully oblivious that neither realizes their slow steps have positioned them (in the most casual of fishing attire) right in front of *the* church in town just as the Sunday service is letting out. The result is an obvious comedy scandal, particularly since Theodora's conservative aunts and the even more conservative members of the town's women's society (particularly the wonderful busybody played by Spring Byington) all seem to be spilling out of the church at the same time.

During the production of *Theodora* the actress and her husband were going through the paperwork necessary to adopt their baby. Coincidently, a baby also plays a prominent part in the picture's finale—which is unusual for the genre. Pets, especially dogs, usually play the surrogate children in screwball comedy. *Theodora* had a bit of both. Near the end of the film, when the unmarried Dunne returns to her character's small town as an outed sex novelist, she is holding a friend's baby. Given the X-rated reputation of her work, everyone assumes the child is Theodora's. Douglas' commercial artist, there finally to declare his love, is taken aback at the sight of the baby. In every ensuing scene he cradles his dog Jake, just as Dunne does the baby, the contrast in bundles underscoring the antiheroic male position, "I'm just a boy playing at being a husband."

Besides the parallels between Dunne's real life and *Theodora*, what was supposed to be a difficult situation (screwball comedy) for her was made more palatable by a good working relationship with the gifted director and novelist Richard Boleslawski. Of course, after the actress' tense experience with Whale on *Show Boat*, she was predisposed to have a better experience with Boleslawski. Working in favor of a good production was the fact that this was the first screwball comedy for both Boleslawski and Dunne, as well as most of the cast. Thus, the director was not walking into an experience (like Whale on *Show Boat*) where he felt like the only rookie on the production. The actress and the director also bonded by both being on the outs with Columbia. Dunne had irritated the studio by her reluctance to play Theodora. Years later she recalled that Boleslawski had been in Columbia's doghouse, too. And Irene was much taken with the fact that her director was the proud father of a baby boy— already nicknamed "Bolie." She was forever peppering Boleslawski with questions about his new child.

An added factor in making *Theodora* a pleasant shoot was the intellectual excitement Boleslawski brought to any production. He was especially interested in actors and interpreting parts. In fact,

Boleslawski had started out as a stage actor under the great Stanislavsky at the Moscow Art Theater. Even when Boleslawski moved on to directing, he recognized the merits of maintaining his fascination with the performer. Fittingly, this multitalented artist had also authored the book *Six Lessons of Dramatic Art*—an analysis of the Stanislavsky method of acting.

This Soviet connection also helps explain *Theodora*'s occasional editing homage to director and film theorist Sergei Eisenstein (1898–1948). Eisenstein was most famous for what has come to be called "intellectual montage," where two seemingly unrelated film clips are juxtapositioned (edited) together to create some new meaning. For instance, in Eisenstein's *October* (1928) he suggests a character is pompous by cutting from this figure to that of a peacock. Boleslawski not only borrows the technique (unusual for comedy) in *Theodora*, he even utilizes another bird motif. For example, during a montage of small-town gossipy women spreading rumors by phone he intercuts images of brainless chickens clucking away in a barnyard. Screwball comedy had never before had such a Soviet touch. But Boleslawski never let his intellectualism get in the way of a disarmingly democratic touch which oozed everyman charm: "I'm afraid I'm just a papa at heart. That's why I like working informally. I . . . wonder if we are not becoming a bit too arty for art's sake."[32]

Needless to say, *Theodora* was a great experience for Dunne, and it was more than reflected in the sterling reviews both she and the picture received. *Variety*'s take was probably the most entertainingly positive: "A comedy of steady tempo and deepening laughter, 'Theodora' is certain to attract big trade and strong word-of-mouth ballyhoo."[33] The publication went on to observe that the "Painstaking direction of Boleslawski brings out the nuances, sequence by sequence. . . . [This direction] and Miss Dunne's playing . . . is a high point of light and shade farce."[34]

Despite the actress' former concerns about screwball comedy, *Theodora* actually had critics calling her a premier comedienne. For example, the *New York Daily News* stated, "The star flashes across the screen in a series of amusing situations which she handles with sufficient deftness to put her in the front ranks of Hollywood comediennes."[35] The *New York Times* said, "Mr. Douglas and Miss Dunne are a splendid comedy team," while the *Brooklyn Daily Eagle* preferred to focus credit on Irene, acting "Honors go chiefly to Miss Dunne, who enters well into the spirit of the story."[36] And the *Motion Picture*

Herald's critique of opening-night viewers said it all: "It kept preview audiences giggling and occasionally giving way to good old fashioned belly laughs during its [entire] ninety minutes running time."[37] (The actress would also receive her second Best Actress Oscar nomination for the role.)

The only mild knock against Columbia's *Theodora* was an accident of timing—the movie opened the same year as the studio's other runaway hit comedy, *Mr. Deeds Goes to Town* (1936). With some story parallels (smalltown types succeeding in New York City) and the same studio producing, it was natural for *Theodora* critics to make the comparison. For instance, one reviewer described the film as "being a feminine counterpart of 'Mr. Deeds,'" while another credited Columbia with "dreaming of a distaff edition of 'Mr. Deeds Goes to Town.'"[38] While both movies now qualify as bona fide comedy classics, the general consensus then and now usually gives the edge to director Frank Capra's *Deeds*.

Part of this advantage (beyond the perennial plus of having come out first) is, however, based in a basic *difference* between the two pictures.[39] *Deeds* is a populist film, a comedy genre anchored in a morality play of good versus evil. Because the genre often showcases the underdog common person in the battle of his or her life, there is ultimately a deadly serious tone to the story's finale. In contrast, *Theodora* is a screwball comedy—a genre that takes nothing seriously. This is America's version of farce, which is tied to exaggerated slapstick situations. Most screwball films merely spoof the traditional romantic comedy, especially as they have an eccentric heroine dominate the proceedings. While neither genre is inherently superior to the other, stories with a more serious tone traditionally receive greater kudos than *mere* comedies.

Something along these lines was at work here. There was the high drama-oriented *Deeds*, versus silly screwball *Theodora*, from that genre about eccentricity. Capra's take on populism further accented the difference, given that the plight of his heroes was invariably intertwined with that of the nation, from *Deeds* providing a blueprint for the depression, to *Mr. Smith Goes to Washington* (1939) going after political corruption in the Senate. But in 1936 it was just the always insightful *Variety* that seemed to get this difference, noting "'Theodora' may [only] superficially be compared to the 'Mr. Deeds' character."[40]

Regardless of the *Deeds*—*Theodora* comparison, the number one story related to the latter film was Dunne's emergence as a comic player. As the *New York Herald Tribune* baldly stated, "Miss Dunne is surprisingly good as a comedienne."[41] The following year (1937), with an inspired assist from writer/director Leo McCarey, Dunne would elevate the screwball comedy bar even higher.

NOTES

1. Elizabeth Wilson, "The First True Story of Irene Dunne's Baby!" *Screenland*, June 1937, 21, 86.

2. Ibid., 20.

3. Dunne described one such incident in Dorothy Calhoun's "Irene Dunne Leads Two Lives," *Motion Picture Story Magazine*, September 1935, 77.

4. "Long Distance Hubby 'Perfect' to Marlene," *New York Daily News*, May 10, 1937, 3.

5. Calhoun, 79.

6. Betty Boone, "Inside the Stars' Homes," *Screenland*, July 1936, 15.

7. Ibid.

8. James Curtis, *James Whale: A New World of Gods and Monsters* (Boston: Faber and Faber, 1998), 269.

9. Ibid., 269–270.

10. Frank S. Nugent, Review of *Show Boat*, *New York Times*, May 15, 1936, 29.

11. Douglas Gilbert, "Song and Sentiment Pageant in 'Show Boat' at Music Hall," *New York World-Telegram*, May 15, 1936, 27.

12. Review of *Show Boat*, *Variety*, May 20, 1936.

13. Eileen Creelman, Review of *Show Boat*, *New York Sun*, May 15, 1936, 29.

14. Ibid.

15. Curtis, 279.

16. Kate Cameron, "A Lavish 'Show Boat' Sails into Music Hall," *New York Daily News*, May 15, 1936, 54.

17. Review of *Show Boat*, *Variety*.

18. "Irene Dunne Collection," 10 boxes of material, Cinema and Television Library, University of Southern California, Los Angeles.

19. "'Showboat'—And Shows in General," *Screen Play*, July 1936, 22; Review of *Show Boat*, *Screen Book Magazine* (July 1936).

20. Review of *Show Boat*, *Screenland*, June 1936, 53; Review of *Show Boat*, *Hollywood Reporter*, April 27, 1936.

21. Beulah Livingstone, "The Story of Irene Dunne," *Table Talk*, September 21, 1936, 14.

22. John McManus, "Magnolia of the Movies," *New York Times*, May 17, 1936, sec. 9, p. 3.

23. Homer Dickens, "Carole Lombard: Her Comic Sense Derived from an Instinctual Realism," *Films In Review*, February 1961, 73.

24. Calhoun, 39.
25. "The Queen Mary Returns to Britain," *New York American*, June 6, 1936, 1.
26. "Stars on the Gangplank," *London Daily Express*, June 11, 1936, 1.
27. *Queen Mary* news item, *Screenland*, October 1936, 58.
28. Ibid.
29. Curtis, 282.
30. "'Show Boat' of 1936," *London Times*, June 11, 1936, 14.
31. Ibid.
32. "Dunne," *Detroit Free Press*, October 10, 1936.
33. Review of *Theodora Goes Wild*, *Variety*, November 18, 1936, 12.
34. Ibid.
35. Kate Cameron, "A Good Time Is Had by All at Music Hall," *New York Daily News*, November 13, 1936, 64.
36. Frank S. Nugent, Review of *Theodora Goes Wild*, *New York Times*, November 13, 1936, 27; Winston Burdett, "'Theodora Goes Wild,' with Irene Dunne, Opens at the Music Hall," *Brooklyn Daily Eagle*, November 13, 1936, 23.
37. Review of *Theodora Goes Wild*, *Motion Picture Herald*, November 14, 1936.
38. Burdett, "'Theodora Goes Wild,' with Irene Dunne . . . "; Nugent, Review of *Theodora Goes Wild*.
39. See my books: *Screwball Comedy: A Genre of Madcap Romance* (Westport, Connecticut: Greenwood Press, 1986); *Populism and the Capra Legacy* (Westport, Connecticut: Greenwood Press, 1995); *Romantic Versus Screwball Comedy: Charting A Difference* (Lanham, Maryland: Scarecrow Press, 2002).
40. Review of *Theodora Goes Wild*, *Variety*.
41. Howard Barnes, "'Theodora Goes Wild'—Music Hall," *New York Herald Tribune*, November 13, 1936, 23.

SIX

Dunne's Leo McCarey Connection—Focus on *The Awful Truth*

McCarey was "the most dear sweet man."[1]

—Irene Dunne

You can really call Irene Dunne the first lady of Hollywood, because she's the first real *lady* Hollywood has ever seen.[2]

—Leo McCarey

Filmmaker Leo McCarey immeasurably changed Irene Dunne's life, professionally and personally. Their friendship was rooted in three films (*The Awful Truth*, 1937, *Love Affair*, 1939, and *My Favorite Wife*, 1940) and some 1950s television work related to the Catholic Church. As already noted, Irene later credited the critical acclaim of McCarey's *Ruggles of Red Gap* (1935) for bringing him to her attention. While the director had hardly been a Hollywood comedy secret prior to *Ruggles*, his greatest previous accomplishments had been underappreciated, from teaming and molding Laurel and Hardy to megaphoning the Marx Brothers' classic *Duck Soup* (1933). That is, comedy producer Hal Roach had funneled off the credit for the former event, and the Marx Brothers' most inspired film was unfortunately way ahead of its time; shockingly, *Duck Soup* was initially a critical and commercial failure.

While McCarey had, however, found more visible box office and critical success with other films, including *Six of a Kind* (1934, with W. C. Fields and Burns & Allen) and *Belle of the Nineties* (1934, with Mae West), *Ruggles* is what put him on the proverbial map. For instance, the *New York Post*, after comparing the picture to the work of Charlie Chaplin and Mark Twain, said, "on a par with the greatest achievements in screen comedy . . . we could use up endless type in admiration of Leo McCarey . . . but this thing has to stop somewhere."³ Along similar lines, the *New York World-Telegram* observed, "if this review smacks of superlatives, blame it upon the hearty and wholesome fun Leo McCarey has brought to the outrageously funny adventures that befall Ruggles."⁴ The reviews were so consistently strong that Paramount incorporated a broad statement along those lines into its ad campaign for the movie—"We're Not Saying a Word! . . . We don't have to! For today all the critics are raving about 'RUGGLES OF RED GAP.'"⁵ This print material ran with a photo of Charles Laughton's Ruggles with a shushing finger to his mouth. (Laughton himself insisted that McCarey was "not only a great director . . . but the greatest comic mind now living."⁶)

Unlike Dunne's revelation that *Ruggles* brought McCarey to her serious attention, history has not recorded the Irene event that first impacted the director. But since he had a decidedly musical side, it is quite possible that Dunne's *Roberta* (1935, a simultaneous smash with *Ruggles*) was the catalyst. Certainly the fact that many reviews for each picture noted the parallel success of the other film (see previous chapter) quite possibly contributed to Dunne coming to McCarey's attention. But one might also make a case for another 1935 picture, *Magnificent Obsession*, making Dunne's first distinctive impact on the director. That is, in a later-acclaimed McCarey/Dunne collaboration, *Love Affair* (1939), the director recycles a melodramatically pivotal scene from *Magnificent Obsession*. In each movie, therefore, Dunne's character is struck by a car and seriously injured—with the remaining balance of both films chronicling a try for romance.

Regardless of just what first brought Dunne to McCarey's critical attention, when the duo came together for *The Awful Truth* they soon realized how much they had in common. First, both were passionate about their Irish ancestry. McCarey would later do two pictures (*Going My Way*, 1944, and *The Bells of St. Mary's*, 1945) that would forever link him to this heritage. For Dunne, being Irish was an extension of her beloved father, and rare was the interview where her Emerald Isle connection was not mentioned. The actress credited everything from common sense to a "quick temper" to her Irish background.⁷ Sometimes, instead of just peppering her every magazine profile, there was enough Irish background to dominate the articles, such as the 1936 *Motion Picture Story Magazine* piece—"It's the Irish in Her."⁸ One can even find a 1937 Dunne quote that credits being Irish as the cause for her sudden full embrace of comedy:

> Being a person who wants to enjoy living, I want to laugh. The Irish in me has never been given a chance. I've been labeled the "cool" Miss Dunne, the "dignified" Miss Dunne, so consistently that no one seems to realize that I can do something else besides look cool—or cry.[9]

(One is, of course, also tempted to credit McCarey with being the un-named Irish director who gave Irene the practical mantra-like tip of saying to herself before a scene, "corned beef and cabbage"—in order to keep in mind she must act natural.)

Being strong Catholics was a second major connection which drew McCarey and Dunne together. Besides both artists having childhoods immersed in the church (Irene attended a convent school; Leo had a favorite aunt who was a nun), McCarey and Dunne were active in Catholic causes and charities throughout their adult lives. But as with their shared Irish component, McCarey's church affiliation was more apparent in his films than hers. Again one thinks of *Going My Way* and *The Bells of St. Mary's*, both of which star Bing Crosby as Catholic priest Father O'Malley. Crosby would win a Best Actor Oscar for the former picture, and forever after-wards Father O'Malley would symbolize what was good about the church. A March 4, 2002, issue of *Newsweek* even saluted McCarey's priestly ideal in the midst of the then-current Catholic pedophilia scandals.[10] Other McCarey pictures closely tied to the priesthood in-clude *My Son John* (1952) and *Satan Never Sleeps* (1962).

As a footnote to both *Going My Way* and the close McCarey-Dunne friendship, one should add that the director personally took the actress to a screening of the film, followed by supper. When Hol-lywood columnist Hedda Hopper spied them at Lucey's restaurant and inquired about the picture, Dunne was "still wiping tears from her eyes [and] said, 'Hedda, it's the best thing I've seen.'"[11]

Of the three joint McCarey-Dunne productions, only *Love Affair* showcases a churchly presence. Though much more subdued than the aforementioned priestly films of the director, the Catholic faith of the figure playing Charles Boyer's grandmother (so pivotal to the Boyer-Dunne "love affair") is beautifully realized—both as a charac-ter, and in the church setting that best defines her (a nearby chapel).

Paradoxically, one key difference in how McCarey and Dunne lived their life in conjunction with the church seemed to bring them closer together. First, the actress was the most idealistically self-sacrificing of individuals, from the most proper of marriages, to a public and private persona forever associated with the image

of a lady. The church helped fuel that discipline. In contrast, McCarey
was a hard-drinking Irishman whose bottle buddies included
W. C. Fields and author Gene Fowler. Indeed, some of McCarey's
epic drunks might have been the inspiration for the comic Irish
drinking scenes in the cinematic world of director John Ford—for
example, the numerous entertaining bouts with the bottle in Ford's
The Quiet Man (1952), including the epic fisticuffs between John
Wayne and Victor McLaglen, where the participants even pause at
a pub for an all-important drink. Coupled with this, the handsome
McCarey (sometimes described as "a poor man's Cary Grant") also
had a roving eye for the ladies, though his marriage usually kept
him from acting on these impulses. Thus, the church periodically
became a sanctuary, or a retreat, for a director modestly bothered
by his lapses.

So how did this McCarey-Dunne contrast bring them closer together? For the actress, there seems to be a sense she was both
amused by the director's periodic bad-boy antics, and maybe a little
envious she could not follow suit. For instance, though 99% of her
interviews from the 1930s suggest she avoided most Hollywood social engagements while her husband was still living in New York
City, one admission early in her West Coast tenure suggested she
briefly flirted with embracing a more sophisticated Noel Cowardish
lifestyle—"whenever a man took me out to an opening . . . he [my
husband] isn't jealous. He knows that I have to go out occasionally
and he wants me to have a normal social life. I hope he goes out with
woman friends, too."[12] While Dunne quickly realized this would *not*
work for her and husband Frank Griffin, she still found this conti-
nental lifestyle interesting in others, à la McCarey.

Conversely, while the director's behavior did not always follow
the straight and narrow, he often had major Catholic guilt over his
lapses. Thus, he greatly admired Dunne's discipline in avoiding
weak behavior. Moreover, their differences here were probably also
softened by the flirtatious nature of both. In fact, after studying their
comments about each other, and a 1975 phone interview with the
actress, one is tempted to suggest there was a platonically modest
romance going on.[13] The always insightful period *Photoplay* author
Adela Rogers St. Johns, who specialized in getting more personal
admissions from her subjects, certainly reinforced the McCarey-
Dunne closeness in a 1944 article:

I found that the woman—maybe the person—that Leo admired most in the world was Irene Dunne. Not just because of her superlative performances . . . But because—well, she was inspirational, she had a crazy sense of humor—sure—but . . . he'd underline her patience and her good cheer and how she'd take any kind of a mad joke on the set but always came back at you . . . and still he couldn't quite find the answer . . . [to her classy uniqueness].[14]

Maybe McCarey was scrambling for a definition of class my grandfather once shared with me years ago: "To be an aristocrat, you must simply act like an aristocrat every day. The title is nothing."

A third major tie between McCarey and Dunne was their joint fascination with music, as well as some shared frustrations along those lines. That is, Irene had most wanted to be an opera singer, while Leo originally aspired to be a songwriter. (McCarey's celebrated O'Malley, besides being the most musical of priests, was a frustrated songwriter!) Both Dunne and McCarey had grown up in musical homes, with a piano for a centerpiece. The director continued that tradition on the sets of his films, playing the piano between scenes to both relax the cast and fuel his ideas for improvisation. One of these comedy riffs actually involved said piano and Dunne—her "Home On The Range" duet with Ralph Bellamy in *The Awful Truth*.

Fittingly, in two of the McCarey-Dunne collaborations (*The Awful Truth* and *Love Affair*) he cast her as a singer. Even their non-music-orientated *My Favorite Wife* manages to have the actress sing in the shower! And of course, their solo film careers (especially as already demonstrated by Dunne's *Roberta* and *Show Boat*) were frequently all about music. Interestingly enough, when McCarey remade *Love Affair* as *An Affair to Remember* (1957, though sadly without Dunne), the formerly unsuccessful songwriter managed to use some of his compositions in the film.

A fourth McCarey-Dunne connection was their shared sentimental nature. While cinema history would later judge their greatest triumphs to be in comedy, both artists were more partial to their melodramatic outings. McCarey's favorite was his *Make Way For Tomorrow* (1937), the tragic love story of an elderly couple. No less a film legend than Orson Welles would later say of this movie, "It would make a stone cry." By the end of her career Dunne's favorite film was *Penny Serenade* (1941), a sometimes weepy about adoption and the loss of a child. But a close second for both artists was their joint effort—the melodramatic romantic comedy *Love Affair*. Mc-Carey and Dunne credited this teary tendency to their Irish backgrounds. In fact, Dunne would sometimes later affectionately refer to McCarey as "an Irish sentimentalist." The director also acquiesced in the actress' personal belief, as noted earlier, that the sad story stayed with one's fans longer than any other kind. One senses that McCarey, again like Dunne, put a higher premium on melodrama because comedy came so easily for him.

A fifth key link between McCarey and Dunne was similar work habits. She later told an interviewer that the director "was very good about sitting down and wanting to talk things out."[15] The actress then went on to describe, with a certain sense of exhilaration, one of their quasi-improvisational *Awful Truth* collaborations: "The scene, if you remember, where . . . [I play] the part of the nightclub dancer, who is supposed to be Cary's [Grant] sister? That was really all written right on the set."[16]

Dunne's auteurist nature (recognizing the significance of the director) bears repeating at this point to better demonstrate the homework she had done on McCarey prior to their first film together, *The Awful Truth*. Early in the production her costar, Cary Grant, was nearly frightened off the shoot by the director's casually improvisational style. With McCarey coming in each day with notes on scraps of paper for possible scenes, Grant was convinced they were heading for disaster. The actor even approached Columbia studio chief Harry Cohn about buying back his contract for the movie, which hardly endeared him to McCarey. But it was Dunne who convinced Grant that this was the director's inspired style. She told her costar, "if he would just stay with it, he would give a wonderful performance, which he did. It upset him that McCarey didn't have a script. I was able to calm him down."[17]

Comically, the movie went on to be such a success that Grant made three later pictures with McCarey. But what made Dunne's act of faith in the director so impressive is that, like Grant, this was her first McCarey movie, too. As she always did in both life and cinema, the actress had thoroughly researched the situation.

A final connection between McCarey and Dunne might just be labeled a "compendium"—a series of modest parallels that, when roped together, constitute a sixth link between them. First, they shared a common wedding anniversary. And on at least two occasions, when Dunne's husband was out of town, the actress celebrated the date with the McCareys. Second, both artists remained married to the same person for nearly forty years, often leaning upon the film advice of that low-profile partner. Third, each of them had a single daughter on whom they doted. Indeed, it turns out that McCarey also doted on the actress' child, who was adopted less than a year before they made *The Awful Truth*. Fourth, while the image of both artists was often tied to laughter, on screen and off, both were capable of playing hardball. Former MGM studio head Dore Schary once said of McCarey, "He's funny, entertaining [and he would] cut your balls off if he had to."[18] Though no one is suggesting that Dunne would have been capable of this degree of toughness, she did not survive and prosper in Hollywood without a healthy dose of moxie. Plus, as noted earlier, journalist Adela Rogers St. Johns credited the actress with the potential for ruthlessness, though this admission appears in an overwhelmingly positive profile of Dunne.[19]

One might even use a final McCarey-Dunne parallel as a transition device for their first film together—both needed a hit. Each of their previous movies, McCarey's *Make Way For Tomorrow* and Dunne's *High, Wide and Handsome* (1937), were exceptional yet greatly underappreciated works. Though both had their period champions, the pictures were too nontraditional for most audiences of the 1930s. For example, the *New York Post's* otherwise positive take on McCarey's film found it so inherently tragic their review opened with the warning, "I don't think you will enjoy it. I don't think anyone could . . . if the familiar Hollywood standards of the happy ending are at all correct, not many people are going to want to see it."[20]

The knock against Dunne's *High, Wide and Handsome*, a musical set in the Pennsylvania oil fields of the 1850s and directed by the acclaimed Rouben Mamoulian, was that the picture could not decide between being a Hammerstein-Kern musical and a drama about industrial America. Thus, while the *New York Daily News* praised the movie as being "as purely a piece of Americana as the Declaration of Independence," the more typical East Coast response was reflected by the *Post's* concern, "It's not wholly satisfactory as a musical romance . . . [mixed with a] violent struggle between railroad magnates and farmers for control of the oil fields."[21] The unintendedly funny title for the latter review, "Musical Romance About First Pennsylvania Oil," also demonstrates why the picture had credibility problems.[22]

The reviews were routinely kinder on the West Coast. But critics were still mystified as to how to define the film. For example, while the *Hollywood Reporter* called it a "pioneering production," they suggested a "new word [genre] will have to be coined even to describe this operetta treatment of a dramatic episode from American history."[23] The *Los Angeles Examiner* was of the same opinion but with more of a comic touch—"the picture fits no previous category of screen entertainment. Frankly . . . [it] has everything, including the kitchen sink."[24] Maybe the lack of an obvious genre kept viewers away, because the movie was not a commercial hit. Coupled with the picture's high cost, the film was also soon being kidded by entertainment industry insiders for its poor performance at the box office. For instance, broadcast personality Walter Winchell even managed to add a punning dig at the expense of the movie's director (Rouben Mamoulian). When asked how much the picture cost, Winchell cracked, "One Mamoulian nine hundred thousand dollars."[25] A diplomatic Dunne later only confessed to thinking, "Give me a comedy—quick."[26] *The Awful Truth* would prove to be just the box office *quick* fix she was after.

The McCarey-Dunne collaboration with *The Awful Truth* was greatly assisted by the addition of Cary Grant. Though he initially had doubts about the project, his screwball gifts of physical comedy and verbal repartee were just then starting to blossom. Unlike McCarey and Dunne, both coming off disappointing film outings, Grant's last release was the critical and commercial megasmash *Topper* (1937, a fantasy screwball comedy of instant classic proportions). Part of Grant's story doubts about *The Awful Truth*, beyond McCarey's improvisational style, was that he was coming from a movie whose ghostly screwball comedy narrative was so familiar to *everyone*—being an adaptation of Thorne Smith's popular novel. Plus, since McCarey had not yet done a film in this genre, maybe Grant felt he, the experienced actor, had more of a handle on screwball comedy. Regardless, things would come together on this film.

In fact, Hollywood dates the birth of Grant's film persona to *The Awful Truth*. No less an artist than writer/director Garson Kanin later said, "How much of that [Grant] personality was directed into him by Leo McCarey, I'm not prepared to say . . . [but] he polished that [*Awful Truth*] personality, and he plays it over and over and over again—each time more skillfully."[27] The power of the McCarey mentoring was that his storytelling mannerisms were so infectious that his performers often ended up aping this director. In my phone interview with Dunne over forty years after the making of *The Awful Truth*, she still literally bubbled over with admiration for McCarey's unintended knack for getting performers to mimic his mannerisms.[28] Thus, Grant's screen penchant for everything from flirtatiously self-deprecating humor to the amusingly expressive use of his hands and eyes were all signature trademarks of McCarey long before they became synonymous with the actor.

Though the credits for *The Awful Truth* say it is based upon a play by Arthur Richman, McCarey actually improvised a marital farce out of a series of misunderstandings with his own wife. The director later told Peter Bogdanovich the movie was, "in a way, the story of my [antiheroic] life—though the few scenes about [suggested] infidelity, I hasten to add, were *not* autobiographical—they were imagination only."[29] The picture opens with Jerry Warriner (Cary Grant) at his New York City men's club getting a sun lamp tan. Jerry is supposed to have taken a solo vacation to Florida but he really stayed in the city to play cards with "the boys." This is the kind of secret "boys night out" from the wives McCarey used to routinely cook up for Laurel and Hardy. Besides getting a tan, Jerry attempts to further his Florida subterfuge by gifting his wife Lucy (Dunne) with a basket of oranges.

After this prologue, Jerry brings home several friends for brunch to ease into the small talk that defines many marriages. But he finds his wife has not yet returned from a previous day's engagement. Eventually, Lucy comes in with her handsome French voice instructor (Alexander D'Arey). His car broke down, so their explanation goes, and they were forced to spend the night at some wayside inn. Neither Jerry nor Lucy believe their separate stories. But again in the Laurel and Hardy tradition, only the male's alibi falls apart upon closer inspection. That is, Dunne's character points out that Florida has been suffering through an unprecedented rainy period—so isn't his tan curious?! Plus, detail-conscious Lucy also notices that his Florida oranges are stamped *California!* The couple quickly begins divorce proceedings, and the rest of the picture involves getting them back together, a classic screwball case of what scholar Stanley Cavell calls the "Hollywood Comedy of Remarriage."[30]

Film historian Gerald Mast once described Charlie Chaplin's ability to construct a story from a random collection of sketches as putting "beads on a string." Not surprisingly, especially since McCarey also came out of silent comedy (à la Laurel and Hardy) and greatly admired Chaplin, Leo also embraced this "beads on a string" approach. Thus, the divorce proceedings are reduced to an inspired courtroom scene that essentially comes down to a custody fight over their dog, Mr. Smith, a pooch already famous as Asta of *The Thin Man* films. Or, when Jerry attempts to crash what he assumes is a romantic tryst between his ex-wife and her voice instructor, he comically stumbles into an innocent music recital.

The secret of McCarey's success in these and countless other casually constructed scenes was to maintain an entertainingly warm collaboration with his performers. Writer Sheridan Gibney later described McCarey's directing style as being "very patient and understanding and sympathetic. Always joking, keeping them [the actors] in good humor . . . what he finally got [on every film] was the best the actor had to give."[31] After being complimented on her *Awful Truth* performance, Dunne said:

> I have a confession to make. For the first time since I've been in pictures, I felt like giving my salary back to the producer. I had such fun making it . . . when the day's work was over none of us wanted to go home . . . it was a riot every minute we were on the picture.[32]

This description meshes nicely with the memories of another Dunne costar from *The Awful Truth*, Ralph Bellamy. He had initially approached McCarey about the absence of a script even before the production started:

> When I went to Leo's house, he met me with his perpetual gleeful grin and dancing eyes. . . . He said nothing much about the story or the part. He just joked and said not to worry—we'd have lots of fun, but there wasn't any script. . . . There never was a script. Each morning Leo would appear with a small piece of brown wrapping paper . . . and throw us lines and business. . . . We were quickly won over to him and had the fun he'd promised. And we made the film in six weeks, a record for that kind of picture.[33]

Bellamy went on to say that "after four or five days, we realized he [McCarey] was a comedy genius."

Another key to McCarey's "genius" was being a masterful comedy doctor. When *The Awful Truth* was eventually sneak previewed, the audience response was not all it could be. McCarey decided the problem was that the movie opened on too somber a note (the im-

mediate divorce); viewers were not certain it was a comedy. So Mc-
Carey went back and shot the most inventive of solutions. He has
Dunne's Lucy call the family lawyer about her plans for a divorce.
This older fatherly figure attempts to counsel Lucy about staying the
marital course. But each time he starts to say, "Marriage is a beautiful thing" his own wife interrupts him that supper is ready and getting cold. This causes the lawyer to briefly curb his conversation
with Lucy and speak sharply to his wife about not bothering him.
McCarey, following an old comedy axiom, then has this routine
repeated three times. With each interruption, the lawyer is amusingly harsher to his wife. The comedy payoff comes when his final
attempt to say, "Marriage is a beautiful thing" is juxtaposed with the
comeback to his wife—"Shut your big mouth." If there had been
viewer confusion before about whether this was a comedy, no questions remained after this addition. *The Awful Truth* went on to be a
monster critical and commercial success.

The reviews even topped the previously cited raves for McCarey's
Ruggles of Red Gap and Dunne's *Theodora Goes Wild*. Critiques do not
get any better than the *New York Daily News'* opening: "About every
person in New York who goes to the Music Hall [theater] this, and
maybe next week, will report that 'the Awful Truth' IS THE FUNNI-
EST PICTURE I EVER SAW."[34] Running this kudos a close second
was the *New York Daily Mirror's* claim, "Topping both 'It Happened
One Night' and the prize 'Mr. Deeds,' this new 'The Awful Truth' is
the best of the flighty [screwball] comedies."[35]

This usurping of Capra's *Mr. Deeds* was rewarding to both Dunne
and McCarey for diverse reasons. With Dunne, it was payback for
the *Theodora* review which praised the picture as second only to
1936's other comedy classic—*Deeds*. For McCarey, *Truth* was often an
affectionate spoofing of friend Capra's *Deeds*. For instance, Ralph
Bellamy's funny failed attempt to read his romantic poetry to a distracted Irene Dunne (Cary Grant is tickling her from behind the
door) parodies the recitation of Gary Cooper to Jean Arthur in the
previous year's *Deeds*.

Consistent with this bettering of a watershed Capra work, most
of the critical praise for *Truth* was filtered through hosannas for
McCarey. Consequently, *Time* magazine said, "Resourceful, humorous director Leo McCarey . . . takes a couple of derby hats [another
footnote to Laurel and Hardy], an ingratiating wirehaired fox terrier,
and three players without any special reputations as comedians and

spins . . . the gayest screen comedy the season has seen."[36] The *Hollywood Reporter* stated, "McCarey brilliantly dominates every minute of his production."[37] And the *New York Sun* was quick to point out that McCarey had done a masterful job of making a tasteful film that flirted with a then-controversial subject (adultery); his "direction has skillfully eluded all problems of censorship, concocting a comedy that is sometimes naughty but always nice. 'The Awful Truth' is as merry as sleighbells."[38]

Praise for McCarey notwithstanding, Dunne received superlative notices, too, with the greatest compliment coming from the *New York Mirror*: *The Awful Truth* "establishes Miss Irene Dunne as Hollywood's supreme comedienne."[39] *Variety* comically observed, "She tops that [winning *Theodora*] performance by almost an Alp [a mountainous amount] in 'Awful Truth.'"[40] *Time* said the film "establishes her with her [comedy pantheon] peers, Claudette Colbert and Jean Arthur."[41] The *Hollywood Reporter* matched this praise with an insightful take on her screwball character's approach to comedy—"Irene Dunne, as the unwilling divorcee with a mocking sense of humor, gives her most alluring and adroitly finessed portrayal."[42] Fittingly, Dunne would receive her third Oscar nomination as Best Actress for playing Lucy Warriner. McCarey would win the statuette for his direction, with the movie also receiving nominations for Best Picture and Best Supporting Actor (Ralph Bellamy). Period conjecture suggests Grant missed a nomination because of a reputation for difficulty, such as attempting to bail out of McCarey's production. Irene Dunne remembered,

> Cary used to be very apprehensive about nearly everything in those days. So apprehensive in fact he would almost get physically sick. If the script, the director, an actor, or a particular scene displeased him, he would be greatly upset.[43]

Be that as it may, McCarey's unorthodox style provoked an Oscar-caliber performance from Grant. For example, in one scene the director told Dunne to open the door of her apartment and discover Grant standing there and say with surprise, "Well, if it isn't my ex." He did not tell Grant what to reply, but the actor ad-libbed one of the film's best-remembered lines, "The judge says this is my day to see the dog."[44]

The beauty of *The Awful Truth* is that it remains as comically entertaining today as it was in 1937. Thankfully, this was something Dunne lived long enough to see. In a rare 1985 interview the actress admitted, "Many of these early melodramas [I starred in and] we took so seriously don't play well at all today. I took my two grand-children to see 'Cimarron' once, and it was laughable in places. On the other hand, 'The Awful Truth' stands up marvelously."[45] The American Film Institute seconded that notion at the end of the twentieth century, selecting *The Awful Truth* as one of the 100 funniest films ever made. And more recently, AFI placed the movie on its list of the 100 greatest love stories.[46]

For this viewer, the ultimate topper occurs at the picture's close, when the Warriners become a couple again at their mountain cabin. The extended scene is both poignant and sexually provocative, with a touch of Chaplin, too. Grant and Dunne have gone to bed separately but in adjoining rooms. The latch on the connecting door is broken and with each opening of this divider they move closer to a reconciliation. The clock over the door (their divorce is final at midnight) has mechanical figures which are reminiscent of Chaplin playing at being a fun house wooden character in *The Circus* (1928). At fifteen-minute intervals McCarey's figures (a boy and a girl) both exit and separately reenter said clock. Meanwhile, the passage of three quarter-hour segments also showcase Dunne and Grant's comic diversity, from his physical shtick assistance to getting the door open (a cat briefly blocks it), to some wonderful Dunne double-talk—"Things are just the same as they always were, only you're the same as you were too, so I guess things will never be the same again." Eventually, however, the couple seem ready to reconcile just as it is time for the third (comedy's rule of three again) shot of the clock figures. Naturally, the face of the clock reads midnight, and on this comic occasion, the boy figure breaks precedent and reenters the clock with the girl figure. Love triumphs without the entanglements of marriage. As the *New York Daily News* said at the time, "The Warriners' get-together . . . is priceless."[47]

Luckily for Dunne, there would be further get-togethers with both Grant and McCarey in her future.

NOTES

1. Irene Dunne, telephone interview by the author, Los Angeles (June 1975), author's files.

2. Stephen Birmingham, "Irene Dunne," *McCalls*, August 1964, 100.

3. Thornton Delehanty, "Charles Laughton and Others in 'Ruggles of Red Gap,'" *New York Post*, March 7, 1935, 14.

4. William Boehnel, "'Ruggles of Red Gap' Grand and Hilarious," *New York World-Telegram*, March 7, 1935, 21.

5. *Ruggles of Red Gap* movie ad, *New York Daily News*, March 7, 1935, 45.

6. Paramount Press Release, "Biography of Leo McCarey," April 1, 1937, in the Leo McCarey file, Margaret Herrick Library, Academy of Motion Picture Arts and Sciences, Beverly Hills, California.

7. Sonia Lee, "Discovering the Glamour in Irene Dunne," *Motion Picture Story Magazine*, March 1937, 78; Elizabeth Wilson, "Projections," *Silver Screen*, November 1936, 74.

8. Leon Surmelian, "It's the Irish in Her," *Motion Picture Story Magazine*, July 1936, 38, 68, 70.

9. Lee, 78.

10. Kenneth L. Woodward, "Bing Crosby Had It Right," *Newsweek*, March 4, 2002, 53.

11. Hedda Hopper, "Praise for Picture," *Washington Post*, March 31, 1944.

12. Janet Burden, "Parted—But Happily Married," *Motion Picture Story Magazine*, July 1932, 77.

13. Dunne, telephone interview.

14. Adela Rogers St. Johns, "Thank You, Irene Dunne," *Photoplay*, September 1944, 36.

15. James Harvey, "Irene Dunne Interviewed by James Harvey," *Film Comment*, January–February, 1980, 29.

16. Ibid.

17. Nancy Nelson, *Evenings with Cary Grant* (New York: William Morrow, 1991), 98.

18. Patrick McGilligan, *Film Crazy: Interviews with Hollywood Legends* (New York: St. Martin's Press, 2000), 197.

19. Rogers St. Johns, "Thank You, Irene Dunne."

20. Archer Winsten, "Tragedy of Old Age at New Criterion Theatre," *New York Post*, May 10, 1937, 15.

21. Wanda Hale, "'High, Wide and Handsome' A Real Thriller," *New York Daily News*, July 22, 1937, 44; Archer Winsten, "Musical Romance About First Pennsylvania Oil," *New York Post*, July 22, 1937, 15.

22. Winsten, "Musical Romance about First Pennsylvania Oil."

23. "'High, Wide and Handsome' Colorful Entertainment," *Hollywood Reporter*, July 22, 1937.

24. Dorothy Manners, "'High, Wide and Handsome' Has Premiere at Carthay Circle," *Los Angeles Examiner*, August 13, 1937.

25. "How Stars Face the Facts of Flops!" *Screenland*, June 1938, 88.

26. Ibid.

27. Nelson, 98.

28. Dunne, telephone interview.

29. Peter Bogdanovich, *Who the Devil Made It: Conversations with Legendary Film Directors* (New York: Ballantine Books, 1997), 412.

30. Stanley Cavell, *Pursuits of Happiness: The Hollywood Comedy of Remarriage* (Cambridge, MA: Harvard University Press, 1981).

31. McGilligan, 160.

32. Hedda Hopper rough draft column on Irene Dunne, in the Irene Dunne file, Margaret Herrick Library.

33. Ralph Bellamy, *When the Smoke Hit the Fan* (Garden City, New York: Doubleday, 1979): 129–130.

34. Wanda Hale, "'The Awful Truth' Now at Music Hall," *New York Daily News*, November 5, 1937.

35. "Conquest and 'Awful Truth,'" *New York Daily Mirror*, November 5, 1937, 39.

36. *The Awful Truth* review, *Time*, November 1, 1937, 45.

37. "'Awful Truth' Comedy; Certain of Good Boxoffice," *Hollywood Reporter*, October 6, 1937.

38. Review of *The Awful Truth*, *New York Sun*, November 5, 1937.

39. "Conquest and 'Awful Truth.'"

40. Review of *The Awful Truth*, *Variety*, October 20, 1937, 12.

41. Review of *The Awful Truth*, *Time*.

42. "'Awful Truth' Comedy; Certain of Good Boxoffice."

43. Geoffrey Wansell, *Haunted Idol: The Story of the Real Cary Grant* (New York: William Morrow, 1984), 121–122.

44. Ibid.

45. John McDonough, "Screening a Star: A Rare Interview with Irene Dunne," *Chicago Tribune*, May 12, 1985, sec. 13, p. 9.

46. "AFI Gets Passionate with Another 100-Best List," *USA Today*, June 12, 2002, 4-D.

47. Hale, "'The Awful Truth' Now at Music Hall."

SEVEN

Hollywood as Home and More Ties with McCarey

I guess it was easier for her to change her name than for her whole family to change theirs—Irene Dunne to Cary Grant on the questionable singing act of Dixie Belle Lee (Joyce Compton) in *The Awful Truth* (1937).

The Academy Awards ceremony for 1937 (March 10, 1938) found Dunne's nominated performance for *The Awful Truth* up against Janet Gaynor in *A Star Is Born*, Greta Garbo for *Camille*, Barbara Stanwyck in *Stella Dallas*, and Luise Rainer for *The Good Earth*. The heavy favorite was Garbo, who had already won several other critical awards for her performance, including the New York Film Critic's prestigious Best Actress prize.

The surprise winner, however, was Luise Rainer, who became the first performer to win back-to-back Oscars. (The year before she had won for *The Great Ziegfeld*, 1936, beating out, among other nominees, Dunne's title character in *Theodora*.) But Rainer's wins were tainted by questions; revisionist historians now suggest the actress' statuettes were orchestrated by the head of her all-powerful parent studio (MGM's Louis B. Mayer). He was able to force block voting by studio employees. As 1936 Oscar nominee Gladys George (for *Valient Is The Word For Carrie*) privately observed the night of the ceremony (March 4, 1937) but *before* the Best Actress announcement, "I thought I might be a dark horse but Luise Rainer won. She's going to win next year, too . . . Mayer's trying to build her up and thought an Oscar would help."[1]

Ironically, if the goal had been to make an American screen star out of the Austrian star, it was not to happen, despite the then unprecedented winning of two consecutive Best Actress Oscars. The rest of her brief Hollywood career was a disappointment, and she had returned to Europe by the late 1930s. Paradoxically, while Dunne would never win an Academy Award, her career would flourish into the 1950s, with two additional nominations. Irene's response to losing yet again in 1938 was a breezingly modest, "Oh, I didn't think I had a chance. Things like that don't happen to me. I've been up [nominated] three times . . . [now]. If I did a 'Zola' [*The Life of Emile Zola*, a serious drama, won the Best Picture Oscar that year] I might have a chance."[2] (The jinx sometimes associated with winning an Oscar, where a performer's subsequent films do not measure up, dates from Rainer's short-lived career.)

While Rainer's days in Hollywood were made equally difficult by an unhappy marriage to egotistical writer Clifford Odets (which ended shortly before her return to Europe), Dunne's career blossomed after her husband's 1936 move west. Whereas Odets could be so self-centered as to state, without a trace of intentional humor, that he wanted a separate bedroom to preserve his creative energy, Dunne's Dr. Griffin did everything possible to advance Irene's film position. This one-time dentist later observed, "We co-operate in everything. When it became a question of whose career was the most important, we decided that both of us would work towards getting her to the top." Coupled to this sacrifice he movingly added, a man "can be just as proud of her [his wife's] success as she is and inside he can take a bow himself for whatever help he's been."[3]

While Dunne's husband had always helped manage her career and sizeable income, after he joined her in Hollywood there was suddenly more opportunity for all those little normal things their previous bicoastal marriage had minimized, from their joint love of weekend travel outings to playing golf together. Like her fellow Hollywood Hoosier Carole Lombard, who often bettered her then companion Clark Gable in athletic events, Dunne often challenged her husband on the fairways—scoring holes-in-one on two separate outings!

After previously spending so much time apart, Dunne and Griffin now made every effort to be together. Thus, the doctor would go on movie location shoots with the actress, while she would accompany her husband Frank on business trips. Besides the many interests they shared (see the opening of chapter 2), the final glue to their bond was Dr. Griffin's dryly self-deprecating sense of humor about being married to a famous film star. His favorite comic metaphor along these lines was to liken Dunne to a feature film, and himself to a modest "coming soon" movie trailer! He was also fond of saying, with tongue firmly in cheek, his wife's career paled his into insignificance. "And I've been insignificant ever since."[4]

The Oscar ceremony of 1938 notwithstanding, the year's most memorable event for Irene and Frank was finalizing the adoption of their daughter Mary Frances "Missy" Griffin. At that time one had to maintain custody of the child for a year prior to making the adoption official. The couple acted to finalize the proceedings in early 1938. The actress observed at the time:

> We could have signed those papers in Los Angeles but I dreaded the reporters and cameramen who would wait outside the judge's chambers. In New York [where the adoption originated], we were assured everything could be done quickly and quietly, with the dignity which had come to mean so much to the doctor [Dunne's husband] and to me.[5]

But while things were quiet "outside the judge's chambers," no one had shared this privacy promise with the New York press. When the new family (and the child's nurse) returned to their Manhattan hotel, they were met by a media feeding frenzy. Unlike some period stars who thrived on publicity, such as Dunne's close friend Carole Lombard, Irene had always avoided the press. For Dunne media publicity was a necessary evil to being a movie star but she wanted none of that for her daughter. As Irene noted shortly before the New York trip, "She's [Missy] too young to have her pictures in the paper."[6]

Paradoxically, the misinformation that came out of the Manhattan hotel incident, such as the melodramatic fabrication that Missy was an orphan, resulted in an arranged article with *Photoplay* magazine (June 1938) to set the record straight. The piece (still with *no* pictures of her daughter) was entitled "The True and Tender Story of Irene Dunne's Daughter," and allowed the actress to continue to work through her mother Adelaide's late 1936 death, which had ironically paralleled the Griffins' initial adoption of Missy. Thus, Dunne revealed in the article that the same day that her mother died she had told the actress:

> She's one of the sweetest children I've ever seen. I'm glad you have her. It's a little difficult now for all of you. You're all strange. But wait, you'll suddenly find she belongs here. And then you'll be surprised that you ever found life good enough without her.[7]

Dunne had worked through a great deal of grief to be able to share such a story. In a later article (1939) the actress revealed a rare assessment of her ever-so-influential mother:

> She never was a 'yes' mother. She was always quick to criticize. Yet she was equally quick to see the good points in others. She gave me inspiration, faith and, when I needed it most, confidence. She was . . . delighted with my profession.[8]

As is often the case with an unexpected death, Irene was initially struck by the dark-comedy absurdity of how quickly one can pass from the living to the dead. In a letter written to a friend shortly after Adelaide's death she revealed, "I shall not go into the details of Mother's passing only to say that she was out in the car laughing & talking & eating candy when the stroke came."[9] Still, baby Missy was a comfort for the actress, who later observed, "Somehow it was as if one life had gone out and another had come in."[10] Besides wanting to love and care for this daughter, the actress was movingly aware of a key gift from children—they "give you another life to live . . . I can share again with Mary Frances *first* raptures, hers."[11] The adoption is yet another reminder that Dunne's life was never only about the movies. She did her acting amid the myriad of events and emotions which chronicle any life shared with others.

As if reflecting the 1938 finalization of their family life (via the adoption), Dunne's only film that year was fittingly entitled *The Joy of Living*. The movie again fell into the category of screwball comedy, with the *New York Daily News* even observing, she "does a variation of her Theodora role in 'Theodora Goes Wild.'"[12] The review's title said it all, "Irene Dunn [sic] Goes Wild Again in 'Joy of Living.'"

This time, however, the actress played a star of stage, screen, and radio who is victimized by a parasitic family. Her free-spirited leading man, (Douglas Fairbanks, Jr.) helps trigger the actress' signature transition to screwball craziness, just as Melwyn Douglas helped the transition along in *Theodora*. But unlike subsequent scenes in that movie, or her zany makeover in *The Awful Truth*, Dunne's *Joy of Living* character does *not* fully get to return this freeing-up phenomenon to her leading man. Possibly, this contributed to the movie's mixed reviews and lackluster performance at the box office. (Of course, things were not helped by period censors—the Hays office—taking away the movie's more racy original title—*The Joy of Loving*.)

The film and its players were not without period champions, how-ever. The *Daily News* called Dunne "a most persuasive and ingratiat-ing comedienne," while the *New York World-Telegram* said Dunne and Fairbanks "employ their engaging sense of comedy in a pleasant manner in the brisk and sophisticated farce."[13] And the *Hollywood Reporter* observed that *Joy of Living* "holds its own in this popular class [screwball comedy] of amusement."[14] Unfortunately, these were minority reports. Indeed, the *New York Times* seemed to be reviewing an entirely different movie: "it might be classed as escapist entertain-ment. [But] Somehow its entertainment value escaped me."[15] A pun-ning *Variety* was kinder, yet still disappointed: "a cast of fine players try valiantly but their joy of living is somewhat limited."[16]

As far as fathoming its failure, however, the *New York Herald Tribune*'s review was the most thought-provoking. It felt the movie had "something of the quality of 'The Awful Truth' but it needed more Leo McCarey characterization.[17] The key component of the characterization McCarey had molded for Dunne in *The Awful Truth* was the ability to impact and/or dominate the leading man by way of her eccentricity. This factor, as previously noted, was decidedly absent from the *Joy of Living*. But regardless of one's take on the pic-ture, the single item period critics agreed upon was Dunne's inspired way with a song. Making her *Joy of Living* character a pro-fessional entertainer enabled Dunne to legitimately sing several songs in the course of the film, something with which the *New York Post*'s reviewer was especially taken.[18]

Barring a private secretary doing all the pasting, Dunne saw this McCarey-orientated *New York Herald Tribune* review, because the critique turns up in her aforementioned scrapbooks, now housed at the University of Southern California.[19] Of course, it is unlikely that any pivotal reviews got by this consummate professional, since she subscribed to a newspaper and magazine clipping service from 1935 until the 1950s. Predictably, she returned to the McCarey fold with her next picture—the monster critical and commercial hit *Love Affair* (1939). But Dunne was always most direct about the sway McCarey had over her. In early 1938 she told Hollywood columnist Sheilah Graham, "I've just finished another comedy, *Joy of Living*, but [I] feel the time has come for something more serious. Of course, if Leo McCarey . . . wants me to make another comedy, that's something else again."[20] This reunion with McCarey had almost happened much earlier.

Late 1937 press coverage of Hollywood had Dunne reteaming with both McCarey and Cary Grant in a film production of *Holiday*.[21] After the huge success of *The Awful Truth* the public was clamoring for a reunion of the trio. When it did occur (1940's *My Favorite Wife*), they had another major hit on their hands. But lightning did not strike again on *Holiday*; the film would become a Katharine Hepburn vehicle. Hepburn literature often states that the actress was largely responsible for putting together the 1938 *Holiday* package, getting Columbia head Harry Cohn to both hire George Cukor to direct, and sign Cary Grant to costar with Hepburn.[22] More recent revisionist research would, however, suggest that Cukor was answerable for putting Hepburn in the film. Regardless, Dunne was not to get the part, which became one of the great regrets of her career. She later confessed to "crying her eyes out over the lost role."[23]

Ironically, *Holiday* would undoubtedly have fared better at the box office with Dunne. Though Hepburn received good reviews, she was then suffering through a difficult period, when the public seemed to have lost interest in her career. In fact, Hepburn and several other period stars (including Fred Astaire and Mae West) were laboring under the claim they were "box office poison." *Holiday*'s mediocre commercial returns were also probably hurt by a plotline that had Cary Grant walking away from being a millionaire simply because he wanted an extended "holiday." For a Depression audience, many of whom had already experienced an economically forced "holiday," the idealism of a 1920s play probably seemed ludicrous. And a previously unexplored explanation for *Holiday*'s disappointing commercial returns might be attached to a public upset that one of its then-favorite performers (Dunne) was unceremoniously dumped from a coveted part, only to be replaced by an actress in disfavor.

A final factor in *Holiday*'s less-than-stellar box office brings one back to the equally disappointing reception accorded Dunne's *Joy of Living*. That is, by 1938 the genre of screwball comedy was becoming passé. After seeming to peak the previous year with an assortment of classics, from *The Awful Truth*, to Cary Grant's *Topper*, or Carole Lombard's *Nothing Sacred*, the year 1938 is peppered with a series of less-than-well-received screwball attempts. For instance, Lombard had one of her rare failures in the genre with *Fools For Scandal*, which opened in New York the same March week as *Joy of Living*. Even 1938's *Bringing Up Baby*, now considered one of screwball comedy's definitive works, proved to be a disappointment at the box office. The genre was definitely in decline. And while there would be the occasional exception in years to come, such as the McCarey-Dunne *My Favorite Wife*, the genre's last period hurrah would come with several early 1940s vehicles by writer-director Preston Sturges, starting with *The Lady Eve* (1941).

The passing of this genre by the late 1930s provides a perfect segue into Dunne's 1939 reconnection with McCarey. Their joint venture, *Love Affair*, was a departure from a screwball comedy—a sometimes comic, sometimes poignant *romantic comedy*. Having recently completed a text on the difference between these two genres, I should posit the following differences.[24] First, the screwball outing places its emphasis on *funny*, while the more traditional romantic comedy accents *love*. That is, the screwball variety embraces the ludicrous—American farce, complete with slapstick. In contrast, romantic comedy is more reality-based, with little or no physical comedy. (The *Love Affair* relationship of Dunne and Charles Boyer is the kind of story where time seems to stop, because nothing else appears to matter. What a contrast with *The Awful Truth*, where there are custody fights over family pets.)

Second, and consistent with farce's anything-goes atmosphere, screwball comedy spoofs the romantic process; love comes across as hardly more significant than a board game. Conversely, romantic comedy frequently embraces sentimental and/or melodramatic story developments completely alien to screwball comedy. (Dunne's *Love Affair* character being struck by a car is a classic example of this point.) Third, screwball comedy is usually defined by both its dominatingly zany heroine, and a complementarily crazy supporting cast. Romantic comedy has a less controlling, more serious heroine, with character actor support which tends to be more funny than flakey. (Instead of Dunne's celebrated screwball tendency to *go wild* and dictate terms, her *Love Affair* heroine actually keeps news of a crippling accident from Boyer, for fear his devotion would be born of pity instead of love.)

A fourth contrast between the genres involves the dating ritual itself. In the screwball category, the eccentric heroine frequently finds herself in a triangle with the sought-after male and some life-smothering other woman. The heroine's mission is to free the male from the rigid life-sucking female. This is not to say romantic comedy cannot have a third party, but conflict for this genre is more apt to occur over character differences, rather than over another character. (Instead of Dunne rescuing Cary Grant from a stuffy blue blood in *The Awful Truth*, *Love Affair*'s burning issue is whether Boyer will ever find out why Dunne did not meet him at the top of the Empire State Building.)

A final contrast between the genres involves pacing. Screwball comedy escalates near the close, such as Dunne's patented tendency to *go wild*. Contrastingly, romantic comedy often slows to a snail's pace at the close, as the audience agonizes over whether the couple will ultimately get together, such as *Love Affair*'s celebrated cliffhanger, where Boyer must figure out Dunne's condition on his own.

Romantic comedy's one-foot-in-reality base suited McCarey better than the ludicrousness of screwball farce. In fact, the director had anticipated the public losing interest in screwball comedy well before 1938. In a 1937 interview the *New York Sun*'s film critic found that, "However the public may feel about charmingly insane [screwball] people on the screen, Leo McCarey is fed up with them."[25] Thus, even in *The Awful Truth* McCarey consciously attempted to anchor the zaniness in a plausible premise—Dunne's character sincerely wants her husband (Cary Grant) back. And just as *The Awful Truth* was triggered by real events in McCarey's life, *Love Affair* had a personal catalyst, too. Returning with his wife by ship from a European vacation, he was inspired by a film idea just as their ship approached the Statue of Liberty. Turning to his spouse, who had suggested the trip so he could recharge his creative batteries, McCarey said:

> Suppose you and I were talking to each other when the boat sailed from England and we got to know each other on the trip. We felt ourselves inseparable. By the time the trip was over, we were madly in love with each other but by the time the boat docked we have found out that each is obligated to somebody else. [After relating this to Peter Bogdanovich he then added] that was the story of [*Love Affair*] the picture.[26]

With McCarey's hit track record, several prominent period actresses, including Greta Garbo and Helen Hayes, were interested in playing the female lead. But the director went with his favorite actress, Dunne, a choice strongly supported by his wife, also a major Irene fan. Dunne's memory of the subsequent shoot was pure McCarey, with "lots of it [improvisation. And] He kept handing us [the performers] pieces of paper all the time with new dialogue. So there wasn't much sense in ever learning anything—you only had to unlearn it."[27]

As was McCarey's habit, he hand-tailored the *Love Affair* heroine for Dunne, which included making her a nightclub entertainer in order that Irene could sing during the picture. McCarey also gave the actress the freedom to choose an all-important signature song for the film. Dunne's pick was an old standard, "Wishing," with the movie's young

Dunne's maternal touch in *Penny Serenade* (1941), opposite Cary Grant.

Dunne in her dressing room just prior to shooting the "burlesque bit" in *The Awful Truth* (the film magazine is the Spanish publication *Cine-Mundial*).

The actress' career-making turn in *Cimarron* (1931), opposite Richard Dix.

Dunne's mentoring of Robert Taylor helped make the *Magnificent Obsession* (1935) his breakout film.

Leo McCarey (right) on the set of *Ruggles of Red Gap* (1935), with the film's title star Charles Laughton (left) and popular period humorist Irvin S. Cobb.

Dunne and her river Romeo, Allan Jones, in *Show Boat* (1936).

Provocative novelist Dunne flanked by her small town aunts, Elizabeth Risdon (right) and Margaret McWade, in *Theodora Goes Wild* (1936).

McCarey (left), Dunne, and Alexander D'Arcy on the set of *The Awful Truth* (the "slant board" allowed Dunne to rest without wrinkling her gown.)

Dunne and director Rouben Mamoulian on the set of *High, Wide and Handsome* (1937).

Part of the extended hat routine in *The Awful Truth*, with Dunne, Grant, and movie star pooch Asta, anwering here to the name "Mr. Smith."

McCarey recycling shipboard reality in *Love Affair* (1939), with Dunne, Charles Boyer, and the all important Empire State Building in the mist.

Playing Boyer's grandmother, Maria Ouspenskaya doubles as both a symbol of and a catalyst for love. Pictured here with Dunne and Boyer in *Love Affair*.

Dunne and screen children, Mary Lou Harrington and Scotty Beckett, in *My Favorite Wife* (1940).

Dunne and Grant's inspired screen rapport was based on a comparable chemistry in real life, pictured here with *My Favorite Wife* co-star Randolph Scott.

Dunne and Grant abroad in *Penny Serenade*.

Preston Foster about to put the romantic rush on Dunne in *Unfinished Business* (1941).

Dunne and Spencer Tracy in the deleted *heavenly* conclusion from *A Guy Named Joe* (1943).

Dunne and her stand-in Kathryn Stanley on the set of *The Awful Truth*.

Dunne's stunning beauty, on the set of *A Guy Named Joe* (1943).

Dunne and her screen son, Richard Lyon, in *Anna and the King of Siam* (1946).

Dunne and Elizabeth Taylor as a potential screen daughter-in-law in *Life with Father* (1947), with ZaSu Pitts.

A new twist on the work
ethnic, Dunne as the title
character in *I Remember
Mama* (1948).

By the time of her Filmex salute (1979), Dunne rated *Mama* and *Love Affair*
(pictured here with Boyer) as her best films.

On screen or off, Dunne exuded a joyful charm—pictured here after a 1941
screening of *Penny Serenade*.

choir making their rendition both a highlight of the picture, and a catalyst for other period artists to record "Wishing." Moreover, the song selection also nicely demonstrated how, at this point in their joint careers, Dunne and McCarey were seemingly on the same creative page. Years later, when Peter Bogdanovich did what amounted to a lengthy deathbed interview with McCarey, the significance of Dunne's song selection was underlined. The director's emphysema limited his responses to short answers. But Bogdanovich's elegantly insightful summation of McCarey's positions, such as his thoughts on "Wishing," were invaluable. Thus, he asked the director, "You once said that people think of you as a sophisticated director but that actually you aren't; that you really believe that song in *Love Affair*—that 'wishing can make it so.' Is that true?"[28] To this McCarey gave a strong "yes."

Unlike some watershed works, which are neglected or not appreciated upon their initial release (such as McCarey's own *Duck Soup*), *Love Affair* garnered pure scrapbook press coverage. *New York World-Telegram* critic William Boehnel's take on the picture was typical of its glowing marks: "I found it the most absorbing and delightful entertainment of its kind that I have seen in a long time—a beautifully acted and directed offering full of taste and distinction."[29] Reviewers seemed to risk running out of superlatives. For instance, another period critic called it "a picture of such exquisite beauty that it is a joy to the beholder. It is a tender, poignant film, sentimental without being gooey, funny but not goofy [screwball]."[30] Peppered throughout these raves was an ongoing appreciation of a comic artist too little known today. For example, the *New York Times'* Frank S. Nugent observed, "Leo McCarey, who directs so well it is almost anti-social of him not to direct more often, has created another extraordinarily fine film in 'Love Affair.'"[31]

The brass ring for the critic with the most entertaining take on McCarey's *Love Affair* accomplishment goes to *Screen and Radio Weekly's* Clark Wales:

> Recommending a Leo McCarey production is something like recommending a million dollars or beauty or a long and happy life. Any of these is a very fine thing to have and the only trouble is that there are not enough of them.[32]

Wales also intuitively noted one of McCarey's most inspired gifts—the director's ability to capture slice-of-life realism: "As in all McCarey pictures, the greatest perfection is in the little, human scenes in which people do commonplace things, or carry on commonplace talk with superb, complete naturalness."[33] This McCarey touch was the catalyst for the celebrated French director Jean Renoir observing, "McCarey really understands people," and George Bernard Shaw sending McCarey a fan letter after seeing his *Make Way For Tomorrow* (1937).

Love Affair's "naturalness" is most movingly manifest in the scenes involving the visit by Dunne and Boyer to his grandmother, played by the Russian-born character actress Maria Ouspenskaya. Though only "commonplace things" are addressed, the matter-of-fact affection revealed between grandparent and grandson has the poignancy of a loving home movie. The viewer almost feels like he should look away—as if an act of eavesdropping is taking place. These magic moments are also memorable because they serve as the foundation for McCarey's love story—Dunne likes playboy Boyer but it is not until she sees him through the eyes of this loving grandmother that he becomes relationship material.

Interestingly enough, Maria Ouspenskaya played movie critic on *Love Affair*, too. In a rare 1939 interview she had great praise for both McCarey and Dunne, which was also a rarity, since this notable character actress seldom found anyone or anything commendable. Thus, she credited the director with creating an "atmosphere of work that is inspirational. Every person connected with the film but everyone!—actor, electricians, and cameramen loved their work and did not want to break away from that atmosphere."[34] But she saved her greatest tribute for Dunne—"the sweetest woman with whom I have ever acted. She is an actress to her finger tips and radiates a charm I have never found in all my 25 years of acting."[35]

Dunne's *Love Affair* clippings from traditional journalistic sources were equally impressive. Indeed, the *London News* felt compelled to rehash her past triumphs, too:

> She has ranged from the drama of such films as "Cimarron" to the singing heroine of "Show Boat" and "Roberta," and to the "pixilated" comedy of "Theodora Goes Wild"; nor has her assurance ever failed her or the charm of her personality diminished in any of the spheres she has invaded.[36]

In contrast, the *New York Telegraph* simply cut to the *Love Affair* chase—"Certainly this Terry McKay of Miss Dunne's is one of the greatest things she has ever done on the screen, a polished and genteel woman of the world."[37] And the *New York Herald Tribune* chronicled her range within *Love Affair*—"Miss Dunne is versatile and utterly persuasive, pointing up the comedy of the early sections, singing a few songs engagingly and realizing all the tragic overtones of the conclusion, when, having been crippled, she refuses to see the man she loves."[38]

The *New York Times* played a McCarey-Dunne balancing act in its praise of *Love Affair*. The newspaper's critic defined the movie's "formula" for success as "comedy plus sentiment plus X (which is Mr. McCarey himself)."[39] But despite the director's importance, the *Times* felt almost as large a measure of significance should be attributed to Dunne and costar Charles Boyer—"the facility with which they have matched the changes of their script—playing it lightly now, soberly next but always credibly, always in character, always with a superb utilization of the material at hand."[40]

Besides all the pluses attached to being in a hit movie, an added *Love Affair* bonus for Dunne was the start of a long-term friendship with Boyer (1897–1978). After Cary Grant, the French star would become the actress' favorite leading man. The phenomenal popularity of *Love Affair* would lead to two Dunne-Boyer reteamings—*When Tomorrow Comes* (1939) and *Together Again* (1944). Boyer had been McCarey's first choice for *Love Affair*'s male lead because the actor was already established as one of the screen's "great lovers." Two earlier Boyer films in particular, *History Is Made At Night* (1937, sometimes considered Hollywood's most romantic title) and *Algiers* (1938) put him on the cinema map as a movie lover. (His *Algiers* screen character Pepe Le Moko would even seem to have inspired Warner Brother's later cartoon character Pepe LePew, the amorous French skunk so taken with romance, and possessor, like Boyer, of a deep, velvety, French-accented voice. In fact, this cartoon character was always wanting to take his love interests to the "Casbah," which is a key district of Algiers in the Boyer movie.)

The public so enjoyed the 1939 teaming of Dunne and Boyer that *Photoplay* that year devoted a double article to how the two screen lovers would describe each other—"CHARLES As Seen By Irene Dunne" and "IRENE As Seen By Charles Boyer." Though some might suggest this was merely the work of a publicist, Dunne's responses are so privately insightful that one cannot help believing she was directly involved. Regardless, Dunne and Boyer were encouraged to use the popular arts as the foundation of their descriptions, after a 1930s party game. The actor's word picture of

Dunne keyed upon architecture: "a gracious house . . . atop a hill."
But Boyer was most entertainingly insightful when he focused on
a special area of this house as a metaphor:

> Of course, the best room would be the music room, a cool place with
> great windows opening on a garden. Great music, and the best of good
> swing, and things by Gershwin would sound there always. The
> acoustics would be perfect. Guests in this house would be relaxed and
> happy but they would have to mind their manners.[41]

This is a poetically succinct picture of Dunne—the gracious but proper
lady, whose great passions were music and her floral gardens.
(Dunne's early 1930s correspondence suggests that California's biggest
selling point was not the movies but year-round flower gardens!)

In contrast, Dunne's metaphorical "reading" of Boyer was most
elegantly revealing of her when she so knowingly compared him to
a painting. That is, Boyer would be:

> A portrait of an actor—naturally—and of a gentleman, painted by Ma-
> tisse. The background would be Monet, and Degas would contribute
> some dim figures in a corner, for balance. Are busts ever carved by
> sculptors out of quartz? Charles could be a Rodin bust in black quartz.[42]

The fact that Dunne was describing a Frenchman was only part of the
catalyst for this description. Outside of New York, Paris was her favorite city, and the qualified-to-be-an-art-instructor Dunne dearly
loved the French Impressionist painters, several of whom are referred
to in her description of Boyer. Consequently, the friendship of Dunne
and Boyer was based in their sophisticatedly cultured backgrounds.

When one factors in these parallels with the partylike atmosphere
McCarey brought to a film set, it is no wonder Dunne especially
enjoyed the shooting of *Love Affair*. And while the picture would
always hold a special place in the hearts of McCarey and Dunne, on
numerous later occasions Boyer would credit *Love Affair* with being
his personal favorite of all his films. Cary Grant so loved the picture
that he was instrumental in convincing McCarey to remake the
movie some eighteen years later as *An Affair to Remember* (1957, with
Grant costarring with Deborah Kerr).

Interestingly enough, as much as *Love Affair* meant to Dunne, the
actress later confessed she personally would have done things differ-
ently, after the accident on the way to the Boyer rendezvous. With com-

ically romantic passion she observed, "If I had been in that girl's place, far from hiding [for fear of pity], I would have trundled my wheel chair up and down the sidewalks of New York *looking* for Mr. Boyer."[43] Irene's equally fervent explanation also spoke volumes about her tenacity: "For if I have learned anything in my life, it is to hold fast, with heart and both hands, to the vital, precious, and important things if, and when, they come to you. They may not come again."[44]

This qualifier notwithstanding, part of the film's uniqueness was just standing out in such a stellar Hollywood year (1939). This date is now considered the high point of the American studio system, with dozens of classics appearing, from *The Wizard of Oz* and *Gone With The Wind*, to *Stagecoach* and *Gunga Din*. Yet, *Love Affair* would be one of the select seven films nominated for the Best Picture Oscar. (The other six movies were *Dark Victory*, *Gone With The Wind*, *Goodbye, Mr. Chips*, *Mr. Smith Goes To Washington*, *Ninotchka*, and *Of Mice and Men*, with *Wind* taking home the 1939 statuette on February 29, 1940.) The following chapter will examine Dunne's own Best Actress nomination for *Love Affair*, as well as her other film outings for 1939–1940. Once again McCarey looms large.

NOTES

1. Mason Wiley and Damien Bono, *Inside Oscar* (New York: Ballantine Books, 1993), 72.

2. An *Awful Truth*/Oscar clipping from 1938 (incomplete citation), in the "Irene Dunne Collection," Box 4, Scrapbook 12 (April–June 1938), Cinema and Television Library, University of Southern California, Los Angeles.

3. Joe Hyams, "Irene Dunne's Husband: 'Be a Trailer,'" *New York Herald Tribune*, March 20, 1958, sec. 3, p. 12.

4. Ibid.

5. Adele Whitely Fletcher, "The True and Tender Story of Irene Dunne's Daughter," *Photoplay*, June 1938, 20.

6. Ida Zeftlin, "The New Side to Irene Dunne," *Motion Picture Story Magazine*, November 1937, 70.

7. Fletcher, 21.

8. Caroline S. Hoyt, "Irene Dunne's True Life Story" (Part 2), *Modern Screen*, January 1939, 79.

9. Irene Dunne to Fritz Ernst, December 22, 1936, "Charles Davidson Collection of Irene Dunne Letters."

10. Fletcher, 21.

11. "Side-Lights on a Star," *Modern Screen*, September 1939, 70.

12. Kate Cameron, "Irene Dunn [*sic*] Goes Wild Again in 'Joy of Living,'" *New York Daily News*, May 6, 1938, 50.

13. Ibid.; William Boehnel, "'Joy of Living' Offers Sophisticated Farce," *New York World-Telegram*, May 6, 1938, 25.

14. "'Joy of Living' Heavy on Slapstick, But Full of Fun," *Hollywood Reporter*, March 18, 1938.

15. Frank Nugent, review of *Joy of Living*, *New York Times*, May 6, 1938. 27.

16. Review of *Joy of Living*, *Variety*, March 23, 1938.

17. Howard Barnes, "'Joy of Living'—Radio City Music Hall," *New York Herald Tribune*, May 6, 1938, 19.

18. Archer Winsten, "'Joy of Living' Opens at Radio City Music Hall," *New York Post*, May 6, 1938, 21.

19. "Irene Dunne Collection," 10 boxes of material, Cinema and Television Library, University of Southern California (Los Angeles).

20. Sheilah Graham, "Hollywood Today," *Chicago Daily News*, March 25, 1938.

21. For example: Louella O. Parsons, "Cary Grant Gets Lead in 'Holiday': Irene is Slated for Top Spot, Too," *Philadelphia Inquirer*, December 24, 1937, 9.

22. For instance: Gary Carey, *Katharine Hepburn: A Hollywood Yankee* (New York: Dell, 1983), 100–101.

23. Margie Schultz, *Irene Dunne: A Bio-Bibliography* (Westport, Connecticut: Greenwood Press, 1991), 13.

24. Wes D. Gehring, *Romantic vs. Screwball Comedy: Charting the Difference* (Lanham, Maryland: Scarecrow Press, 2002).

25. Eileen Creelman, "Leo McCarey Tells of Directing Irene Dunne in a New Comedy, 'The Awful Truth,'" *New York Sun*, November 3, 1937.

26. Peter Bogdanovich, *Who the Devil Made It: Conversations with Legendary Film Directors* (New York: Ballantine Books, 1997), 417.

27. James Harvey, "Irene Dunne Interviewed by James Harvey," *Film Comment*, January–February 1980, 29.

28. Bogdanovich, 418.

29. William Boehnel, "'Love Affair' Seen as Outstanding Film," *New York World-Telegram*, March 17, 1939, 23.

30. Kate Cameron, "Exquisite Romance on Music Hall Screen," *New York Daily News*, March 17, 1939, 48.

31. Frank S. Nugent, review of *Love Affair*, *New York Times*, March 17, 1939, 25.

32. Clark Wales, *Love Affair* review, *Screen and Radio Weekly*, March 1939, 5, in the "Irene Dunne Collection," Box 4, Scrapbook 14 (February–May 1939), Cinema and Television Library, University of Southern California, Los Angeles.

33. Ibid.

34. Regina Crewe, "Mme Ouspenskaya, back from Coast, Offers Helping Hand to Fledglings," *New York Journal*, March 19, 1939.

35. Ibid.

36. Michael Orme, "The World of the Kinema," *London News*, April 29, 1939, 760.

37. Leo Mishkin, "'Love Affair' a Music Hall Winner; Irene Dunne, Charles Boyer Superb," *New York Telegraph*, March 18, 1939, 2.

38. Howard Barnes, "'Love Affair'—Music Hall," *New York Herald Tribune*, March 17, 1939, 16.

39. Frank S. Nugent, review of *Love Affair*, *New York Times*, March 17, 1939, 26.

40. Ibid.

41. "IRENE as Seen by Charles Boyer," *Photoplay*, October 1939, 24.

42. "CHARLES as Seen by Irene Dunne," *Photoplay*, October 1939, 25.

43. Faith Service, "My Screen Selves and I," *Silver Screen*, August 1944, 60–61.

44. Ibid., 61.

EIGHT

The End of a Decade, and One Last Film with McCarey

She's the twinkle of diamond heels going down a theater aisle . . . But the person wearing them might just possibly be chewing bubble gum. There's an irrepressible youthfulness about Irene.

—Charles Boyer on Dunne (1939)[1]

After the watershed *Love Affair*, Dunne's other two pictures for the year, *Invitation to Happiness* and *When Tomorrow Comes* (both 1939), were decidedly disappointing. One should quickly add that they were often entertaining but just not on a par with the McCarey film. The weaker of the two, *Invitation*, was a variation upon a popular period theme—a relationship born of a prizefighter and a lady. What begins as a quasi-romantic comedy about two people from different sides of the track turns melodramatic as Albert "King" Cole (Fred MacMurray) neglects his society wife (Dunne) and child (Billy Cook) in an endless quest to get a title fight.

Invitation reunited Dunne with her *Cimarron* director, Wesley Ruggles. And while the actress received her standard excellent notices (*Variety* said, "Miss Dunne switches to a straight dramatic role . . . and does a most capable job."[2]), most critics felt Ruggles, to quote the *New York Herald Tribune*, "was scarcely in top form."[3] Still, the director had such a solid track record, and a tendency to salvage memorable scenes in even mediocre movies, that many critics were kind. For instance, the *New York Times'* Frank S. Nugent observed, "But, of course, no Ruggles film ever is really bad. They always have a saving grace of humor . . . and a compassionate understanding of people."[4]

109

Consequently, Nugent said, "We confess a delightful appreciation of the scenes in which Miss Dunne and [her screen father] face the advent of . . . [a baby], and that in which she claims her triumph over King Cole's pre-marital blonde."[5] Some critics, however, skirted the issue of director and merely focused on praising Dunne. This was especially true of heartland reviewers, such as the *Detroit Free Press'* James S. Pooler, "We don't know what there is about Irene Dunne that gives . . . her pictures a lift above average but in 'Invitation' you'll find fine performances, emotions to clog your throat and a neatly contrived story."[6]

Dunne's third film for 1939 featured a reteaming with *Love Affair* costar Charles Boyer in the melodramatic *When Tomorrow Comes.* Though it was an improvement upon *Invitation*, the Boyer connection triggered more frequent comparisons with *Love Affair*—which found it wanting in comparison to that film, too. Indeed, rare was the *When Tomorrow Comes* review which did not kick off with hosannas for the McCarey picture. For instance, here is critic William Boehnel's opening for his *New York World-Telegram* take on *When Tomorrow Comes*: "Having helped to make 'Love Affair' the finest love story of the year, Irene Dunne and Charles Boyer now lend their engaging talents to a middling-fair-tear-jerker."[7]

The *New York Daily New's* Kate Cameron observed, "The stars who made 'Love Affair' the most delightfully romantic picture of the year have done much to make this a tender . . . tale of a frustrated love."[8] But the title of her review was even more succinct on the subject—"Another Love Affair For Dunne and Boyer." On the business side, the always film industry–savvy *Variety* stated what was probably the key catalyst for the quick Dunne-Boyer reteaming—"Pair's click in 'Love Affair' is still fresh to give added b.o. [box office] impetus for the profit side."[9] West Coast reviewers were less distracted by the preceding greatness of McCarey's *Love Affair*. For example, the *Los Angeles Examiner* critique stated, "I don't know any more romantic pair on the screen than Irene Dunne and Charles Boyer."[10]

However, *When Tomorrow Comes* was not a McCarey rehash. The movie reunited Dunne with director John Stahl, who megaphoned her in the melodrama hits *Back Street* (1933) and *Magnificent Obsession*. And *When Tomorrow Comes* owes more than a little to the earlier weepy. Again, there is a love affair complicated by the man's marriage. But this time Dunne's character does *not* go the kept woman route of *Back Street*. Besides a censorship code by then in place (since

1934), Irene's screen persona had become too dominant to kowtow to a married man.

Still, *When Tomorrow Comes* pushes all the standard melodrama buttons, from class differences (a concert pianist and a waitress), to a problem marriage with extenuating circumstances (Boyer's screen wife has bouts of insanity!). And as a metaphorical take on the couple's agitated psychological state, the lovers are even caught in the proverbial terrible storm. (But in defense of this plot device, the eastern seaboard had actually been hit by a hurricane the previous fall—1938.) Regardless, *When Tomorrow Comes* successfully returned Dunne to the genre (melodrama, the stereotypical "woman's picture") on which her early career was launched. Indeed, the *New York Times'* review of *Tomorrow* opened with a popular culture reference to the gender-specific nature of this genre—the film "was met by a solid phalanx of women at the Rivoli yesterday."[11]

As a final footnote to *Tomorrow*, despite the film's general pigeonholing in melodrama, it boasts a scene that was quite possibly the catalyst for Jack Nicholson's later celebrated "chicken salad sandwich" speech in *Five Easy Pieces* (1970). Just as Nicholson had to get comically creative with his waitress, Boyer tried to order American cheese from waitress Dunne—but Luncheon Number 4 required that said cheese could only be part of the apple pie dessert order. While there is not the veiled hostility which Nicholson displayed towards his server, the Boyer-Dunne encounter is still an entertaining example of the same point—the absurdity of all the petty rules which encumber us.

Ironically, with today's hindsight, Dunne's biggest 1939 film news, after the hit *Love Affair*, was *not* the disappointing *Invitation to Happiness* and *When Tomorrow Comes*. Instead, it was actually a movie she did not make. In May of 1939 it was widely reported that Dunne was going to play the woman reporter in director Howard Hawks' screwball comedy reworking of the Ben Hecht-Charlie MacArthur classic, *The Front Page*.[12] Hawks and his leading lady were taking a creative chance with a gender revamping of the original play. For instance, period columnist Dorothy Manners observed, "Right off the bat Irene will have to sell the cash customers and the critics on the idea that a girl reporter can be as exciting as Lee Tracy made [the character of] Hildy in the original . . . play."[13]

Of course, this was the production which would become the celebrated *His Girl Friday* (1940), though the working title in May of 1939 was *The Bigger They Come*. Columbia chief Harry Cohn, whose studio was producing the picture, had originally announced in March that Jean Arthur was going to be Hildy. But the actress and Hawks had not seen eye to eye on their previous film, *Only Angels Have Wings* (1939), and Arthur backed out of *Friday*. Cohn and Hawks were then most interested in Dunne, who tentatively agreed, only to back out, too.

The "why" remains a mystery, though Hawks' definitive biographer documents that Dunne was hardly alone in turning down this inspired movie.[14] The Hollywood who's who that followed Irene's lead and passed on playing Hildy included Ginger Rogers, Claudette Colbert, and Carole Lombard. Even the eventual taker, Rosalind Russell, was initially a reluctant participant. Part of the problem, as noted in the last chapter, was that screwball comedy had become passé by this time. Both Dunne and Lombard had been burned in their previous screwball outings—Irene's *Joy of Living* and Carole's *Fools for Scandal* (both 1938). Even Colbert's 1938 contribution to the genre, *Bluebeard's Eighth Wife*, which had opened simultaneously with the Dunne and Lombard vehicles, had been judged a disappointment, given that it was an Ernst Lubitsch film. Of the aforementioned actresses considered for the Hildy role, only Ginger Rogers had had a successful screwball outing in 1938—the George Stevens picture *Vivacious Lady*, with Jimmy Stewart. If these performers were not spooked by the genre, there was also the professional risk of playing a part originally conceived for a man.

What makes Dunne's rejection of the role most frustrating, however (beyond *Friday*'s ultimately great critical and commercial success), was how hard Columbia seemed to be trying to recapture the magic of the studio's earlier picture, *The Awful Truth* (1937). Not only would Dunne have been reteamed with her *Awful Truth* costars Cary Grant and Ralph Bellamy, *Friday* would embrace the same screwball character configuration. That is, Dunne and Grant would be the comically battlin' former couple, with Bellamy playing the antiheroic third wheel in yet another example of the genre's perennial romantic triangle arrangement of principal characters. (*The Awful Truth* was such a smash hit that Hollywood dealmakers had *immediately* started pitching a Dunne and Grant reteaming. For instance, shortly after *Truth* opened the *Los Angeles Times* ran the story, "Cary Grant Paired With Irene Dunne Again In 'Joy of Loving.'"[15] Of course, the male lead eventually went to Douglas Fairbanks, Jr.—see previous chapter.)

Friday's *Awful Truth* connection would eventually be another reminder for Dunne of the talisman-like effect McCarey seemed to have on her career. Certainly 1939 had been peppered with such references, from the hit *Love Affair*, to most reviews of *When Tomorrow Comes* being measured against the McCarey film. Moreover, early 1940 developments further reinforced Dunne's connection with the director. She would receive her fourth Oscar nomination as Best Actress for her *Love Affair* performance.

At this point in her career, one-half of these nominations were tied to McCarey pictures—*The Awful Truth* being the first example. Unfortunately, come Oscar night (February 29, 1940) she would again lose to a foreign actress (England's Vivien Leigh in *Gone With The Wind*, 1939). But the quality connection associated with McCarey films loomed large in Dunne's world. And 1940 would see them joining forces yet again with *My Favorite Wife*. But before examining this film, another *Love Affair* Oscar nomination merits consideration, with regard to Dunne's admiration for McCarey.

The actress had always been greatly taken with the director's casting of pivotal character actors. (Indeed, screenwriter Sheridan Gibney was later on record as saying McCarey's greatest gift was being a "brilliant caster" of *all* parts.[16]) Regardless, no one was more central to the success of *Love Affair* than the Oscar-nominated Best Supporting Actress Maria Ouspenskaya, who played Charles Boyer's grandmother in the picture and served, as previously noted, as an indirect matchmaker. But this grandmother also accents the sentimental depiction of love in an additional manner often associated with romantic comedy: she is an ongoing symbol of the eternal purity of love. Long widowed, she remains very much in love with her late husband, something which is warmly communicated to those around her without any degree of mawkishness. Plus, in death her promise of a special scarf for Dunne is what brings the couple back together—Boyer delivers it and finally discovers why Dunne did not make their Empire State Building rendezvous.

Besides being central to *Love Affair*, as these older poignant figures often are in romantic comedy, Ouspenskaya's performance is all the more moving given the actress' convincing naturalness in the part. This was a fact not lost on period reviewers. *New York Post* critic Archer Winsten observed, "This role is so deeply felt, so brilliantly paced and projected, that it will be remembered when parts ten or twenty times as big have long been forgotten."[17] The *Brooklyn Eagle* reviewer added, "Her playing of Boyer's grandmother . . . is a joy to watch—delicate, sincere and eloquently restrained."[18] One is, of course, reminded of the central elderly couple in McCarey's *Make Way For Tomorrow* (1937), who are tragically separated at the movie's gut-wrenching conclusion. One could, in fact, credit McCarey with helping make these older symbols of long-lasting love an integral part of romantic comedy. The best modern example of the genre's use of elderly corroborative witnesses for a sentimental celebration of love (testimonials, if you will) occurs in *When Harry Met Sally* (1989). Peppered throughout the movie are a series of interviews with older couples briefly but warmly chronicling their love stories. In each instance, they are fittingly seated on a love seat looking straight at the camera—ready to share. Moreover, making the final duo Harry and Sally further suggests the permanence of their relationship. That is, the viewer identifies them with all the preceding golden-aged testimonials to love. Again, this was part of the McCarey gift which so fascinated Dunne, also an obvious student of the sentimental.

Besides the significance of 1939's *Love Affair*, the year was also memorable in a more subtle but no less important way—the actress who had sometimes been portrayed as "Icy Irene" in private had seemed to finally win over *all* of the press. Credit the transition to her by then celebrated gift for comedy and/or an accompanying ease with the Fourth Estate. If one were pressed to pinpoint a pivotal interview, this author would opt for a provocatively entitled 1939 piece, "She's No Lady," which is disarmingly funny:

> I watch my weight, too, and I'll bet you won't get many of them [actresses] to admit that. Why is it that many women who have divine figures like to pretend that they're God-given? Gosh, I haven't had a potato since I played in "Cimmaron" [1931].[19]

Regardless, given McCarey's period Midas touch, he was soon able to entice Dunne back to the fading genre of screwball comedy. The property was *My Favorite Wife* (1940), the long-awaited *Awful Truth* reunion of McCarey, Dunne, and Cary Grant. Once again magic happened. Reviewers fell over themselves praising the movie, sometimes to comic effect. For example, the *Los Angeles Examiner* entertainingly shared, "here is a rogue of a picture, sophisticated, sparkling, gay, and so hilarious it will make the worst grouch in all Kingdom Come forget he's mad?"[20] Accounts now differ as to whether McCarey was actually scheduled to direct, or simply to produce and play story guru. But a near-fatal automobile accident kept him from officially wearing the director's hat (that credit went to Garson Kanin). There were, however, soon hospital conferences and McCarey quickly became a fixture on the set. And once the picture initially wrapped, McCarey was responsible for both tweaking the picture in the editing process, and then writing some new material (including a second comic courtroom scene—drawing loosely from McCarey's background in law).

Despite a *My Favorite Wife* storyline that involves a missing wife (Dunne) showing up just after she has been declared legally dead and her husband (Cary Grant) has remarried, there are enough *Awful Truth* parallels (including an in-the-country conclusion) that period critics correctly tagged this a McCarey picture. For instance, the period's greatest but still underrated film critic, the *New Republic*'s Otis Ferguson, even called *My Favorite Wife* a "nonsense-sequel to *The Awful Truth.*"[21] But then, this was a standard period slant, as exemplified by the *New York Sun*'s casual story line aside, "None of this has anything to do with its [the film's] very obvious resemblance to another McCarey comedy, 'The Awful Truth.'"[22] Surprisingly, the normally staid *New York Times* was the most poetically upbeat about crediting McCarey with the critical and commercial triumph that was *My Favorite Wife*:

> This is briefly to report the discovery of a new island yesterday—a little island of joy at Fiftieth Street West and Sixth Avenue North, where Leo McCarey's "My Favorite Wife" floated into the ken of audiences at Radio City Music Hall . . . this is the sort of refuge we can all find pleasure in these days.[23]

Fittingly, given that Dunne was McCarey's favorite actress, the *Times* also suggested that the actress was the best embodiment of the director's comic gift for creating "the prolonged and amorous tease." Their praising litany of Dunne traits along these lines included "her luxurious and mocking laughter, her roving eyes and come-hither glances—mere man is powerless before it."[24] Despite it being a screwball comedy, McCarey also managed to slip in some of his signature sentimentality. Again, it fell to Dunne to deliver along these lines, such as reconnecting with screen children her character had not seen in seven years. The *New York World-Telegram* critic acknowledged the actress' gifted versatility: "Irene Dunne gives a performance masterful in its wealth. It is full of laughter, but it is also tinged with fear and pathos."[25]

While period critics seemed to appreciate the significance of the McCarey-Dunne collaboration, the actress' equally winning rapport with Cary Grant has yet to be fully explored, beyond the most cursory of comments. For instance, near the close of the *Boston Post's* review of *My Favorite Wife*, almost as an afterthought, the critic blandly states "Miss Dunne and Mr. Grant make the perfect team for romantic comedy . . . and they are both charming people."[26] Yet, I would posit that among screwball heroines, Grant was probably at his best opposite Dunne, a fact no doubt assisted by the presence of McCarey. Grant's other romantic teamings in the genre (including Katharine Hepburn, Constance Bennett, and Rosalind Russell) are also winning arrangements. But his couplings with Dunne are bolstered by their special give-and-take—which smacked of being affectionate equals, despite the genre's propensity to have the heroine dominate.

Dunne's lady mother hen persona, moreover, both onscreen and off (critic Pauline Kael once called her "the ancestor of Julie Andrews"), provided the perfect parental contrast for Grant's often childlike shtick—McCarey borrowings which remind us of Laurel and Hardy. For instance, in *My Favorite Wife* Grant has just had a pep talk with Dunne on how to tell his second wife their marriage is off. As he rehearses his lines little boy style near the hotel stairs between his two rooms (for wives one and two), Grant is very demonstrative with his hands, including a "we can still be friends" sort of outward handshake thrust of his right arm. At this exact moment a suspicious hotel clerk appears, and Grant milks the scene to comic perfection. Amusingly leaving his extended hand outward like an inanimate prop, he looks first at the clerk, then returns his gaze to said hand, followed by yet another stare at the clerk. Stan Laurel could not have executed the scene more comically, though it was actually a little routine McCarey sometimes used among friends.

In Kael's imaginative *New Yorker* profile of Grant, "The Man From Dream City," which remains the key essay examination of the actor, she beguilingly describes screwball comedy as a genre which "turned love and marriage into vaudeville acts and changed the movie heroine from sweet clinging vines into vaudeville partner."[27] This screwball comedy-as-vaudeville metaphor is best realized in the teaming of Grant and Dunne. Indeed, the all-important *Awful Truth* even finds Dunne literally recreating a nightclub/vaudeville routine which had occurred earlier in the picture.

The in-film audience for her performance includes several people at a social gathering, but Dunne's focus is entirely on Grant for two reasons. First, she is obsessed with winning her soon-to-be-ex-husband back. Second, her recreated vaudeville turn is dependent upon the fact that only she and Grant had already seen it performed by another . . . and found it wanting. Thus, Dunne's ongoing comic asides during the number reflect their winsome rapport, with regard to a past shared experience as well as documenting how far she will go (public humiliation) to get him back. Moreover, with Dunne's routine being so Grant-directed, it makes the performance reminiscent of Kael's vaudeville *team* reference, with regard to screwball couples.

In addition, the Grant-Dunne screwball package beats other teamings in the genre for another reason also associated with McCarey. Celebrated French director Jean Renoir affectionately observed of his friend, "No one knows people like McCarey." The implied meaning here is that no director created such likeable screen characters as McCarey, no small accomplishment in a genre where eccentric behavior can often prove abrasive to many viewers. For instance, while Howard Hawks' *Bringing Up Baby* (1938) is now considered a pivotal example of screwball comedy, modern audiences (especially my college students) often find Katharine Hepburn's nonstop manic manipulation of Cary Grant irritating to the point of distraction. There is a similarly smothering component to many of Carole Lombard's screwball heroines, a trait Hepburn no doubt borrowed from in *Baby*.

In contrast, Dunne's duels with Grant in *The Awful Truth* and *My Favorite Wife* are invariably crowd-pleasers. No small part of this is creating those aforementioned likeable characters. The always insightful film critic and historian Richard Schickel best dissects this pleasing Dunne persona in his essay, "Irene Dunne: A Secret Light," which is the best single source (long or short) available on the actress. He observed:

> She always knew how to put a man in his place but at the same time leave him room to maneuver out of it . . . [such as joining] her in good-natured laughter at the all-too-transparent stratagems . . . [of the anti-heroic] male animal.[28]

Coupled with this but appearing later in his essay, Schickel knowingly adds, "Maybe one didn't—doesn't—meet many women like Irene Dunne . . . but because her [comic] reactions . . . were so unforced, so free of mannerisms, one felt—feels—comfortable in her presence, as one often does not with a more overtly 'screwball' like Lombard."[29] I am reminded of my maternal grandmother's ultimate compliment after meeting someone significant—he or she "still acted common." This was at the heart of Dunne's ever-so-likeable persona.

The mother hen component of Dunne's screen character (rein-forced in private life by her 1936 adoption of a baby) is probably most pleasingly presented in the country conclusion to *My Favorite Wife*, when Dunne and Grant drive to their mountain cabin with their two screen children in tow. The frustrated Grant is still faced with the which-wife-should-I-choose problem. (The film had opened with Grant marrying Gail Patrick shortly before the surprise return of first wife Dunne—missing for the past seven years in the South Pacific.) After putting their children to bed, Grant finds him-self in a child's bed stored in the attic, surrounded by toys. He is ob-viously on the verge of making his decision in Dunne's favor but he is too frazzled by this point to know how to express it. Moreover, at bedtime Dunne does not hurt her cause any by attractively and yet forcefully assigning separate rooms—she to the *master* bedroom, he relegated to the attic.

The effect of Grant's trek upstairs is that of a small boy sent to his room without supper. It is heightened by the nursery surroundings of the attic and the little bed in which he must sleep. The setting is a scaled-down version of the children's bedrooms in McCarey's cele-brated Laurel and Hardy short subject *Brats* (1930), in which the duo play double roles as fathers and little boys.

Grant gets ready for bed with toys literally hanging from the low ceiling. As he crawls into the squeaky bed, knocking things down, the viewer's eyes focus on two specific toys—a doll beside the bed and a toy cannon just underneath. (Without being overly metaphor-ical, this reduction of male to toy cannon nicely describes *My Favorite Wife* and numerous other screwball comedies.) As if to accent the childlike focus while revealing Grant's thoughts, the doll falls and says "mama." With this suggestion, he does, in fact, get up and go to "mama's" (Dunne's) bedroom.

After Grant has made the long trek down to her room, she rein-forces the earlier suggestion of the supperless child by asking in the most motherly of ways, "Are you hungry?" Needless to say, the true answer is something of a yes and a no; but Grant replies in the most appropriate of little boy styles that he cannot sleep. There are no "nice mattresses" in the attic as there are here—referring to the spare bed in Dunne's room. Using a bit of the aforementioned "amorous tease," she coyly says that, then, he can sleep on the unoccupied one. After his face has sufficiently lit up, like a little boy's at Christmas, she tells him he would be most welcome to take the mattress upstairs.

The crestfallen man-child that is Grant then takes the mattress out of the room, but McCarey's camera remains with Dunne. Grant returns in seconds complaining that the mattress does not fit, adding quietly in befuddlement, "I'm stuck. This could go till doomsday. I'm stuck but I don't care what people think." After this pointed regression, we once again see the two in their separate beds—with both anxious to end the separation. Grant must somehow express to Dunne that she truly is *my favorite wife*. But because of his long puzzlement over the decision and this complete childhood regression, which itself could be seen as the actualization of a little boy ego that refuses to admit a mistake, Grant seems to be literally struck dumb—unable even to communicate with normal speech patterns.

When you note this verbal incapacity of Grant's, you also remember that "'Do it visually'" was McCarey's byword. Grant therefore can be expected to perform some very comically symbolic act to resurrect his marriage to Dunne. Moreover, whatever symbol is chosen to represent the uniqueness of this day should be commensurate with a red-letter day in childhood. Grant is obviously operating with the mindset of a child, and it is only natural that he should communicate as such. (A key point to keep in mind, however, is the earlier suggestion by Grant that he take an ocean cruise alone to help him choose his favorite wife—a cruise which would last until Christmas.)

After individual shots of Grant and Dunne in their separate beds, the camera remains on Dunne. With a creative use of off-camera sound (another Laurel & Hardy connection), the viewer then hears Grant's attic bed collapse, another crash, the squeak of the attic door, and finally jingle bells. Grant then bursts in dressed as Santa Claus and cries "Merry Christmas!" Since Christmas is probably the most anxiously awaited moment of childhood, Grant's happiness over this apparent reconciliation proves to be a most effective communication, as well as suggesting the aforementioned possible reconciliation date. Just as in childhood, Grant plays his game by dressing up as someone else and imagining it to be a different time. And, despite the fact that "goodnight" is then written across the screen, ending the film with Grant's Santa Claus entry maintains the asexual nature of the child. Paradoxically, while Dunne continues to double as a mother hen, there is also a sexiness to her here, as there was with the similar close of *The Awful Truth*, which belies the actress' real-world Republican conservatism. One is reminded of film scholar Maria DiBattista's entertainingly breezy take on

Dunne—"She may have been a morally unimpeachable, happily wed Catholic woman in private life but on screen she courted impropriety like a pagan."[30]

A charming modern-era variation upon the child-husband and mother-wife of McCarey's *My Favorite Wife* occurs in Blake Edwards' *Micki & Maude* (1984), where diminutive leading man Dudley Moore also finds himself with two wives. But the inventive new twist for *Micki & Maude* is that both wives (Ann Reinking and Amy Irving) are keepers, à la Irene Dunne. Consequently, Moore has a more legitimate reason for being indecisive than Grant, whose second wife is the beautiful but witchy Gail Patrick. *Micki & Maude* is also more of a comically twisted modern tale, since child-man Moore enters into the second relationship while his first wife (Reinking) is very much around. (In Grant's case, first wife Dunne had been reported missing at sea.) Regardless, it seems most fitting that Edwards has created a new variation upon *My Favorite Wife*, since McCarey was his early comedy mentor, and Edwards' real-life wife is Julie Andrews— whom Pauline Kael had later compared to Dunne.

The May 1940 world premiere of *My Favorite Wife* took place in the city of Dunne's birth—Louisville. Her Hoosier hometown of Madison lost out because sports fan McCarey wanted the opening to coincide with the famous Kentucky Derby, an event he had never before experienced.[31] (Moreover, the trip would come at studio expense!) Regardless, Irene was at the center of the premiere, accompanied by her husband, Dr. Frank Griffin, mentor McCarey, and her *My Favorite Wife* costar Randolph Scott—who was Dunne's shipwreck companion, prior to finding her way back to screen civilization and Cary Grant. During this trip the actress also made a point of giving Frank his first tour of nearby Madison, enabling him to meet some of her Indiana friends and relatives.

Wife was Dunne's only 1940 film outing, but there had nearly been another teaming with Charles Boyer in the Warner Brothers' melodrama *All This and Heaven Too* (1940). But when the studio's pivotal star Bette Davis came back from a suspension the part went to her. Dunne also had a chance that year to return to Broadway in the musical *Lady in the Dark*, which had originally been written for Gertrude Lawrence by Moss Hart, Ira Gershwin, and Kurt Weill. After Dunne turned the property down, Lawrence reconsidered and she soon had a major hit on the "Great White Way." If you couple that with the fact that both *All This and Heaven Too* and *His Girl Friday* were runaway successes, Dunne took some professional lumps during 1940.

Ever the planning professional, however, late that year Dunne joined several clients of Hollywood agent Charles Feldman in forming Group Productions, a company which would receive funding and a release outlet through 20th Century-Fox.[32] She was aligned in this enterprise with her friend and costar Charles Boyer, actor Ronald Colman, and directors Lewis Milestone and Anatole Litvak. The goal for Group Productions was increased creative autonomy and an attempt at greater profits—risking minimal salaries against a sizable percentage of the profits. (One should add that Dunne was already in Hollywood's upper tax bracket. For instance, she was paid $100,000 for *My Favorite Wife*, plus a percentage of the profits.)

Though Group Productions would ultimately prove to be a disappointment for Dunne, her first film release of 1941 was anything but that—a final teaming with Cary Grant would prove to be yet another critical and commercial smash. But this time it was *not* a screwball comedy.

NOTES

1. "IRENE as Seen by Charles Boyer," *Photoplay*, October 1939, 24.

2. Review of *Invitation to Happiness*, *Variety*, May 10, 1939.

3. Howard Barnes, "'Invitation to Happiness'—Paramount," *New York Herald Tribune*, June 8, 1939, 16.

4. Frank S. Nugent, review of *Invitation to Happiness*, *New York Times*, June 8, 1939, 31.

5. Ibid.

6. James S. Porter, "Irene Dunne Play Is Par Even for Her," *Detroit Free Press*, June 17, 1939.

7. William Boehnel, "Love and Thrills in Two Pictures," *New York World-Telegram*, August 17, 1939.

8. Kate Cameron, "Another Love Affair for Dunne and Boyer," *New York Daily News*, August 17, 1939, 44.

9. Review of *When Tomorrow Comes*, *Variety*, August 16, 1939.

10. Louella O. Parsons, "Irene Dunne and Charles Boyer Engaging in Romantic Film, 'When Tomorrow Comes,'" *Los Angeles Examiner*, August 11, 1939.

11. Frank S. Nugent, review of *When Tomorrow Comes*, *New York Times*, August 17, 1939, 16.

12. For instance, see: Dorothy Manners (subbing for Louella O. Parsons), "Irene Dunne to Play Girl Reporter: 'Front Page' Revised and Retitled," *New York Journal American*, May 23, 1939, 9.

13. Ibid.

14. Todd McCarthy, *Howard Hawks: The Grey Fox of Hollywood* (New York: Grove Press, 1997), 282.

15. "Cary Grant Paired with Irene Dunne Again in 'Joy of Loving,'" *Los Angeles Times*, October 15, 1937, 10.

16. Patrick McGilligan, *Film Crazy: Interviews with Hollywood Legends* (New York: St. Martin's Press, 2000), 160.

17. Archer Winsten, "'Love Affair' Opens at Radio City Music Hall," *New York Post*, August 17, 1939.

18. Herbert Cohn, review of *Love Affair*, *Brooklyn Eagle*, March 17, 1939, 11.

19. Martha Kerr, "She's No Lady," *Modern Screen*, October 1939.

20. "'My Favorite Wife' Is Riot of Laughter," *Los Angeles Examiner*, April 30, 1940.

21. Robert Wilson, ed., *The Film Criticism of Otis Ferguson* (Philadelphia: Temple University Press, 1971), 302.

22. Eileen Creelman, "A Bright Farce, 'My Favorite Wife,'" *New York Sun*, May 31, 1940, 22.

23. Bosley Crowther, review of *My Favorite Wife*, *New York Times*, May 31, 1940, 15.

24. Ibid.

25. William Boehnel, "New Film Sparkling Comedy," *New York World-Telegram*, May 31, 1940, 12.

26. "'Favorite Wife' at Memoria," *Boston Post*, June 21, 1940.

27. Pauline Kael, "The Man From Dream City," *The New Yorker*, July 14, 1975, 54.

28. Richard Schickel, *Matinee Idylls: Reflections on the Movies* (Chicago: Ivan R. Dee, 1999), 79.

29. Ibid., 80.

30. Maria DiBattista, *Fast-Talking Dames* (New Haven, Connecticut: Yale University Press, 2001), 205.

31. "Madam Queen," *Modern Screen*, May 1947, 44+.

32. Margie Schultz, *Irene Dunne: A Bio-Bibliography* (Westport, Connecticut: Greenwood Press, 1991), 15.

NINE

A Last Picture with Cary Grant, Followed by Her Final Screwball Outings

With a good director and, say, Cary Grant, comedy can be a hilarious occupation. We used to laugh ourselves into inertia at noontime rushes . . . of "The Awful Truth."

—Irene Dunne just after the release of *Penny Serenade* (1941).[1]

For an Irene Dunne-Cary Grant picture, *Penny Serenade* was a departure. Instead of the screwball world of *The Awful Truth* (1937) and *My Favorite Wife* (1940), *Penny Serenade* was a romantic comedy that frequently embraced melodrama. Told in flashbacks cued by memorable songs in a couple's past, the film chronicled a troubled marriage twice rescued by the adoption of a child. The weepy component of the film was further enhanced by an accident that not only causes a Dunne miscarriage but also prevents her from being able to ever bear children. This tear factor is then topped by a story direction that has the couple losing their first adopted child to illness.

One should hasten to add, however, as Dunne did for a *New York Sun* interview, "The picture, although its story is drama, has more laughs than most comedies."[2] Much of the humor is drawn from the comic misadventures of childrearing, such as the midnight feeding where Grant thinks the baby is missing, whereas Dunne has merely taken the infant back to bed with her. There is also comedy connected to Grant's attempt to start and sustain a small-town newspaper, with the chuckle factor further enhanced by his assistant, the gifted character actor Edgar Buchanan.

This attention to McCarey-like comic detail was no accident. *Penny Serenade* director George Stevens had started out in film as

123

McCarey's cameraman on Laurel and Hardy silent short subjects. In fact, in later years Stevens played unofficial comedy historian in assessing the impact of this comedy team on screwball and romantic players like Dunne:

> The beauty of the Laurel and Hardy shorts . . . was their absolute deliberation [reduced pacing] . . . the Laurel and Hardy concept [with an assist from McCarey] moved into other films . . . with Cary Grant, Roz Russell, Irene Dunne doing the late take and even the double take.[3]

In the aforementioned *New York Sun* interview with Dunne, the actress even compared the occasional improvising of Stevens with that of McCarey. But she also qualified the two directors' reputations for being spontaneous on the set. With a laugh Dunne observed, "They don't always have it written down, but they have an awfully good idea [of what is going to happen]."[4]

Consequently, while the reviews and the box office for *Penny Serenade* were uniformly excellent, the take on which genre should be highlighted in the picture varied drastically from critic to critic. The *New York Daily News* keyed on melodrama: "Buckets of tears are being shed at the Music Hall over the touching domestic adventures of Roger Adams and his wife, Julie. . . . Such human, ordinary people, like ourselves."[5] The melodrama position was also seconded by the *Hollywood Reporter*—"In the basic simplicity of its deep emotional appeal, 'Penny Serenade' deserves to be ranked with the most memorable films of recent years."[6] The *New York Post* took a romantic/family film slant: "It will touch you, especially if you are susceptible to love, marriage, babies, and little children."[7] And the *New York Sun*'s follow-up review, after the interview with Dunne, keyed on comedy: *Penny Serenade* "is also very funny. Irene Dunne and Cary Grant, one of Hollywood's best comedy teams . . . [have no] difficulty in sliding from first comedy to a heartbreaking scene or ending a poignant moment with a laugh."[8] But in one case, a genre value judgement (to the detriment of comedy) is made.[9] This otherwise rave review from the *Los Angeles Examiner*, preserved as it was in Dunne's private papers, suggests the kind of critical bias that may have contributed to the actress' general preference for straight drama:

> Her versatility is surprising for we have seen her in so many of these frivolous comedies that it's hard to realize . . . what a fine dramatic actress [she] is and how human she makes [her *Serenade* character] Julie Adams.[10]

Penny Serenade had been a lengthy but very enjoyable shoot for Dunne. She thought highly of director Stevens, and Grant would always be her favorite costar. The feeling seems to have been mutual; the actress was later fond of sharing that Grant "once said I had the best timing for comedy of any actress he ever knew." Then a somewhat embarrassed Dunne added, "He also said—and I don't know that we should put this into print—that I was the sweetest-smelling actress he ever knew."[11] But one need not just depend upon the actress' memory. "Cary Grant told [*My Favorite Wife* director] Garson Kanin that Dunne was his favorite leading lady partly because she was always so inventive and delightful on the set; doing a movie with her was less like work than like a long and always surprising 'flirtation.'"[12]

The *Penny Serenade* production was drawn out for two reasons. Working with babies (sets of twins to maximize a production schedule) frequently prolonged the making of a movie. Plus, Stevens tended to shoot a great deal of footage. He would later be famous for epics like *A Place in the Sun* (1951) and *Giant* (1956), both of which earned him Best Director Oscars. According to Dunne, while McCarey worked very quickly, "Stevens was just the opposite, very slow. But he came well prepared . . . we would have rehearsals on the set, and . . . discuss details of how a scene would be played."[13]

Despite *Penny Serenade*'s excellent critical and commercial reception, the picture would garner only one major Oscar nomination—a Best Actor nod to Cary Grant, his first. (Shockingly, the actor would be nominated only one other time in his long and unique career—for *None But The Lonely Heart*, 1944.) Like Dunne, he would never win the statuette, though he would later receive an Honorary Oscar (1970). Grant's competition for his *Penny Serenade* performance included Orson Welles in the now celebrated *Citizen Kane* and Robert Montgomery in the screwball fantasy *Here Comes Mr. Jordan* (both 1941). But the ultimate winner, Gary Cooper in *Sergeant York* (1941), was a harbinger of things to come. Alvin York was a World War I hero whose story was being told to help prepare the United States for the approach of World War II. By the time of the Oscar ceremony honoring 1941 films (February 26, 1942), America was already entangled in the Second World War. Indeed, the country's first prominent war casualty was a movie star—Dunne's fellow Hollywood Hoosier, Carole Lombard. The actress had died in a plane crash returning home from the United States' opening war bond rally (in Indianapolis).

Whereas a home state (Indiana) and a film genre (screwball comedy) had formerly linked Dunne and Lombard, they were now tied by the war effort. Later in 1942 Irene would take part in a tour as part of the motion-picture industry's billion-dollar war bond sales campaign. The highlight for Dunne took place in her beloved New York City on September 8, 1942, where she urged a Times Square crowd of thousands to buy bonds. The macabre centerpiece of the rally featured the coffins of Hitler, Hirohito, and Mussolini. The purchase of a bond gave the buyer the privilege of driving a nail into the coffin of one of these perpetrators of World War II. A punning *New York Times* headline for the event nicely captured the dark comedy thrust of the rally—"Coffin Nailers Busy Boxing Axis Rulers."[14]

During this Times Square rally Dunne received a good-luck token from Miss Lee Yachine, a then-famous Chinese aviator. (In the 1930s Asia's China had first felt the military wrath of Japan.) Fittingly, for the music-loving Dunne, song was an integral part of the event. The crowd was entertained by both the popular period musician Will Osborne and his band, and by Liu Liang-mo, the originator of community singing in China. Liu's featured song was one that he used in China to help build the morale of the people during the war with Japan.

In a career development which might seem paradoxical to events like bond rallies, Dunne's two 1941 films just prior to our entry into the Second World War fall under the genre umbrella of screwball comedy. But had not this comedy approach become passé in 1938? Yes, it had. However, pivotal entertainment formats often die hard, especially when the occasional exception demonstrates renewed clout at the box office. Two classic examples of this occurred in 1940—both with Dunne connections. First, there was her missed opportunity with the now-celebrated *His Girl Friday*. Second, there was Irene's costarring involvement in the equally funny but underrated *My Favorite Wife*, orchestrated by and similar to Leo McCarey's pivotal screwball classic, *The Awful Truth*.

Another reason for the modest early-1940s revival of screwball comedy is its link to the natural cycle of any genre. As an entertainment formula exhausts its many storylines, the final harbinger of the end is a decided gravitation towards parody. It is as if to say, "We have exhausted every possible plotline; all that is now left to do is make affectionate fun of the waning genre itself." A later textbook example of this occurred to the Western in the latter half of the 1960s (culminating with 1972's *Blazing Saddles*). One might also plot a similar graph with the horror film during the late 1990s and the spoofing closure of *The Scream* trilogy (1996, 1997, 2000).

This parody signpost for the end of a genre cycle as we know it is not always an obvious phenomenon. That is, there are essentially two kinds of film parodies—the broad and obvious puncturing of a genre (à la *Blazing Saddles* or any other Mel Brooks spoof), and a more subdued approach that manages comic deflation with an eventual reaffirmation of the subject under comic attack, such as the trio of *Scream* movies. These latter parodies of reaffirmation are not so blatant. They are often confused with the genre being undercut. Thus, the *Scream* pictures mix broad spoofing with graphically horrific death. This produces a provocative tension between genre expectations (in this case, horror—to be scared) and a parody that is comic without deflating the characters involved. This is in contrast to the more traditional horror parody of a *Young Frankenstein* (1974), in which, for example, Marty Feldman's entertaining Igor, with those "pop" eyes and roving hump on his back, cannot be taken seriously, nor is the viewer ever worried about danger to his person.

While one cannot rate either of these spoof approaches as superior to the other, the reaffirmation style would seem to offer a more fascinatingly complex take on the genre of parody. With regard to early 1940s screwball comedy, no one artist better showcased period reaffirmation than inspired writer/director Preston Sturges. This is best exemplified by his *The Lady Eve* (1941) and *The Palm Beach Story* (1942).

The former film works as a summing up of the screwball genre that pushes the envelope so far (zany heroine Barbara Stanwyck nearly drives antiheroic Henry Fonda clinically crazy with her comic revenge) that the movie easily qualifies as basic reaffirmation spoofing. But Sturges' parody pièce de résistance is *The Palm Beach Story*. From its inspired opening, which is really the stereotypical "happy ending" of the typical screwball comedy, Sturges inventingly examines whether this genre's standard couple really does have a future. More specifically, *The Palm Beach Story*'s harried pre-credits sequence culminates with a wedding service and the on-screen title: "And they lived happily ever after—or did they?" Then several years dissolve across the screen starting with 1937—coincidently, the aforementioned high point of screwball comedy. When this reaffirmation parody gets to 1942, the viewer sees the proverbial "rest of the story."

Neither of Dunne's final two screwball outings, *Unfinished Business* (1941) and *Lady in a Jam* (1942), are in a reaffirmation parody class with these highlighted Sturges films. But while *Unfinished Business* was a critically acclaimed period hit, *Lady in a Jam* was popular with neither reviewers nor the public. Both movies were megaphoned by celebrated 1930s director Gregory LaCava, who had helped define screwball comedy with the masterful *My Man Godfrey* (1936). Given that Dunne always keyed upon the director, it is easy to see why she teamed up with LaCava twice late in his career. Indeed, as an early 1941 profile of LaCava in the *Chicago News* observed, "any star in Hollywood would drop everything to get into a LaCava picture."[15] (Nearly ten years earlier he had also directed her in the melodrama *Symphony of Six Million*, 1932.)

Besides LaCava's kudos for comedy, which also included a New York film Critics Best Director award for *Stage Door* (1937), he had a working style Dunne would have found similar to Leo McCarey's. In fact, movie critic Andrew Sarris' pioneering 1968 auteur study, *The American Cinema: Directors and Directions, 1929–1968*, places both McCarey and LaCava in the second highest category—just after "Pantheon Directors." Moreover, Sarris' opening description of LaCava for the director's citation could easily double for McCarey— his "best films . . . reveal a flair for improvisation and a delicate touch with such expert comediennes as . . . Ginger Rogers and Irene Dunne. . . . [He] was most effective when he could work between the lines of his scenarios and against the conventions of his plots."[16]

LaCava's own take on his McCarey-like system, or the lack thereof, was as follows—"I believe that . . . our spontaneous thoughts are the best ones, so I carry the IDEA of the story in my head and construct the action and dialogue as we go along."[17] Given his improvisational style, more than one critic also enjoyed the title *Unfinished Business*. For example, the *Detroit News'* Harold Heffernan comically volunteered, "To those who understand, or try to understand LaCava's system of directing a movie, the title is probably the most fitting one could dream up for one of his productions."[18]

Regardless, period reviewers sometimes found parallels between the work of LaCava and McCarey. In *New York Daily News* critic Kate Cameron's rave critique of *Unfinished Business*, she compared the picture to *Love Affair*: "The stories are dissimilar in plot but both Leo McCarey . . . and LaCava have managed to inject considerable droll wit into the movement of tales based on frustrated romance."[19] Still, as comedy historian James Harvey observed decades later, "Similar as the two filmmakers' methods were, LaCava never really matched McCarey's talent for snatching coherence from chaos. . . . McCarey's genius for making a brilliant whole out of a succession of loosely related scenes [as he does in *The Awful Truth*]."[20]

Like *The Lady Eve*, *Unfinished Business* would seem to be something of a screwball comedy summing-up, at least as it pertained to earlier Dunne roles in the genre. Thus, at the beginning of *Business*, she is something of the naïve small-town girl of *Theodora Goes Wild*, despite doubling as a provocative novelist in the latter movie. Also, like *Theodora*, she is quickly bowled over romantically by a sophisticated male (Preston Foster) who just as quickly exits her life. As in McCarey's *The Awful Truth*, *Business* casts Dunne as a singer defined, in part, by her music—just as the actress was in real life. (Both LaCava and McCarey modeled characterizations on the actual performers, with LaCava once stating, "When I direct them [actors] I tell them to use their own personalities, not to assume someone else's."[21]

Unfinished Business' eventual dovetailing into melodrama, where Dunne's character marries Preston Foster's brother (Robert Montgomery) on the rebound, also borrows a sentimental component from McCarey's *Love Affair*. But with entertaining predictability, Dunne ultimately manages to both take charge and pull it all together, as is her custom in comedy. *Business'* story demands did, however, stretch the believability factor for her character. The *New York Times'* review comically summarized this tendency in its review: "Under the circumstances, the actors do exceedingly well. Miss Dunne, even though she must combine the naiveté of Cinderella with the devastating wit of a Dorothy Parker, is charming."[22]

The *Times'* praise was typical of the critical hosannas received by *Business*. The *New York World-Telegram* observed, "It isn't enough to say that Mr. LaCava is a fine director. That is too mild. There is a flawless sense of timing, a wealth of inventive incident, a preception of character, a gusto, and a keen appreciation of the way people talk about everything he does."[23] The *World-Telegram's* celebration of the picture's naturalness (more shades of McCarey) was further embellished by *Time* magazine: "Much of the charm of *Unfinished Business* is its lack of what passes for acting in Hollywood. For the most part, its characters are just people . . . human and natural."[24] The *New York Daily News*, under the headline "Rivoli Reopens With A Delightful Picture," credited *Business* with being "as smoothly finished a production as we have seen this season."[25] And one might quote the *New York Post* as providing a fitting topper to all this praise—"LaCava has polished it [*Unfinished Business*] until it shines like a rare jewel luminous from within."[26]

Moving beyond these superlative picture overviews, the takes on individual performers were equally impressive. Critic Kate Cameron's comments, from the *New York Daily News*, were typical: "I don't believe that Irene Dunne, Robert Montgomery, Preston Foster, or Eugene Pallette, to mention only the top-ranking members of the cast, have ever appeared to better advantage."[27] The signature scene, both then (1941) and for today's viewer, is the initial romantic encounter between Dunne and Foster. For instance, period *Variety* said, "There are several decidedly human touches that clearly stamp the LaCava technique . . . [starting with] Foster's pickup of Miss Dunne on the train."[28]

Decades later auteur critic Andrew Sarris would credit the same sequence as a pivotal example of LaCava's creative ability to maximize sexual innuendo during a prime period of censorship: "The seduction scene of Irene Dunne and Preston Foster in *Unfinished Business*, like that of Jean Arthur and Joel McCrea in [George] Stevens' *The More the Merrier* [1943], demonstrates the conflict between Hollywood's erotic images and its laundered scripts."[29] Though Sarris compares LaCava here to Stevens, the analogy would work equally well with McCarey—especially the inherently sexy suggestiveness in the country conclusions of *The Awful Truth* and *My Favorite Wife*.

Paradoxically, another signature element of *Unfinished Business* (Montgomery's drinking scenes) serve as an ironic transition to the problematic LaCava-Dunne collaboration *Lady in a Jam*. Period accountants, if they offered an excuse for this later film's flatness, stated, "It is only fair to add that private advisers [contacts] indicate Mr. LaCava was ill when the picture was made."[30] But the problem was LaCava's alcoholism. Sadly, while this was another trait he shared with McCarey, Dunne's favorite Irish director managed to go on the wagon while his movies were in production.

In a perverse twist befitting two filmmakers who both called the hard-drinking W. C. Fields friend, LaCava had actually used alcohol as a comedy catalyst for much of his career. This is best demonstrated by LaCava's greatest film, *My Man Godfrey*, where a boozing-party atmosphere was maintained on the set throughout the production . . . to enhance the equally boozing-party atmosphere of the picture. Pulitzer Prize–winning author Robert Lewis Taylor entertainingly documented this approach in his celebrated 1949 biography of the co-median, *W. C. Fields: His Follies and His Fortunes*: "LaCava announced . . . it might be fun to maintain a sort of party atmosphere on the set. Accordingly, he arrived each day with many bottled drinks, canapés, and other equipment usually reserved for the cocktail hour."[31] (In La-Cava's *Stage Door* the date who comes to take out Lucille Ball's char-acter is named Mr. Dukenfield—W. C.'s real name.)

In a later interview I had with LaCava's friend and sometimes pro-ducer, Pandro S. Berman, this award-winning filmmaker shared that "Greg [LaCava] was most off-the-cuff creative when he was drinking. And his career only stalled when his doctors told him to go on the wagon in the 1940s."[32] Berman's comments notwithstanding, LaCava's drinking seems to have been a liability on *Lady in a Jam*. However, in the director's defense, the film was not without its period champions. For example, the *New York Herald Tribune* credited the movie with sometimes having "the same brilliant regard for mood, cumulative ex-citement, and three-dimensional characterization which made 'My Man Godfrey' one of the happiest comedies of our time."[33] Even the brutally direct *Variety* said the picture "has enough comedy to achieve its elemental purpose."[34] And the *Hollywood Reporter*, sounding more like the business-orientated *Variety*, entitled its review "'Lady in Jam' Plenty Silly But Irene Dunne Will Sell."[35]

The story finds Dunne playing a zany heiress who cannot compre-hend she has blown her fortune. Her guardian (Eugene Pallette) places Dunne under the care of a psychiatrist (Patrick Knowles), with this odd couple then visiting her eccentric grandmother (Queenie Vassar) out West for health reasons. Plus, Ralph Bellamy is thrown into the mix to loosely reprise his Western third wheel from *The Awful Truth*. Contemporary critic Leonard Maltin's recent capsule re-view of the film represents an insightful summary: "Thirties-type screwball comedy doesn't really hit bull's-eye, with wacky Dunne convincing psychiatrist Knowles to marry her to cure her ills."[36]

What Maltin's even-tempered look at the picture does not note is the vitriolic nature of many *Lady in a Jam* period reviews. While the *New York Times* was the most comically damning—"'Jam' has no more pulse than a dead duck"—there was plenty of negative criti-cism from which to choose.[37] What disappointed reviewers most of-ten zeroed in on was LaCava's normally celebrated off-the-cuff style. For instance, the *New York Post* said, *Jam* "has the worst kind of spon-taneity. You might say that it is spontaneously and offensively dull.

The LaCava [improvising] method, struggling with a clinker in its grate, proves itself not infallible."[38] The *Los Angeles Examiner* even tried to make a joke out of the director's failed spontaneity: "The only explanation for the present slump is that the usual LaCava cuff [from off-the-cuff] must have gone to the laundry."[39] Overall, among the critiquing dissenters, only *The New Yorker* managed to add a touch of class (in Dunne's favor) to their pan—"On the whole, the picture shouldn't happen to Irene Dunne. After all, she once played Theodora."[40]

The actress was devastated by the picture, and concerned for La-Cava, whose career would end badly in the 1940s after walking off a later picture. The amazingly wonderful reviews for *Unfinished Business* (Dunne would later observe, "We thought we had another *My Man Godfrey*") had resulted in a no-brainer about rejoining LaCava on *Lady in a Jam*. But *Jam*'s failure would result in Dunne now keying upon World War II–related movies, just as her private life was often tied up with whatever she could do to help the country's war effort. Even if screwball comedy had not become passé, the actress was ready for more serious film fare.

NOTES

1. Beth Twigger, "Eighteen Inches from Camera, Well, Let Irene Dunne Tell of It," *New York Herald Tribune*, May 18, 1941, sec. 6, p. 3.
2. "Irene Dunne Talks of 'Penny Serenade,' Which Opens Today at the Music Hall," *New York Sun*, May 22, 1944, 15.
3. Patrick McGilligan, *Film Crazy: Interviews with Hollywood Legends* (New York: St. Martin's Press, 2000), 80.
4. "Irene Dunne Talks of 'Penny Serenade. . . .'"
5. Kate Cameron, "'Penny Serenade' Is Most Affecting Film," *New York Daily News*, May 23, 1941, 46.
6. "Col's 'Serenade' Emotional Smash for Dunne and Grant," *Hollywood Reporter*, April 17, 1941.
7. Archer Winsten, "'Penny Serenade' Opens at Radio City Music Hall," *New York Post*, May 23, 1941, 15.
8. Eileen Creelman, "'Penny Serenade,' with Irene Dunne," *New York Sun*, May 23, 1941, 24.
9. Copies of most of the previous reviews are included in the actress' personal scrapbooks: "Irene Dunne Collection," 10 boxes of material, Cinema and Television Library, University of Southern California, Los Angeles.

10. "Human Touch in 'Serenade' Wins Praise," *Los Angeles Examiner*, April 17, 1941, in the "Irene Dunne Collection," Box 4, Scrapbook 21 (April–May 1941), Cinema and Television Library, University of Southern California.

11. For instance, see: Joyce Haber, "The Sweet Smell of Irene Dunne," *Los Angeles Times*, March 16, 1975, Calendar Section, 33.

12. James Harvey, *Romantic Comedy in Hollywood: From Lubitsch to Sturges* (New York: Da Capo Press, 1998), 234.

13. John McDonough, "Screening a Star: A Rare Interview with Irene Dunne," *Chicago Tribune*, May 12, 1985, sec. 13, p. 8.

14. "Coffin Nailers Busy Boxing Axis Rulers," *New York Times*, September 9, 1942, 26.

15. Harold Hoffernan, "Comedy by LaCava: Off the Cuff," *Chicago News*, March 14, 1941.

16. Andrew Sarris, *The American Cinema: Directors and Directions, 1929–1968* (New York: Dutton, 1968), 95.

17. "He Makes Hits Sans Scenarios," *San Francisco Bulletin*, October 25, 1941.

18. Harold Hoffernan, "The LaCava Technic Hurdles Word Hitch," *Detroit News*, March 13, 1941.

19. Kate Cameron, "Rivoli Reopens with a Delightful Picture," *New York Daily News*, September 2, 1941, 42.

20. Harvey, 334.

21. Quentin Reynolds, "Give Me *Real* People," *Colliers*, March 26, 1938, 53.

22. Bosley Crowther, review of *Unfinished Business*, *New York Times*, September 2, 1941, 20.

23. William Boehnel, "'Unfinished Business' a Nifty Comedy Drama," *New York World-Telegram*, September 2, 1941, 12.

24. Review of *Unfinished Business*, *Time* magazine, September 15, 1941.

25. Cameron, "Rivoli Reopens with a Delightful Picture."

26. Archer Winsten, "'Unfinished Business' Reopens the Rivoli," *New York Post*, September 2, 1941, 9.

27. Cameron, "Rivoli Reopens with a Delightful Picture."

28. Review of *Unfinished Business*, *Variety*, August 27, 1941.

29. Sarris, 95.

30. Archer Winsten, "'Lady in a Jam' Opens at Loew's State Theatre," *New York Post*, September 11, 1942, 34.

31. Robert Lewis Taylor, *W. C. Fields: His Follies and His Fortunes* (1949; reprint, New York: Signet Books, 1967), 169.

32. Pandro S. Berman, interview by Wes D. Gehring, Hillcrest Country Club, Beverly Hills, California, June 1975, author's files.

33. Howard Barnes, "'Lady in a Jam'—State," *New York Herald Tribune*, September 11, 1942, 17.

34. Review of *Lady in a Jam*, *Variety*, July 1, 1942.

35. "'Lady in a Jam' Plenty Silly But Irene Dunne Will Sell," *Hollywood Reporter*, June 26, 1942.

36. *Lady in a Jam* entry in *Leonard Maltin's Movie & Video Guide: 2003*, ed. Leonard Maltin (New York: Signet Book, 2002), 761.

37. Bosley Crowther, review of *Lady in a Jam*, *New York Times*, September 11, 1942, 25.

38. Winsten, "'Lady in a Jam' Opens At Loew's State Theatre."

39. Dorothy Manners, "LaCava in a Slump Says Critic on 'Jam' Film," *Los Angeles Examiner*, July 17, 1942.

40. Review of *Lady in a Jam*, *The New Yorker*, July 22, 1942.

TEN

Keying on the War Years

I don't think it [*The White Cliffs of Dover*, 1944] smacks of propaganda, but if it does then I'm glad. I feel everything possible should be done to cement the friendship between two nations that are most alike and speak the same language.[1]

—Irene Dunne

As briefly noted last chapter, Irene Dunne gave patriotic time and effort to the United States' cause from the very beginning of our involvement in World War II (1941–1945). She was also a founding member of Clark Gable's Hollywood Victory Committee, which organized filmland's efforts to both sell bonds and entertain servicemen. Dunne's first USO show dated from a 1941 Hollywood Bowl appearance, while she was part of a celebrity bond tour, "Stars Over America," in 1942. (Film clips of the actress performing at USO shows were included in the patriotic short subject *Show Business at War*, 1943, and in the feature *Follow The Boys*, 1944.)

Her favorite war-related activity was visiting hospitalized servicemen, which involved everything from making small talk and writing letters, to singing their favorite songs. There were also frequent appearances on the Armed Forces Radio Network, where she joined other stars entertaining and thanking the troops for their efforts. (These broadcasts were heard by Americans in uniform around the world.) Maybe her most moving war-related effort was the January 15, 1944 Long Beach, California christening of the Liberty ship *Carole Lombard*. The vessel honored Dunne's fellow Hollywood Hoosier, Lombard, who had died tragically in a 1942 plane crash following the first bond rally of the war. What made the ceremony especially poignant was a keynote address by the victim's husband, Captain Clark Gable. The actor, who had recently returned to the United States after six months in action with the U.S. Eighth Air Force in Europe, had maintained his composure during the speech. But after Dunne broke the bottle on the ship he could no longer contain his grief and openly wept. Irene comforted the star she had always admired but had never appeared with in a movie. (Occurring within one day of the two-year anniversary of Lombard's death, the christening ceremony was broadcast on radio coast to coast.)

After the disappointing screwball comedy *Lady in a Jam*, most of Dunne's film work during World War II would also reflect America's involvement in the global conflict. The actress might have been commenting on this career change when she told a Pennsylvania war bond rally, in the fall of 1942, "You folks have probably seen me traipsing around on the screen in comedies . . . Today I want you to know I have a new assignment. This is no time for comedy. I'm now a saleswoman, I sell bonds."[2] Of her war-related films made during the conflict, none fit the battle billing more than the fantasy drama *A Guy Named Joe* (1943). The actress plays a ferry command pilot stationed in Great Britain and romantically involved with a bomber pilot played by Gable's close friend, Spencer Tracy. During his last mission he patriotically crashes his disabled plane into a German warship and dies. But Tracy's pilot discovers the war continues in the afterlife. His heavenly mission is to now guide green Air Force cadets through their flying basics. (This plays upon the old superstition that pilots never die.) Tracy's first assignment is to help a wealthy but fearful young flyer (Van Johnson).

The story conflict ironically occurs shortly after Tracy has helped Johnson's confidence level both in the air and on the ground—the young flyer becomes interested in Dunne. Tracy is naturally jealous, especially after the new couple become engaged. He attempts to get Johnson in trouble by encouraging him to perform some daredevil stunts. Paradoxically, this only helps Johnson privately and professionally; it reminds Dunne of the chance-taking Tracy, and it convinces the Air Force top brass that this cocky young man is the right flyer for a dangerous mission.

Several additional plot twists now occur. Recalled to heaven, Tracy decides to let Dunne find happiness on earth. In contrast, a still grieving Irene decides she cannot live without Tracy. She calls off her engagement with Johnson and secretly decides to replace him on the secret mission. If Dunne were to die in this lone bomber assignment, all the better—she could join Tracy in heaven. Indeed, this was how the original picture ended. Thus, Dunne's surviving script concludes with the following description of the heavenly couple—"Hand in hand they start AWAY from [the] CAMERA toward Advanced Headquarters, walking with heads up, steps brisk. The mist grows lighter, the light brighter, as they recede from our view."[3]

Sneak preview audiences, however, found this conclusion too much of a downer, and Dunne is allowed to live and find happiness with Johnson. Tracy is tied into this closely by playing guardian angel to Dunne during that dangerous final mission and emotionally releasing her to love again. Ironically, this sensitive screenplay, which is so patriotically religious, was authored by the gifted Dalton Trumbo—later famous (or infamous) for being one of the *Hollywood Ten*—artists sentenced to jail time for contempt of Congress. The 1947 charge was refusing to testify before the House Un-American Activities Committee about possible membership in the Communist Party. (If ever a screen credit constituted a defense against a ludicrous charge, *A Guy Named Joe* fit the bill.)

Strangely enough, as entertaining as the film proved to be, the behind-the-scenes events on this movie proved even more provocative. Tracy "took an immediate dislike" to Dunne—finding her "too prudish."[4] Unfortunately, despite his on-screen populist persona, the real Tracy could be mean-spirited. Consequently, both he and the film's action director, Victor Fleming, would sometimes kid Dunne to the point of tears. Just as things had reached an intolerable situation (there was even talk of taking Irene off the picture) Van Johnson was seriously injured in a motorcycle accident.

Near tragedy, however, brought out the best in Tracy. MGM wanted to replace Johnson (so popular with wartime bobby-soxers) and reshoot his scenes. But Tracy would have none of it. He threatened to walk unless studio chief Louis B. Mayer shut down the production until Johnson's recovery. But to Mayer's credit, he worked out a compromise with the actor—lighten up on Dunne and MGM would put *A Guy Named Joe* on hold until Johnson could return.

Years later Irene revealed she had given Mayer some added leverage in the negotiating process:

I knew they [MGM] were going to be looking at some film [rushes from *Joe*], and I made up my mind I was going to be my *best*—my best, my best, my *very* best. So they came out of the projection room and Mayer said, "If we're going to replace anybody, let's replace Tracy." Which they never would have done, of course. But I'll always remember that. And we ironed everything out, Tracy and I.[5]

Always the diplomatic lady, Dunne later also downplayed the severity of the conflict with Tracy: "He was my [acting] hero. Then, when we started working, he got the idea that I thought he wasn't a hero anymore. Which was not true."[6]

Joe merits a two-part addendum at this point. First, period coverage of Johnson's accident suggest that Dunne was equally adamant about shutting down the production until the injured actor could return. For instance, the *Chicago Daily News* reported that besides being Johnson's first visitor in the hospital, Dunne told him, "You are going to get well and you are going to finish that picture. It's a great role and you're not going to lose it."[7] (The Dunne-Tracy production relationship might also have improved after their apparent joint demand that Van Johnson be kept in the picture.)

Second, while Dunne later minimized her conflict with Tracy and Fleming, one can be certain the actress handled herself with digni- fied restraint—which was her philosophy. For example, two years earlier Dunne's friend and stand-in, Kathryn Stanley, described the actress being baited by an unnamed director, "Alright, let's turn the lights off and let Miss Dunne get all the acting out of her system. Then maybe we can get the scene."[8] The actress' response, according to Stanley, was to walk off camera and work on her makeup, with- out saying anything. When the stand-in later complimented Irene on her restraint, Dunne said, "I won't let anyone upset me and I wouldn't lower myself to answer back."[9]

Regardless, *Joe* was a tough production for other reasons, too. The original shoot began during an unusually dark and rainy winter sea- son, at a time when the *real* war was not going particularly well for the Allies. And with a set reflecting Great Britain during the winter, there was an actual gloom to the working environment. Topping this off were conflicting Dunne-Tracy working habits. Though Dunne had blossomed in the improvisational world of McCarey, she enjoyed at least a modicum of rehearsal. Tracy, later famous for the most comi- cally basic of acting advice—"know your lines and don't bump into the furniture"—preferred to just do it . . . passing on rehearsal. Finally, when *Joe* shut down after Johnson's accident, Dunne started shooting

The White Cliffs of Dover (1944). However, when *Joe* resumed production, Irene found herself shooting two movies simultaneously!

Joe opened during the 1943 Christmas season and was one of the top-grossing movies of 1943–1944.[10] The picture's initial box office take of over four million dollars was a phenomenal amount for the time. The matter-of-fact showcasing of an afterlife struck a responsive chord with period audiences often coping with their own personal losses. Moreover, Dunne always felt her character's ability to move on (after Tracy's death) was ultimately helpful, a catharsis, for countless women who had lost husbands and lovers during the war. Even today, the film retains a moving poignancy that is not to be denied. One of these later fans was no less a figure than celebrated director Steven Spielberg, who so admired the picture that he remade it as *Always* (1989, with Holly Hunter and Richard Dreyfuss reprising the Dunne and Tracy roles).

Oddly enough, *Joe* only received mixed reviews upon its initial release. While audiences ate up the sentimentality, it was a stumbling block for some period critics, especially on the East Coast. The *New York Post*'s Eileen Creelman seemed most concerned by this tear factor: "The audience is evidently expected to weep throughout the film, even or especially during the lighter moments."[11] But criticism of the sentimentality was not limited to the pans of the picture. For instance, the *New York Daily News*' Kate Cameron observed, "Tracy and Miss Dunne play their parts well and director Victor Fleming has at times given the story a touch of poetic magic that lifts it above the average war film."[12] But then she added, the movie was flawed by a "tedious attempt to be whimsical about death."[13] Ironically, it took a male reviewer, the *Post*'s Archer Winsten, to add a touch of feminist criticism: "Irene Dunne's ship bombing is a tribute to all brave women who think they could do it, too."[14] And his capsule take on the actress' performance in *Joe* might have been lifted from any number of 1943 reviews—Dunne "gives a performance worthy of a better film."[15]

Joe played more effectively for critics from the West Coast and America's heartland. The *San Francisco News* entitled its review, "Engaging War Fantasy: Tracy and Dunne Duo Excels," while the *Hollywood Reporter* correctly predicted the picture's commercial success: "Exhibitors will have reason to rejoice in the extraordinary box office attraction that MGM has ready for release."[16] The *Chicago Daily News* called *Joe* "a relief from the underscored realism of most war pictures."[17] But more importantly, the *Daily News* entertainingly noted an important connection missed by most critics—*Joe*'s producer (Everett Riskin) was also behind the screwball fantasy *Here Comes Mr. Jordan* (1941), another period film where the male lead dies early in the picture and one is confronted with a very business-as-usual afterlife. Thus, the *Daily News* affectionately described the film as "'Here Comes Mr. Jordan' as a G. I. Joe, sprouting a pair of silver wings."[18]

A final footnote to the movie might be labeled the "fountain of youth factor." At *Joe*'s release Irene was forty-five years old, nearly twenty years senior to leading man Van Johnson. This was a rare development, both then and now. Yet no one seems to have ever addressed this fact. Indeed, period reviews were never kinder about her beauty. For example, *Variety* said, "Miss Dunne is nifty to look at," while the *New York Times* observed, "Miss Dunne is as lovely and fetching as we've ever seen her—maybe even a little more so."[19] Of course, as noted earlier, Irene's various studio biographies had her being six years younger. Regardless, when viewing the film one would never guess there is such an age difference. (Maybe the romance was made all the more palatable by the megahit rendition of "I'll Get By" sung by Dunne in the movie. During the summer of 1944 *Billboard* would list the recording as the most-played jukebox record for over a month. And several other artists would cut their own versions of this 1928 song, personally selected by Dunne for the film, with the Harry James and Dick Haymes cover being the biggest hit.)

Dunne's next movie, *The White Cliffs of Dover* (1944), also addressed both the war and Great Britain. But these were story points showcased in a domestic setting that covers thirty years, stretching back to the eve of World War I—told as an extended flashback. Irene's character comes to England for what was supposed to be a brief 1914 visit. Instead, she falls in love with a titled Brit (Alan Marshal) and makes England her permanent home. While the couple is blessed with a son (Roddy McDowall plays the character as a boy and Peter Lawford as a young man), Dunne's husband dies late in the war (1918), before he can see him. Predictably, she vows to never let her boy go to war. She even flirts with returning to America. But in the end Irene remains in her adopted country and ably raises the boy. When war comes again he joins his father's old regiment.

As the flashback returns the viewer to the present (1944), Dunne's character (a Red Cross supervisor) continues to wait for the latest group of wounded servicemen to arrive at her hospital. Borrowing a chapter from Dunne's past melodrama heyday (*White Cliffs'* extended flashback narrative is already reminiscent of 1941's *Penny Serenade*), her son will be part of the latest convoy of wounded. What is worse, Irene soon has to cope with losing him. But the saving grace for Dunne's character, and the movie's effective but hardly subtle closing message, is that the shared patriotic cause of Great Britain and the United States somehow makes her loss palatable. Dunne's surviving script concludes with these lines, "A light of exaltation comes to her eyes with the high resolve to keep the faith. In a thundering crescendo of cheers, a triumph of proud, confident [patriotic] music [is heard, as Allied soldiers pass nearby]."[20]

Not surprisingly, *White Cliffs* had several things in common with MGM's earlier critical and commercial hit, *Mrs. Miniver* (1942), which profiled an idealized World War II British wife and mother in a title part which won a Best Actress Oscar for Greer Garson. Both movies were shepherded by producer Sidney Franklin in an attempt to mix entertainment with a spirited sense of wartime Anglo-American cooperation. Like most quasi-sequels, *White Cliffs* does not match the artistry of *Mrs. Miniver*. But in its own right, *White Cliffs* is a winningly romantic melodrama of patriotic proportions. And period reviews said as much. For example, the *New York Herald Tribune* observed, "At its finest, the picture is an affecting biography of a staunch lady who becomes as English as she once was a Yankee."[21]

The *New York Daily News'* critique even opened like one of the reviews from Dunne's melodramatically focused past: "'The White Cliffs of Dover' is a beautifully made, sensitively acted picture that will appeal mostly to women . . . [especially] in the sequences that deal with a mother's protective love."[22] The *News'* review title was even more melodramatically succinct, "'The White Cliffs of Dover' Tears at the Heartstrings," and was coupled with the highest marks for Dunne—her performance "is one of the finest portrayals she has given on the screen. She runs the gamut of acting, from a thrilled debutante . . . to that of a bereaved wife and widow who watches her only son . . . die."[23] And the *San Francisco News* critic compared Dunne's performance to one of her signature melodrama parts, and credited *White Cliffs* as superior—"never, even in her great success 'Back Street' [1932], has she approached such a gracious, lovely quality of playing."[24] Without noting specific other Dunne films, the *Chicago Sun Times* also seconded the *San Francisco News'* argument that this was the actress' greatest performance.[25] Given these kudos,

White Cliffs would join *A Guy Named Joe* as one of the top-grossing movies of 1943–1944.[26] (The movie also joined a select circle of pictures to ever play New York's famed Radio City Music Hall for seven consecutive weeks.)

Strangely enough, though *White Cliffs* was done, in part, to bolster Anglo-American relations, England's image in the United States was already so positive that one of the rare criticisms of the movie was that it occasionally showed negative British behavior. For instance, the *New York Post* chronicles an early movie scene where debutante Dunne meets some "haughty aristocrats who say, 'I should never have taken you for an American,' meaning to be complimentary. When Miss Dunne strikes back at English people who have hurt her feelings as an American, an American audience cheers."[27] *Post* critic Archer Winsten, whose overall review of the picture was still positive, asked how such negativism could help Anglo-American relations.

The answer lies, of course, in the fact that it makes the movie more realistic than most melodramas. What cause and/or country is without a few flaws? Moreover, such negative examples demonstrate that Dunne is outspokenly proud to be an American—which later gives added credibility to her difficult decision to marry and remain in England. Indeed, the picture is effective at subtly suggesting Britain is a better place for gaining Dunne as a citizen. She is a study in moral courage and dedication as both a spouse and parent. Paradoxically, the precise thing that upsets the *Post* critic is one of the *balanced* elements that a contemporary viewer, especially one cognizant of the patriotic extremes of an earlier at-war society, can find refreshing about *White Cliffs*.

Even Frank Capra's inspired nonfiction film, *The Battle of Britain* (1943, certainly the best of his "Why We Fight" series of documentaries produced for the United States government), creates an image of England on the verge of deification. The idealized extremes of Capra's Oscar-winning documentary series also represents a telling backdrop (catalyst) for the kind of concerns expressed by the *Post* critic. A negative England was just not being done at the time of *White Cliffs*. Indeed, to repeat part of the Dunne quote which opens the chapter, "I don't think it [the film] smacks of [pro-British] propaganda, but if it does then I'm glad."

Obviously, the actress felt strongly about the movie and worked hard to promote it. This activity involved two directly related radio broadcasts. Shortly after the film's May 1944 release Dunne appeared on the *Canada War Bond Show* to recite Alice Duer Miller's poem "The White Cliffs," upon which the movie was loosely based. And in September 1946 Irene and her *White Cliffs* costar C. Aubrey Smith reprised their roles on CBS radio's *Academy Awards* program. These appearances were consistent with Dunne's tendency to appear regularly on 1940s radio. Thus, the same year that *White Cliffs* appeared (1944) the actress surfaced on a half-dozen different broadcasts, ranging from entertainment specifically for servicemen, to radio adaptations of two previous Dunne films—*The Awful Truth* (for CBS' *Goodyear Program*) and *Penny Serenade* (for CBS' *Lux Radio Theatre*).

As a closing comment upon *White Cliffs*, there was also a special appropriateness to Hollywood's designated *first lady* of cinema actually playing an English lady by marriage. Yet, as the *New York Times* insightfully suggested, the actress still managed to give her character an ongoing "glow of American charm." For instance, though she would raise her son to be a proper English lord, the "boy gives evidence of democracy by falling in love with . . . a [commoner's daughter]."[28] Fittingly, *Variety* correctly suggested that Dunne's "excellent performance" would contribute to *White Cliffs* being "an outstanding [box office] grosser [in England] as it will be on this side [of the Atlantic]."[29] As a final footnote to *White Cliffs*, I found a recent conversation with film historian Anthony Slide especially insightful, with regard to comparisons with *Mrs. Miniver*— "As an Englishman, I would rate *White Cliffs* as infinitely superior to *Mrs. Miniver*."

Dunne's busy 1944 also included a third and final teaming with Charles Boyer in the aptly titled feature, *Together Again*. But this was their first coupling in a straight romantic comedy, avoiding the melodramatic overtones of their *Love Affair* and *When Tomorrow Comes* (both 1939). The movie was also Dunne's first non-war-related picture since 1942's unsuccessful *Lady in a Jam*. *Together Again* cast Irene as the widowed mayor of a small Vermont town. Charles Coburn, fresh from an Oscar-winning turn as a matchmaker in 1943's *The More the Merrier*, plays a similar role here as Irene's father-in-law. He is concerned that she is devoting too much time to her job and an eccentric stepdaughter (Mona Freeman). Comically, when lightning hits a statue of Dunne's late husband, knocking off the head, Coburn takes it as a tongue-in-cheek sign from above that Irene again needs love in her life. Consequently, he sends her to New York City to find a new sculptor and, hopefully, romance as well.

Predictably, Boyer is that sculptor—his third teaming with Dunne where he is an artist. (He was a painter in *Love Affair* and a pianist in *When Tomorrow Comes*.) They have an amusingly provocative first meeting when he mistakes her for a model and asks Irene to take her clothes off! This is soon followed by a sexually suggestive scene where Dunne is arrested in a nightclub raid, mistaken for a stripper. As noted in an earlier chapter, though mild by today's standards, the baring of the actress' undergarments was actually big news for 1944—the film "is considered noteworthy on several . . . counts, not the least of which is the fact that in the picture Miss Dunne will exhibit her nether limbs (and undergarments) for the first time cinematically."[30] In the movie an embarrassed Irene quickly leaves New York, only to have Boyer follow her home to small-town Vermont— a variation of Melvyn Douglas' visit to another small-town Dunne setting in *Theodora Goes Wild* (1936).

In fact, the actress herself likened the movie to *Theodora* in a 1944 interview with the *New York Sun*. She also anticipates Jerry Seinfeld's description of his later celebrated sitcom by decades—"It's [*Together Again*] really about nothing. We've made a picture that has nothing to do with anything. It's more like 'Theodora,' I think, than anything else . . . . [But] maybe that's just because of the small town atmosphere."[31] The *Sun* interview, moreover, was broad, reaching into other Dunne-related subject matter. For example, the actress provided yet another reason for traveling: "Hollywood is an extraordinary place. [Still,] you have to get away from it occasionally to appreciate it. If you don't get away you begin to feel it is all too mechanical."[32] Plus, she described director Charles Vidor's "spontaneous" style for the *Together Again* shoot like it was a McCarey or LaCava improvised production: "We never were sure what was going to happen next. There was always something new, something unexpected. Well, that's the way I made 'The Awful Truth' and several other comedies. It's rather fun too."[33]

"Fun" is the optimum word here, since *Together Again* went on to be both a critical and commercial hit. The *New York Daily News* even said, "It is all a lot of fun and is heartily recommended to anyone in need of a relaxing laugh."[34] The *New York World-Telegram* took a similar slant but anchored its review in the often somber period that was World War II: "'Together Again' is a relaxed, timeless comedy, a type very scarce these days when too many movies feel they must have some overtone of war, whether they need it or not."[35] Surprisingly enough, the *New York Times* also echoed this sentiment, despite the *Times* often seeming to prefer issue-orientated art: "A romantic comedy without the faintest trace of topical significance, and all the more engaging because [of] it."[36]

Consistent with these East Coast reviews, the *Hollywood Reporter* was actually comically silly in its happiness over a major movie *without* an ax to grind: "At last, praise heaven, here is a picture which does not try to teach anybody anything. It has no message, no moral. It doesn't give a hoot . . . [who directs] the affairs of the universe."[37] In contrast, the *Pittsburgh Press* was just happy to see its favorite actress in a funny film: "Irene Dunne is back in the type of role she does better than any actress on the screen."[38] And *Variety's* "Miniature Review" might have served as an apt summary for most period critics: "Irene Dunne and Charles Boyer in spritely romantic farce for solid diverting entertainment."[39]

Just as it was a shame Dunne's teamings with Cary Grant were limited to three pictures, fans of the actress would have enjoyed a fourth outing with Boyer. There is an easy rapport between the two. Though less inherently comic than her teaming with Grant, Dunne and Boyer have an undeniable romantic chemistry. Plus, it was just easier working together. Boyer said at the time:

> I like working with Irene . . . we're used to one another. I've a pretty good idea by this time just what Irene's reactions will be—how she likes to play a scene. With an actress who is a stranger, it's all a question of trial and error. It makes one a little uncertain, and the camera can tell the difference.[40]

Moreover, improvisational director Vidor borrowed another trait from McCarey by closely tailoring the *Together Again* parts to both Dunne and Boyer—something often noted by period critics. For example, the *New York Times* described the movie as "entertainment that is eminently suited to its principals' talents."[41]

Dunne's final war period film was an adaptation of Ruth Gordon's play *Over 21* (1945). The movie opened to mixed reviews and so-so box office for two reasons. First, the original stage production (also authored by Gordon) was so associated with that actress' persona, that Irene was in a no-win position. This central role of an army camp–following writer wife of a soldier "was written for an actress to spin all over the place—to [verbally] toss and catch and juggle in a highly individual way . . . permitting a famous lady writer . . . to come up against the low-brow problems of life in a bungalow court."[42] Dunne does an inspired job in this part, especially given that the actress excelled at improvisational situations—something both encouraged by the original text and the return direction of Charles Vidor. (*Together Again* costar Charles Coburn also resurfaced in *Over 21.*) But the movie adaptation of *Over 21* so closely followed Ruth Gordon's Broadway triumph that Dunne was forever in the other actress' shadow.

The second reason the picture was not a major success had to do with timing—*Over 21* was a war-related story which opened just *after* the conflict ended. Even otherwise positive reviews, such as Kate Cameron's *New York Daily News* critique, were taken aback by this development: "It is a bit startling to find oneself . . . suddenly transported back to the early days of the war."[43] And the *New York Post* opened their review by baldly stating, "Like many another picture caught by the war's sudden ending, 'Over 21' . . . must now get along as a film at the Music Hall without benefit of timeliness."[44]

Much of the comedy, moreover, played upon a by then overused early 1940s plot device—the war-related housing shortage, so entertainingly showcased in such earlier movies as *The More the Merrier* (1943) and *Standing Room Only* (1944). These qualifiers notwithstanding, *Over 21* had its period champions. For example, the *Hollywood Reporter* called the film "hilarity to the hilt," with Dunne described as "a shining mistress of comedy, playing with great gusto in a role right up her alley."[45] And *Variety* rated it a "bright film comedy, just as it was a sparkling stage laugh piece . . . the lines and [visual] business that made it click in legit [on Broadway] are equally as potent on celluloid."[46] *Variety* also gave Irene high marks; her "character is slightly superficial, but in Miss Dunne's hands comes out as a choice job of miming."[47] Of course, as was true for most of her career, the actress invariably generated positive notices regardless of the overall tone of the review.

For all of Dunne's wartime successes, from hit movies supporting the Allied cause, to a 1942 award from the United States Treasury Department for selling war bonds, the actress' career during this period was not without disappointments. Other than Katharine Hepburn usurping her reteaming with Cary Grant in 1938's *Holiday*, not being able to play the title role in MGM's *Madame Curie* (1943) was Dunne's greatest professional regret. Universal had originally bought the property for her in 1937. Indeed, an interview/article with the actress that same year had her excitedly observing, "At the moment, I think one of the most fortunate and stimulating things which could have happened to me is to be able to do as my next picture the *Life of Madame Curie.*"[48]

Irene was so driven to play this role that on an earlier trip to France she talked for hours with Curie's daughters, as well as visiting the haunts of this scientist—the Institute de France, the Academy of Medicine, and the Pasteur Institute. An obviously humbled Dunne recalled, "I handled her instruments and test tubes. [I] sat at the very table where she worked. To my mind, she was the greatest woman of this modern age."[49]

Unfortunately for Irene, changes in Universal's front office and the actress' own busy schedule resulted in the project being shelved. The studio later sold the property to an MGM anxious to showcase Greta Garbo in the title role. But when World War II proved to be a catalyst for that actress' early retirement (Garbo's films were most profitable in a Europe then occupied by Nazi Germany), the Curie project was temporarily shelved at MGM, too. However, when Dunne signed on with this studio in the early 1940s she hoped to reclaim this coveted part. Instead, the role went to an actress MGM saw as a younger version of Dunne—Greer Garson. "With a ten-year age difference, Garson seemed the better investment for the studio."[50]

Irene had also planned to star in the American film adaptation of the play *Gaslight*, which had first been brought to the screen in a 1940 British production entitled *Angel Street* in the United States. Columbia had originally bought the play for Dunne (who had a multiple studio arrangement), but as with the Curie project, the property was shelved and later sold to MGM. After she signed with the studio *Gaslight* was announced as a forthcoming film for Dunne. But again she eventually lost the lead to another even younger actress—Ingrid Bergman, who would win her first Oscar for the role of a woman whose husband (Charles Boyer) attempts to drive her mad, in order to discover hidden jewels.

Though it is hard to deny an Academy Award–winning performance, the already well-established rapport between Dunne and Boyer would have made for a most provocative *Gaslight* production, too. Moreover, given that they had played lovers in their previous teamings, a Dunne/Boyer *Gaslight* stood to generate shadowy nuances just not possible with the younger Bergman in the lead. Ironically, an additional wartime missed opportunity for Dunne also involved another possible reteaming with Boyer.

She was to have costarred with the Frenchman in one of the five episodes comprising *Tales of Manhattan* (1942), a charming story which chronicles a dress tailcoat through the lives of several individuals. Dunne's married character was to have had an affair with Boyer, followed by a sophisticated confrontation with her husband. As the episode now stands (with a young Rita Hayworth as the straying wife), Boyer's tour de force performance dominates not only the segment but the whole film. Though Hayworth is given little to do, one assumes Dunne would have been able to embellish said situation from her backlog of sexually suggestive screwball comedies. At the very least, as with a Dunne/Boyer *Gaslight*, the duo would have been showcased in a refreshingly new situation.

For this author, however, the most fascinating wartime "What if?" for Irene involved the actress almost rejoining her favorite director, Leo McCarey, on the critical and commercial hit film—*The Bells of St. Mary's* (1945), the sequel to his multiple-Oscar-winning *Going My Way* (1944). Producing studio RKO wanted Ingrid Bergman to play Sister Superior to Bing Crosby's beloved Father O'Malley. But independent producer David O. Selznick owned Bergman's contract and almost squelched any deal because of high salary demands. And even when these differences were ironed out a Bergman illness nearly scratched the actress from the production.

Given McCarey's longtime admiration for and loyalty to Dunne, the director naturally turned to Irene. The actress later said, "I remember going upstairs and taking a towel and putting it over my head to see how I would look as a nun. But Ingrid got well."[51] Given that Dunne's charity work would later (June 29, 1949) be recognized with the highest possible Catholic honor (the Laetare Medal) for a layperson, to have appeared as a nun in her old friend's film would have been perfect casting.

Professional disappointments are one thing, but the actress nearly suffered a personal tragedy near the war's conclusion. Her husband Frank suffered a nearly fatal heart attack and Irene focused several months entirely upon him as he slowly recovered. His illness further reinforced her ongoing philosophy to never let her career dominate. In fact, she risked losing a much sought-after Hollywood part to care for her husband. That is, Dunne had already been signed to play the title character in 20th Century-Fox's epic production, *Anna and the King of Siam*. When the studio pressured her about a starting date, the actress asked to be released from her contract. Dunne later observed, "As long as my husband was ill, I wasn't going to leave him for five minutes to play any scene; no matter how great."[52] The studio waited.

Irene's ability to look at the bigger (non-Hollywood) picture
also came out in a 1943 *Photoplay* article which asked several
prominent wartime actresses to share "My Secret Dream."
Whereas her acting peers tended towards the self-centered (Ann
Sheridan's dream house), or the just plain goofy (Carole Landis
wanted to be a detective!), Dunne had visions of giving back to
America via politics:

> We are now in the throes of such vast changes that it is impossible to
> speculate on what lies ahead. However, we know there will be impor-
> tant work to be done. . . . This means not only building up a country's
> power but maintaining the highest idealism along with the practical
> [political] execution.[53]

Just as the young budding stage actress Irene Dunne found time
to take in the Democrats' 1924 presidential convention in New York
City, the following chapter explores both her ongoingly successful
movie career *and* increased activity in the world of politics.

NOTES

1. Maggie Schultz, "Hollywood's Great Ladies: Irene Dunne," *Hollywood
Studio Magazine*, January 1988, n.p.
2. "Film Star Irene Dunne Exceeds Million Mark in Sale of War Bonds . . .,"
Wilkes-Barre Record—PA, September 11, 1942, 1.
3. *A Guy Named Joe* script, January 28, 1943, 185, in the "Irene Dunne
Collection," Box 1, Cinema and Television Library, University of Southern
California, Los Angeles.
4. Margie Schultz, *Irene Dunne: A Bio-Bibliography* (Westport, Connecticut:
Greenwood Press, 1991), 108.
5. James Harvey, "Irene Dunne Interviewed by James Harvey," *Film
Comment*, January–February 1980, 30.
6. Ibid.
7. Harold Haffernan column, *Chicago Daily News*, August 9, 1943, in the
"Irene Dunne Collection," Box 5, Scrapbook 12 (April–August 1943).
8. Kathryn Stanley (as told to Sonie Lee), "Irene Dunne as I Know Her,"
Movies, August 1941, 54.
9. Ibid.
10. Cobbett Steinberg, *Reel Facts: The Movie Book of Records* (New York:
Vintage Books, 1978), 342.
11. Eileen Creelman, "'A Guy Named Joe,' Drama of the War, with
Spencer Tracy and Irene Dunne," *New York Post*, December 24, 1943, 7.

12. Kate Cameron, "'A Guy Named Joe' an Air Forces Show," *New York Daily News*, December 24, 1943, 15.

13. Ibid.

14. Archer Winsten, "'A Guy Named Joe' Flies at the Capitol Theatre," *New York Post*, December 24, 1943, 16.

15. Ibid.

16. Emilia Hodel, "Engaging War Fantasy: Tracy Dunne Duo Excels," *San Francisco News*, May 26, 1944; "'Guy Named Joe' Fantasy of Beauty, Action and Delight" *Hollywood Reporter*, December 24, 1943.

17. Carl Guldager, "'A Guy Named Joe' Fights Fanciful War," *Chicago Daily News*, April 3, 1944.

18. Ibid.

19. Review of *A Guy Named Joe*, *Variety*, December 29, 1943; review of *A Guy Named Joe*, *New York Times*, December 24, 1943, 17.

20. *The White Cliffs of Dover* script, January 18, 1943, 156, in the "Irene Dunne Collection," Box 1, Cinema and Television Library, University of Southern California.

21. Howard Barnes, "'The White Cliffs of Dover'—Music Hall," *New York Herald Tribune*, May 12, 1944, 12.

22. Kate Cameron, "'The White Cliffs of Dover' Tears at the Heartstrings," *New York Daily News*, May 12, 1944, 15-c.

23. Ibid.

24. Claude LaBelle, "Irene Dunne Shines at Head of Fine Cast," *San Francisco News*, July 26, 1944.

25. Doris Arden, "'Cliffs of Dover' Touches the Heart," *Chicago Sun Times*, July 2, 1944.

26. Steinberg, 342.

27. Archer Winsten, "'The White Cliffs of Dover' Opens at Radio City Music Hall," *New York Post*, May 12, 1944, 27.

28. Bosley Crowther, review of *The White Cliffs of Dover*, *New York Times*, May 12, 1944, 15.

29. Review of *The White Cliffs of Dover*, *Variety*, March 15, 1944.

30. Fred Stanley, "Hollywood Round-Up," *New York Times*, August 20, 1944, sec. 2, p. 1.

31. Eileen Creelman, "Irene Dunne Talks of 'Together Again,' Columbia Comedy Which Opens Thursday," *New York Sun*, November 21, 1944, 21.

32. Ibid.

33. Ibid.

34. Kate Cameron, "Music Hall Presents Entertaining Film," *New York Daily News*, November 24, 1944, 40.

35. "'Together Again' Pleases," *New York World-Telegram*, November 24, 1944, 25.

36. Review of *Together Again*, *New York Times*, November 24, 1944, 19.

37. "Columbia 'Together Again' Smash for Van Upp, Vidor," *Hollywood Reporter*, November 3, 1944.

38. Dick Fortune, "Dunne-Boyer Film Is Full of Laughs," *Pittsburgh Press*, November 24, 1944.

39. Review of *Together Again*, *Variety*, November 8, 1944.

40. Herb Sterne, "Unrehearsed 'Clinches' Irk Great Lover, Boyer," *Atlantic Constitution*, November 26, 1944.

41. Review of *Together Again*, *New York Times*.

42. Bosley Crowther, review of *Over 21*, *New York Times*, August 17, 1945, 20.

43. Kate Cameron, "Gaiety Is Keynote of Music Hall Film," *New York Daily News*, August 17, 1945, 34.

44. Archer Winsten, "'Over 21' Comes Late to Radio City Music Hall," *New York Post*, August 17, 1945, 12.

45. "Hilarious Comedy Despite Crusade," *Hollywood Reporter*, July 23, 1945.

46. Review of *Over 21*, *Variety*, July 25, 1945.

47. Ibid.

48. Sonia Lee, "Discovering the Glamour in Irene Dunne," *Motion Picture Story Magazine*, March 1937, 79.

49. Ibid.

50. Schultz, *Irene Dunne: A Bio-Bibliography*, 17.

51. Barbara Saltzman, "A Warm Reception for Irene Dunne," *Los Angeles Times*, August 28, 1979.

52. Patricia Clary, "Studio Wanted $50,000 in Time for Irene Dunne," *San Francisco News*, April 24, 1946.

53. "My Secret Dream," *Photoplay*, October 1943, 54.

ELEVEN

A Triumphant Postwar Trilogy, and Political Distraction

I just couldn't go to Heaven without Clare [William Powell]. Why, I get lonesome for him even when I go to Ohio.

—Irene Dunne as Vinnie in *Life With Father* (1947).

The immediate postwar period gave Dunne the opportunity to star in a series of prestige pictures starting with first billing in *Anna and the King of Siam* (1946). Margaret Landon's popular biography of the nineteenth-century governess to the Siamese court had made this part the one most coveted by Hollywood actresses of the mid-1940s—especially a lobbying Bette Davis. But 20th Century-Fox producer Darryl Zanuck and director John Cromwell were sold on Dunne from the beginning.

Cromwell had directed her in three previous pictures, *The Silver Cord*, *Ann Vickers* (both 1933), and *This Man Is Mine* (1934). And in later discussing the many prominent actresses he had directed (who included Katharine Hepburn and Bette Davis), he called Dunne his "special favorite," one who possessed a "great star presence" though she was often "underrated on every count."[1] Given that the character of Anna was an educated proper British widow, Dunne's image of "First Lady" of Hollywood no doubt also assisted her getting the part.

As briefly noted in the previous chapter, her husband's heart attack in the fall of 1945 tested the resolve of Zanuck and Cromwell to keep Dunne in the role, because she would not work until Frank was out of danger. Naturally, Irene offered to relinquish the part. But they stayed with her, despite the $50,000 cost of what amounted to a two-month delay.[2] Their loyalty, however, was well-rewarded.

Anna and the King of Siam was a critical and commercial smash, fueled by a Grauman's Chinese Theater opening which the *Los Angeles Herald-Express* called "the greatest Hollywood premiere since Pearl Harbor."[3] A crowd estimated at 15,000 watched the stars arrive at the gala! These first-nighters included Bob Hope, Shirley Temple, Lana Turner, Paulette Goddard, and California governor Earl Warren, whom Dunne would later nominate for President at the Republican national convention of 1948.

Critics around the country inundated both the picture and Dunne, as well as costar Rex Harrison (in his first American film), with kudos. *Variety* entertainingly described the movie as "socko adult drama," as well as praising Dunne's "superb enactment of Anna, the woman who influenced Siamese history by being teacher and confidante to a kingly barbarian."[4] The *Philadelphia Bulletin* said, "The role of Anna is played brilliantly by Irene Dunne, who looks amazingly young and beautiful and gives her finest performance in many years."[5] Even influential former first lady Eleanor Roosevelt turned complimentary critic when she observed in her widely syndicated newspaper column:

> I enjoyed the movie, "Anna and the King of Siam" very much indeed.
> I think Irene Dunne makes it seem quite reasonable that Anna could
> "get away" with her outrageous behavior [of constantly confronting a
> king] . . . and finally win his regard, admiration, and affection.[6]

Amusingly, a copy of this Mrs. Roosevelt review is prominently displayed in one of Dunne's scrapbooks, despite the longtime Republican actress' propensity to support whoever was running against the first lady's husband.[7]

The movie was a return to the lavish prewar production values Hollywood was capable of giving a historical epic. One only wonders why the film was not shot in color in order to better maximize the scope of the physical set detail. Though the film version of the stage musical, *The King and I* (1956, Yul Brynner's signature work), is now better known, the Dunne original is equally satisfying.

An additional bonus, therefore, for 20th Century-Fox was the propensity of reviewers to reinforce this epic prestige picture image for which the studio was shooting. For example, the *New York Sun* said, "While others moan the lack of fresh material for movies, 20th Century-Fox comes up with the most original drama of many years."[8] The *New York Daily News* added, "It is by far the best picture turned out by Darryl Zanuck's studio in years and is one of the most original and delightful pictures to be presented at the Music Hall during this or any other year."[9]

For Dunne, *Anna* was the first of a trilogy of postwar triumphs in which she would star—all of which were adapted from best-selling books and/or plays keying upon earlier period settings. *Anna* was followed by *Life With Father* (1947) and *I Remember Mama* (1948). But before addressing these follow-up classics to *Anna*, one should briefly take stock of Dunne's personal life. For instance, for all her professional accomplishments and political drive, she could still play the free spirit at parties, such as her complexly comic ability to sit at a piano playing "The Sailor's Hornpipe" with her right hand and Rachmaninoff's "Prelude" with her left, while simultaneously singing "I'll be down to get you in a taxi, Honey." Party favorites such as these help better explain why the comedy duo of Abbott and Costello kept trying to convince Dunne to make a picture with them during the war years, though they were equally impressed with her then "queen of screwballs [screwball comedy]" status.[10] (Dunne and the team had become well acquainted on a war bond tour.)

By 1946, the year *Anna* opened, the actress' daughter, Mary Frances, was ten years old and acting as her mother's "technical advisor" on pictures. Dunne shared at the time, "She's very frank. If she thinks one of my pictures is silly, she tells me so. She's the only one to do that. Other people tell me how wonderful I am. I have great confidence in her judgement."[11] Mary Frances' interest in her mother's films had also been another catalyst for doing *Anna*; Dunne felt a historical epic might be more educational for her daughter than a mere comedy. (Of course, sometimes the daughter could assist with the educating. On *Together Again*, 1944, she had helped teach her mother how to jitterbug!)

Given Dr. Griffin's recent heart attack, the always family-conscious Irene attempted to devote even more time to the home front. But her "technical advisor" daughter took it upon herself to monitor this situation, too—sometimes with her own comic touch. For example, when an unusually busy production stretch for *Life With Father* required Dunne's presence for three consecutive days *and* nights, the actress found the following note beside her breakfast plate: "When is the studio going to let daddy and me have some 'Life With Mother'?"[12]

Later that same year (1947) Irene was interviewed on the formula for her happy marriage. She answered with typical Dunne practicality, "It's a large measure of give and take—which is a thing I had to learn and a lot of women aren't inclined to admit."[13] The actress, frequently praised through the years for her stylish clothing, also confessed that her husband, "the doctor," was responsible for picking out her "most becoming outfits and hats." While undoubtedly true, it also demonstrates a Dunne trait frequently mentioned by friends and colleagues—her propensity to direct attention away from herself through compliments to others.

As this text has suggested, Dunne had seldom embraced the high-profile Hollywood life. But because of the attention accorded *Anna*, the actress and her family were thrilled when she was accorded one of the film capital's oldest photo opportunity rituals—preserving her footprints in cement at Grauman's Chinese Theater. *Anna* costar Rex Harrison was also honored, marking the first time, until then, that two performers had been immortalized at the same ceremony.

Fittingly, for an actress who preferred to define herself as a wife and parent, Dunne's celebrated postwar trilogy (*Anna, Life With Father*, and *I Remember Mama*) all were predicated on her creating entertainingly dominant figures of motherhood. The widowed Anna takes her son to 1860s Siam, where she is a teacher and surrogate parent to the King's sixty-plus children. In *Life* she supervises a prosperous 1880s household full of children, all the while managing to let the biggest child (Father) think he is in charge. And Dunne's title role in *Mama* showcases a sentimentally matriarchal Norwegian immigrant family that the mother leads with affectionate insight in early twentieth-century San Francisco.

Ironically, Dunne almost did not join the cast of *Life With Father*. Indeed, she turned the part down . . . several times. Only the persistence of director Michael Curtiz finally wore her down, though she later told the *Los Angeles Times*—"Mother is certainly secondary to Father in it, but I accepted the part because it seemed to be rewarding enough to be in a good picture that everyone will see."[14] However, the secondary status had never really been the problem. Off the record she simply felt "that woman is so silly." But one should first put her character, Vinnie, in context.

Life With Father started out as a series of inspired Clarence Day, Jr. magazine articles about his beloved but cantankerously comic father. Set in the affluent 1880s New York City household of his youth,

Day's amusing sketches do not tell a story as much as they paint a casual character study of his father. The senior Day attempts to rule his wife and large family with an irascible autocratic personality, but an irrational world and a loopy wife really dictate his existence. (Film censors eliminated the modest swearing with which this often foiled figure peppered the air in the play. But gifted screenwriter Donald Ogden Stewart has provided an arsenal of W. C. Fields-like euphemisms, such as "Oh, Gads!" and "What in tarnations!")

Given Father's take-charge manner and his nineteenth-century setting, one might mistakenly place him among America's capable crackerbarrel types. But his continued comic frustrations at the day-to-day business of just getting by better pigeonhole this fun memoir with the antiheroic humor of the then–topically groundbreaking Robert Benchley and James Thurber. Appropriately, several of the Day stories first appeared in *The New Yorker*, both a showcase for this new comedy and the parent magazine for Benchley and Thurber.

Eventually the stories appeared both in book form and as a hit Broadway play. In fact, by the time the screen adaptation took place, *Life With Father* was the longest-running play in Broadway history up to that time—approximately eight years. Consequently, Dunne's initial reluctance to play the story's eccentric female lead might seem odd, especially since the actress was famous for her screwball heroines. But there was a difference. The totally zany screwball leading lady was a Carole Lombard specialty. Dunne merely transformed herself into a screwball at the appropriate time, as best defined by the title of her first excursion into the genre—*Theodora Goes Wild* (1936). Proud of this more cerebral comic heroine, it was natural Irene might be hesitant to play what she perceived to be a pure ditz—whose irrational mindset was just right for the irrational modern world. However, as her aforementioned remark suggests, it was ultimately just too plum a role to turn down—something director Curtiz probably included in his nonstop sales pitch.

The actress also refreshingly admitted at this time (1947), that neither she, nor any performer was infallible: "Actors and actresses don't always know what's best for them. When they think they do, it is usually the beginning of the end."[15] But in this case Dunne (or the persistent Curtiz) turned out to be very right; *Life* was a monster critical and commercial hit. The most diverting hosanna came courtesy of *Box Office Digest*: "This is a picture that begs for the adjective 'swell,' 'delightful,' and then rushes with full confidence for 'great.'"[16] The

New York Daily News' Kate Cameron kept her entertaining praise more comically succinct, calling it "a honey of a picture."[17]

The *Life With Father* tributes to Dunne were equally pervasive and affectionately amusing. The *New York Sun* said, "Irene Dunne, a happy choice for any part, plays Mrs. Day, the lovable, childish woman who always somehow got Father to do what she wanted."[18] *Time* magazine credited Dunne's character with an "infinitely guileful soul . . . winning victories by passive resistance," while the *Motion Picture Herald* called her "clever enough to know how to probe the cracks in his [Father's] armor."[19] Dunne later implied director Curtiz should have received more credit for *Life*, because he greatly assisted her performance by frequently discussing character motivation with her. He did this not to force Vinnie in a certain direction but rather to pump up Dunne's enthusiasm, "because I [still] didn't like the role very much, and he had to placate me and make it more palatable."[20]

Life would also represent several firsts for Dunne. This would be her only teaming with the great William Powell, who played Father. There had been a near pairing during the war, when Irene was handpicked to replace Myrna Loy in the *Thin Man* series, after Loy went into temporary retirement. But her cinema departure proved to be shortlived, and viewers were denied a chance to see Dunne as Nora Charles. Second, *Life* would be Irene's first and only excursion into Technicolor, which as one critic noted, allowed the filmmakers "to show to the best advantage the plushy setting that represents the Day home on [New York City's] Madison Avenue in the early 1880s."[21]

Third, though box office returns for some of Dunne's earlier pictures are unavailable, it would appear that *Life* was also the top-grossing movie of her career. Between a phenomenal viewer turnout and higher postwar ticket prices, the film made an impressive $6,260,000—numbers which easily surpassed such other 1947 hit movies as Claudette Colbert's *The Egg and I*, Gregory Peck's *The Yearling*, Clark Gable's *The Hucksters*, and Cary Grant's *The Bachelor and the Bobby-Soxer*.[22] *Life* magazine comically summed up this box office potential with the observation:

> When the play opened back in 1939, critic Brooks Atkinson prophesied, "Sooner or later everyone will have to see 'Life With Father.'" This film [adaptation] should clean up any remaining pockets of sales resistance.[23]

The last component of Dunne's postwar prestige picture trilogy
was *I Remember Mama*, from John Van Druten's play, based upon
Kathryn Forbes' book, *Mama's Bank Account*. A screen adaptation of
the play had been the pet project of producer Harriet Parsons for
several years. Finding the perfect Mama was proving next to impossible. The original plan was to cast a character actress. But none
of the potential candidates had sufficient box office clout to pay for
the picture. Therefore, the first name performer to be asked was
Greta Garbo. Unofficially retired since *Two-Faced Woman* (1941), she
was still occasionally flirting with comeback vehicles in the late
1940s. After Garbo declined to play Mama, Dunne was approached
about the role. She was captivated by the part and later confessed:

> I love Mama; she has such sensitiveness—she is such a fine person, and
> in her own way, a philosopher. I knew that we must have someone to
> direct . . . who would appreciate all these things, so I said if I could
> have George Stevens, I would play Mama.[24]

Needless to say, Stevens, who had directed Dunne in *Penny Serenade*
(1941), was brought in to megaphone *Mama*. This would be his first
film in the postwar era.

Though casting the glamorous Garbo in the part of a plain, financially pinched immigrant wife and mother might today seem like a
stretch, many people in 1948 had the same take on Dunne in this
role. On screen and off, the willowy beauty was known for her fash-
ionable attire and well-coifed appearance, not unlike that of her
close friend Loretta Young. Yet in *Mama* Dunne would use body
padding (to appear heavier), wear dowdy clothing, and use no
makeup. (Even her two previous period films still had stories which
allowed her to be elegantly stylish in appearance.)

Irene thought the part was too strong, however, to be concerned
about a character actress look. She also spent two months with a dialect coach (Judith Sater) to correctly hone her Norwegian accent.
Dunne became so immersed in getting her character's voice down
pat that she started using her accent at home on the family. Naturally, "technical advisor" Mary Frances enjoyed this development,
too, though history has not recorded whether she offered her mother
tips or merely kiddingly mimicked the accent.

As a praising critic noted at the time of its release, "'I Remember
Mama' has no more plot in the usual meaning of that word than has
'Life With Father.'"[25] But as with *Life*, the series of sketches which

unfold pull the viewer into the most absorbing of character studies. The oldest daughter, Katrin (Barbara Bel Geddes), is going to be a writer. The film opens with the finishing of her book about Mama. As Katrin looks at the finished manuscript, the movie goes into a series of flashbacks. Each of these charming vignettes, even the passing of the irascible Uncle Chris (Oscar Homolka, a first cousin to Clarence Day's Father), is brimming with affectionate humor and a touch of pathos.

Dunne's Vinnie Day was a modern comic figure using an irrational nature to traverse an equally irrational world (like the James Thurber women of his *My Life and Hard Times*, 1933). Conversely, the actress' Mama was a throwback to the rational world of crackerbarrel philosophers—where common sense and perseverance could solve anything. This is what Dunne was suggesting earlier when she described Mama as "a fine person" and "a philosopher." As a comedy genre it falls under the umbrella of populism—the Capraesque world of second chances and belief in the inherent goodness of all people, though sometimes Mama must help the busybody type to see the proverbial light.[26]

My favorite scene in *Mama* is when Dunne uses hard work, a defining trait for both her character and the genre, to solve a basic story point—how to see a hospitalized daughter during restricted after hours. Scrubbing her floor at home out of pure frustration, it dawns on her she might pass as a cleaning lady at the hospital. The plan works, and she essentially scrubs her way to the child's (June Hedin) bed. Director Stevens also savored the scene but not merely for its pathos. He told Dunne that for someone who came to work each day in white gloves, she was quite an impressive floor scrubber.

Stevens' filmmaking reputation for being slow and meticulous held true on this film, too. Producer Parsons later said, "We lost, on the average, a day a week."[27] Stevens was known to film scenes from every possible angle, creating shooting ratios (exposed footage versus the final cut) much higher than the Hollywood norm. But Dunne's later explanation for why they went over budget and schedule was that Stevens "was a perfectionist. He took a lot of preparation with his crew. He didn't do a lot of takes [on *Mama*]."[28]

The perennially even-tempered Dunne also had her only disagreement with Stevens on this picture. He normally allowed the performer a certain degree of freedom in at least sharing his or her slant on a given scene. But in this one instance, Stevens was rather dictatorial in his blocking of a scene for her:

I said, why? He said, "*Do* as I say. Ten steps, then cross [the room]." Well I didn't like that. I have to know *why* I'm doing something. As it turned out, it was just for the cutting. But he wanted to be stubborn, to make me do it without telling me why. So we had a kind of upset [argument].[29]

(Given Dunne's sometimes quasi-method acting need for motivation and Stevens' autocratic response, it is easy to see why there were later fireworks between the director and method-acting fanatic James Dean on the set of *Giant*, 1956.)

Regardless, *Mama* would prove to be yet another critical and commercial success, despite a length of nearly two hours and twenty minutes—the maximum length allowed by New York's prestigious Radio City Music Hall. The *Hollywood Reporter*'s rave review of *Mama* said, "From Radio City Music Hall to the humblest house in the Ozarks, there is not a situation on which the drama can fail to exact its universal appeal."[30] *Variety* added, "With 'I Remember Mama,' RKO is spreading a layer of warm and deeply moving nostalgia that plucks at that special heartstring which echoes strongly at the cash register."[31] Period reviewers probably felt a lot like Louella O. Parsons when she scrambled to praise the picture: "WHAT IS THERE LEFT for me to say about 'I Remember Mama.'"[32]

Dunne's notices were equally impressive. The *New York Daily News* observed, "Irene Dunne's wonderful performance of Mrs. Day in 'Life With Father' is excelled by her superb portrayal of the industrious, canny, big-hearted Norwegian immigrant in 'I Remember Mama.'"[33] *Cue* magazine, which described the picture as "enchanting," said, "This is without doubt her finest role."[34] And *Variety*, calling her "the central pillar of this production," added that, "In holding down the most demanding role of her career, she earns new honors as an actress of outstanding versatility."[35]

One such new honor for Dunne was receiving her fifth Oscar nomination in the Best Actress category. Her competition for the award included: Jane Wyman as a deaf-mute in *Johnny Belinda*; Olivia de Havilland in the pioneering film on mental illness, *The Snake Pit*; Ingrid Bergman as *Joan of Arc*; and Barbara Stanwyck in the film noir thriller, *Sorry, Wrong Number*. Since the Academy dearly loves disabilities, both then and now, Wyman and de Havilland were the clear favorites. But both Dunne's performance and her general popularity made her a sentimental dark horse.

Dunne's close friend Loretta Young encouraged this thinking, since her *Farmer's Daughter* (1947) had been the upset winner in the previous year's Best Actress Oscar race, besting the heavily favored Rosalind Russell in *Mourning Becomes Electra* (1947). *Liberty* magazine even did a tongue-in-cheek article supporting underdog Dunne. Noting she "is long overdue for an Academy Award," the publication posited the hope that she might "do a Truman."[36] (The previous November Harry S. Truman had pulled off one of history's most chronicled Presidential upsets, narrowly defeating Republican challenger Thomas E. Dewey.) *Liberty's* pro-Dunne piece might have been inspired by the period comedian who observed, shortly after the election, "Public opinion polls reach everyone in America, from the farmer in his field right up to the President of the United States, Thomas E. Dewey."

Unfortunately, lightning did not strike twice; Jane Wyman won the Oscar for *Johnny Belinda*. But the positive fallout from *Mama* took four paths. First, for a time, Dunne was everyone's favorite mother. This included winning several screen mother of the year awards, as well as briefly becoming sort of a movieland "Dear Abby."[37] For example, *Silver Screen* magazine carried a special Dunne column for several months called, "Tell Me Your Problem."[38] Second, Dunne's positive screen persona gave her considerable private charity work greater visibility, which resulted in more awards—such as the 1949 Laetare Prize, given to the outstanding member of the American Catholic laity.

Third, the somber subject matter Dunne competed against for the 1948 Oscar caused the actress to lobby her old friend, director Leo McCarey, to dust off his classic melodrama, *Make Way For Tomorrow* (1937), for a remake. Though the original, a poignantly tragic love story about an elderly couple, was not a commercial success, Dunne made a compelling case for late 1940s audiences being better prepared for darker material, such as *The Snake Pit*.[39] Moreover, she sensitively suggested the original *Tomorrow* might have been miscast, with regard to the male lead, comedian Victor Moore. Dunne felt he gave a "splendid performance," but the picture "drew his public, which had been taught to expect merriment at the mere sight of him."[40] Since the part was not played for comic effect, Moore's fans were disappointed and/or stayed away. Plus, the more serious-minded viewer saw comedian Moore's name and stayed away, too. Though nothing came of this *Tomorrow* project, it effectively showcases an actress very cognizant of her art form, both past and present.

Fourth, while Dunne had always been a student of politics, it was not until roughly the opening of *Mama* (summer 1948) that the actress merged this interest with another personal trait—to put one's natural advantages to practical use. Describing this political awakening a few months later, she said:

> I began to perceive that when one is a motion picture player, he has the advantage of a ready-made audience. People in just about every walk of life have seen your pictures and they enjoy talking to you. . . . It seemed a very wonderful advantage, and one that should be put to good use.[41]

Consequently, Dunne was very much a part of the Republican presidential convention that summer (1948) in Philadelphia. She helped lead the demonstration for the candidacy of California governor Earl Warren. Irene then had the honor of giving a five-minute speech seconding the nomination of Warren. Though Dewey, then governor of New York, would ultimately receive the Republican nomination, Warren would be chosen as his vice presidential candidate. This was heady stuff, Dunne later confessed: "I shall never forget the occasion [the convention], when I realized how politics could get into the blood the same as picture-making."[42]

The media-savvy Dunne also had a special epiphany at the convention that was still years away for many political pundits: "It was there at Philadelphia that I learned how television was drawing even closer the nature of the two activities [movies and politics]. For when I heard the question, 'Is he photogenic?' I felt at home immediately."[43] Unfortunately, this sounds a little too Machiavellian. One would prefer Dunne to at least modestly protest the shallowness of any political litmus test that begins with, "Is he photogenic?" But she was a movie star looking to expand her sphere of influence; finding any commonality with her old profession (selling through appearance) must have been comforting.

On her return from the convention, a *Los Angeles Times* reporter asked whether she would "consider" a Cabinet post if so offered from the thought-to-be-sure-thing Dewey. Her honest reply was, "I'm not fitted for a job like that. I'll stick to making motion pictures."[44] But the single-mindedness that had made her an enduring screen star seemed to have been distracted. How else does one explain her having followed three consecutive film classics just prior to the Republican convention with three so-so movies and early screen retirement?

164 *Chapter Eleven*

NOTES

1. Larry Swindell, *Charles Boyer: The Reluctant Lover* (Garden City, New York: Doubleday & Company, Inc., 1983), 115.

2. Patricia Clary, "Studio Waited $50,000 in Time for Irene Dunne," *San Francisco News*, April 24, 1946.

3. Jimmy Star, "'Anna and the King,' in Brilliant Premiere," *Los Angeles Herald-Express*, July 19, 1946, B-1.

4. Review of *Anna and the King of Siam*, *Variety*, June 5, 1946.

5. Laura Lee, "Irene Dunne in Moving Story of the East," *Philadelphia Bulletin*, August 15, 1946.

6. Eleanor Roosevelt, "Eleanor Roosevelt" syndicated column, *Los Angeles Daily News*, July 11, 1946.

7. "Eleanor Roosevelt" column, in the "Irene Dunne Collection," Box 10, Scrapbook 1 (July 1946), Cinema and Television Library, University of Southern California, Los Angeles.

8. Eileen Creelman, "One of Year's Delights," *New York Sun*, June 21, 1946.

9. Kate Cameron, "Music Hall Presents an Enchanting Movie," *New York Daily News*, June 21, 1946, 41.

10. Hedda Hopper, "Queen of Screws," *Chicago News*, April 18, 1942.

11. Irene Dunne studio biography for 20th Century-Fox (1946), in the Irene Dunne Files, Margaret Herrick Library, Academy of Motion Picture Arts and Sciences, Beverly Hills, California.

12. Article without citation, "Irene Dunne Collection," Box 10, Scrapbook 2 (August–October 1946), Cinema Television Library, University of Southern California.

13. Rosalean Doherty, "Irene Dunne Likes Marriage . . .," *New York News*, December 7, 1947.

14. Philip K. Scheuer, "Personality First, Irene Dunne Says," *Los Angeles Times*, August 31, 1947, sec. 3, p. 1.

15. Ibid.

16. Review of *Life with Father*, *Box Office Digest*, August 30, 1947.

17. Kate Cameron, "'Life with Father' Is a Honey of a Picture," *New York Daily News*, August 16, 1947, 21.

18. Eileen Creelman, "'Life with Father' Arrives at the Warner Theater as a Charming, Funny Film," *New York Sun*, August 16, 1947.

19. Review of *Life with Father*, *Time* (August 25, 1947); review of *Life with Father*, *Motion Picture Herald*, August 16, 1947.

20. James Harvey, "Irene Dunne Interviewed by James Harvey," *Film Comment*, January–February, 1980, 31.

21. Cameron, "'Life with Father' Is a Honey of a Picture."

22. Cobbett Steinberg, *Reel Facts: The Movie Book of Records* (New York: Vintage Books, 1978), 343–344.

23. "Movie of the Week: 'Life with Father,'" *Life* magazine, August 18, 1947, 65.

24. Louella O. Parsons, "In Hollywood with Louella O. Parsons," *New York Journal American*, March 28, 1948.

25. Rose Pelswick, "Dunne, Homolka Star in a Beguiling Film," *New York Journal American*, March 12, 1948, 21.

26. See my: *Populism and the Capra Legacy* (Westport, Connecticut: Greenwood Press, 1995).

27. Los Angeles International Film Exposition "Tribute to Irene Dunne" program, in the Irene Dunne Files, Margaret Herrick Library, Academy of Motion Picture Arts and Sciences, Beverly Hills, California.

28. Harvey, 32.

29. Ibid., 31.

30. "'I Remember Mama' Hits Superb Heights on Film: Brilliant Picture Tops Play, Novel," *Hollywood Reporter*, March 9, 1948.

31. Review of *I Remember Mama*, *Variety*, March 10, 1948.

32. Louella O. Parsons, "'Mama' Film Heart Warming," *Los Angeles Examiner*, April 2, 1948.

33. Kate Cameron, "Easter Comes Early to Music Hall Stage," *New York Daily News*, March 12, 1948, 54.

34. Review of *I Remember Mama*, *Cue*, March 13, 1948.

35. Review of *I Remember Mama*, *Variety*.

36. Elizabeth Wilson, "Hollywood's Character Reference," *Liberty*, April 1949, 26.

37. For instance, see "Screen 'Mama' Gets Mothers' Award," *Buffalo Evening News*, February 3, 1949.

38. For example, see Irene Dunne, "Tell Me Your Problem," *Silver Screen*, November 1947, 34–35, 70.

39. Please see Jay Carmody, "Irene Dunne Asks for Remake of Cinema's Saddest Story," *Washington Star*, February 7, 1949.

40. Ibid.

41. Hedda Hopper, "Irene Dunne Becomes Hollywood's Own Good Will Envoy on American Way," *Los Angeles Times*, February 27, 1949, 1.

42. Irene Dunne, "The Twin Cities," *Hollywood Reporter* (19th Anniversary Issue), December 1949.

43. Ibid.

44. "Irene Dunne Returns from Convention Trip," *Los Angeles Times*, July 11, 1948.

TWELVE

Leaving the Screen, and an Active Retirement

I don't know exactly why the public took a liking to me so fast. Popularity is a curious thing. The public responds to a dimple, a smile, a giggle, a hairstyle, an attitude. Acting talent has less to do with it than personality.[1]

—Irene Dunne in retirement

Though actors often flip-flop on their favorite film, Dunne was fairly consistent while she was active in the profession—remaining loyal to her career-making *Cimarron* (1931). Of course, this is not to say there was not occasional wavering. *Penny Serenade*'s (1941) story of adoption remained special because it reminded Dunne of her own adopted daughter, Mary Frances. And her title role in *I Remember Mama* (1948) remained especially dear the rest of her life. Still, in 1948 when the *Saturday Evening Post* asked the actress to author its famous column, "The Role I Liked Best . . .," she chose *Cimarron*.

Though there is undoubtedly a great deal of sentiment attached to any first memorable film, one cannot help thinking there might have been a new factor now fueling Dunne's *Cimarron* selection—her increased interest in politics. After all, her character in the film eventually becomes Oklahoma's first Congresswoman. Moreover, the role had generated the aforementioned praise from Will Rogers—Hollywood's first major star to use his celebrity for political purposes. While Dunne does not directly acknowledge this, she confessed, "The height of the unforgettable [*Cimarron*] experience was the scene where Sabra stands before the townspeople and thanks them for electing her to Congress."[2]

In Dunne's Hollywood return from the 1948 Republican national convention, in which she took an active part, the actress said it was time to get back to films. But she would be off the screen for well over two and one-half years. Besides being bitten by the political bug, Irene was finding it difficult to find any part which would measure up to her celebrated title role in *I Remember Mama*. The only definite for Dunne was a desire to break out of her then-recent run of period mothers. Eventually, she settled on an innocuous comedy with Fred MacMurray—*Never A Dull Moment* (1950).

Dunne plays a New York songwriter who marries a rancher (MacMurray) and has to adjust to life in Wyoming. Unfortunately, her city-girl-goes-west comic problems (rising early, cooking, milking a cow, and so on) are all too familiar. Indeed, MacMurray and Claudette Colbert had already done a similar story in *The Egg and I* (1947). And with a title like *Never A Dull Moment*, many reviewers saw the picture as a basic example of false advertising.

The film was not, however, without a few period supporters. For instance, *Variety* said, "There's a fair amount of diversion . . . to see it through most general situations."[3] The *New York Herald Tribune* observed, "The roles of lady songwriter who falls in love with a . . . likable broncobuster who needs a wife to help him with . . . his ranch are ideally suited to this pair of excellent screen comedians."[4] But many reviews were less kind, with the *New York Times* being the most biting: "a series of rustic encounters that are about as funny as stepping on a nail."[5] Not since *Lady in a Jam* (1942), eight years before, had a Dunne film faired so poorly with the critics.

Luckily, the actress had a quality prestige film in the can, which opened only a month after *Never A Dull Moment*—a fictionalized episode in the life of Queen Victoria, *The Mudlark* (1950). Though the latter film was also a commercial disappointment in the United States, many critics (both here and abroad) were impressed with her portrayal of the queen. More importantly, Great Britain's King George VI (Victoria's great-grandson) "loved" the picture, which he communicated directly to Dunne after a special "Command" screening before the royal family and an audience of 3,200.[6] The story is an account of a meeting in Windsor Castle between the queen and a London street urchin (a "mudlark" being a waif dependent upon scraps left by the tides of the Thames), which helps bring Victoria out of her lengthy period of mourning following the death of her beloved husband, Prince Albert.

More remarkable than this story, however, was the initial British criticism she and 20th Century-Fox received over an American playing an English monarch. Particularly pointed were the remarks of Labor Party member Michael Foote, who found the casting an "insult to the British Empire," as well as another example of the "Americanization" of the English film industry.[7] Seemingly aware of the hyperbole apparent in his statements, Foote was not averse to playing directly for comic effect. For example, in a House of Commons speech he said the last time the British Empire was so insulted was when the Australian "Errol Flynn captured and saved Burma singlehanded [in *Objective, Burma!*, 1945]."[8]

The catalyst for this crisis of casting was that 20th Century-Fox had money frozen in Britain dating back to the war. The studio's head of production, Darryl F. Zanuck, decided to shoot a picture in Great Britain to tap into those funds. The cast, which would include Alec Guinness as Prime Minister Disraeli, would all be English, except for Dunne. She represented a metaphorical insurance policy— potential appeal for an American audience.

When the initial (late March 1950) firestorm of protest occurred, the actress was providentially on an extended European holiday with her husband and fifteen-year-old daughter Mary Frances and was thus isolated from the media. By the time they reached England (mid-May), the casting criticism had somewhat abated. But any remaining doubts about an American playing the queen were quickly put to rest by the press conference called by the ever diplomatic Dunne. The actress completely charmed the British press corps.

The secret to her success was a marriage of humor, dedication, and acting like an everyday person. For example, she shared how hard she was working on the appropriate English accent, knowing that "Queen Victoria would turn over in her grave if I portrayed her with an American accent."[9] Wanting to get the voice right was an extension of Dunne's winning statement, "I am absolutely fascinated by Queen Victoria's character."[10] But even here there was humor, since Dunne confessed to driving her family "mad" with her attention to detail, from perfecting the accent, to studying countless biographies of the queen. The reporter for the *London Evening Standard* was moved to say, "her late Majesty would surely find no fault with . . . Miss Dunne. She is completely without the mannerisms and affectations one associates so often with famous film stars."[11]

The actress' press conference was so down to earth she shared everything, from her daughter's latest interest—to marry a rancher and live in the country (no doubt inspired by her mother's *Never a Dull Moment*), to practical tips on cleaning jewelry (simply rub it with toothpaste). But like any effective negotiator, by the close of this media gathering she gently returned to the reason for the conference—couching her comments in compliments about the practical good sense of just letting her do her job:

> I am so glad that the criticism of my selection for the role has died down. I . . . look upon it as one of the most important roles in my career. [But] after all, it is only acting—and surely an American actress can act the part of an Englishwoman.[12]

Years later Dunne would admit that like many other inherently shy performers, "I loved playing it," because character parts, under pounds of makeup, enable "you [to] really hide."[13] Gordon Bau was responsible for the rubber masks and other makeup that transformed her into Victoria, while costume designer Edward Stevenson, who created the padding for *I Remember Mama*, did more of the same on *The Mudlark*. Thankfully, her performance was appreciated by most critics. For instance, *Variety* said, "The Queen's eventual meeting with the young mudlark is an emotional triumph for both Miss Dunne and Andrew Hale, and is a certain tearjerker for the femme customers [shades of her melodrama reviews]."[14]

Crediting the actress with a "superb performance," the *New York World-Telegram* described the picture as a "beguiling combination of stately pomp and impudent fantasy. This unlikely match has been blended into a pleasant sentimental glow on the Rivoli screen."[15] The *Los Angeles Examiner* called *Mudlark* a film of "great charm, humor, and pathos," while the *New York Post* credited Dunne with an "excellent imitation."[16] Given this multitude of praise, *New York Times* critic Bosley Crowther somehow panned Dunne's pivotal performance as "superficial," yet found the picture "warm and rewarding."[17] But rare is the major reviewer who has so frequently *misread* the movies, or to quote Pauline Kael, the celebrated former film critic for *The New Yorker*, "Bosley Crowther . . . can always be counted on to miss the point."[18]

Regardless, for *Mudlark*'s American premiere, at Los Angeles' Grauman's Chinese Theatre, Dunne borrowed a lesson from the picture's royal "Command" screening in London, where all proceeds went to charity. Consequently, Los Angeles ticket sales for the first night gala went to one of Dunne's favorite helping institutions—the city's St. John's Hospital. This *Mudlark* opening drew a who's who of Hollywood, including Clark Gable and wife Sylvia Ashley; Loretta Young and husband Thomas Lewis; Harold Lloyd and his wife, former actress Mildred Davis; Ethel Barrymore; Joe E. Brown and his daughters; and Pat O'Brien and his wife, actress Eloise Taylor. And in a special promotion for the benefit premiere, Dunne's close friend, Loretta Young, bought the first ticket for the event—which ultimately raised $135,000 for St. John's Hospital.[19]

Unfortunately, the domestic box office for *Mudlark* was disappointing. As much as Dunne enjoyed hiding behind an elaborate makeover, she later attributed the film's mediocre grosses to viewers who were *not* interested in seeing a disappearing act—"My fans hated me with that rubber mask and all that padding."[20] Unhappily, Irene would pull a real cinema disappearing act in two years— which is when her last picture, *It Grows On Trees* (1952), opened. This modest comic fantasy was about a housewife (Dunne) who discovers some backyard foliage is producing five- and ten-dollar bills. The thin story conflict involves her conscientious husband (Dean Jagger, winner of a Best Supporting Actor Oscar in 1950) wanting to turn the money into the police.

Dunne's normally financially pinched character simply wants to be able to cover her bills, or better yet, just have the cash for an occasional escape to the movies. Of course, in 1952 America that made her unusual—most of yesteryear's film fans were now staying home to watch free television. This was another commercial strike against *It Grows On Trees*, which was essentially a studio programmer that would have fared better in the days before the small screen.

Maybe with an imaginative director (normally a Dunne demand), such as fantasy specialist René Clair (see his inventive *I Married a Witch*, 1942), something might have been made of *It Grows On Trees*. Instead, the picture was megaphoned by the successful journeyman, Arthur Lubin. Best known today for directing numerous Abbott and Costello films, as well as the entire output of television's *Mr. Ed* series, he was a competent filmmaker but not someone who could push the creative envelope. Consequently, a great actress' screen career ended in the most lackluster manner. Over a quarter of a century later sports fan Dunne explained her exit from the movies with a baseball analogy:

> I don't know for sure why I retired when I did. I didn't have to quit. Scripts were still coming in. I compare my career to Mickey Mantle's. Like him, I quit while I was still at the top. Maybe it was simply because I didn't think I'd be happy playing second and third leads. I never wanted to be a character actress.[21]

Actually, she improved upon Mantle's retirement. The general consensus, even among Yankee fans, was that the Hall of Famer should have bowed out earlier. Dunne's refusal to play lesser parts, however, certainly rings true. From the beginning her contracts gave the actress preferential billing status. Interestingly enough, in another interview given during her long retirement she both more strongly accented her need to quit "at the top," and added another wrinkle. Again, there is a baseball metaphor—"When my batting average was high, I decided to retire from the screen. I think I could have stayed on and worked into character parts, but there were other things I wanted to do."[22]

"Other things" included ongoing charity work, periodic appearances on television, and continued involvement in Republican Party politics. The latter activity had its biggest payoff when President Dwight D. Eisenhower appointed her (1957) an alternate delegate to the United Nations. When the typically modest Dunne asked "why me?," the President was also frank, "Because we want someone from the West and we want a woman."[23] The actress would call the appointment the "highlight of my life."[24] As a delegate her "biggest thrill" was addressing the UN General Assembly and requesting "$21,000,000 for Palestine refugees."[25] Upon leaving her post in late 1958, Dunne received a letter of commendation from Secretary of State John Foster Dulles. The correspondence read, in part:

> The problems which you handled—involved all the most delicate issues of "colonialism," with all the different meanings that word has for different nations—were the most significant faced by our delegation. I recall, in particular, your fine work in connection with . . . South West Africa.[26]

The general assumption that she would run for elective office never happened, though close film star friends George Murphy and Ronald Reagan made very successful transitions into politics. Murphy would become a United States Senator from California (1965–1971), while Reagan would use his California governorship (1967–1975) as a stepping-stone to the White House (1981–1989). Maybe Dunne's reasoning for not following this political path can be gleaned from yet another retirement interview in which she casually observed, "I drifted into acting and drifted out. Acting is not everything. Living is."[27] Since politics was clearly synonymous with acting for Dunne (see previous chapter), it is not unreasonable to assume that having already moved beyond movies, she would make even shorter shrift of politics.

If "Acting [and politics] is not everything. Living is."—what else constituted *living* for Dunne? In a single word—family. Irene remained very close to her daughter. The 1950s are peppered with memorable—they were in all the papers—moments of significance between an upper-class mother and daughter: the social whirl of the debutante's coming out, the announcement of the formal engagement, the tony wedding, and the celebrity mom becoming a grandma . . . twice. Dunne's daughter even played homage to Mom's film career by taking a small part, as a nurse, in the 1961 remake of Dunne's classic tearjerker *Back Street* (1932).

Of course, family often starts with one's partner. Irene's marriage to Dr. Francis "Frank" Griffin remained a unique love story until his 1965 death from heart-related problems. Remember, this is a woman so committed to her husband that, even as an actress, she would never remove her wedding band—regardless of the part. If Dunne's character was single the ring had to be disguised by makeup and/or skin colored tape. Though they continued to travel extensively in the 1950s (ranging from a visit to the Venice Film Festival, where she was a Hollywood representative, to a nostalgic return to the small town of her youth—Madison, Indiana), Frank's later health problems would restrict the taking of long trips.

Though Dunne walked away from her screen career in the early 1950s, television allowed the actress to occasionally keep her hands in the "business." Part of the attraction was the convenience of a minimal time commitment (versus a lengthy film production). Ironically, her first involvement in this new medium was relatively ambitious—she acted as the hostess of the *Schlitz Playhouse of Stars* for twenty-six shows during the second half of 1952. This half-hour dramatic anthology series appeared Friday nights (9:00–9:30 EST) on CBS. During its eight seasons the program attempted to bring adaptations of literary merit to the small screen, as well as performers not generally associated with television. Irene's position called for her to set up each evening's program in a short prologue and to return at the close for an equally brief epilogue wrap-up.

The openings also allowed Dunne to make a fashion statement, since she frequently appeared in designer gowns. Indeed, this facet of Irene's hostess duties might have contributed to the celebrated stylish entrances of her close friend Loretta Young, when she began hosting her own program the following year. *The Loretta Young Show* (1953–1961) was also a dramatic anthology program, in which Young often starred. But it is still best known for those dramatic designer clothing entrances—a trademark often lampooned by period comedians.

Dunne had consciously avoided appearing in the *Schlitz Playhouse* adaptations, because she wanted to ease into television slowly. Even so, she was no mere clotheshorse for the show. For instance, one prologue had her in a nightclub set seated beside a chimpanzee:

> He kept looking at me, with a gleam in his eyes . . . [and] his actions seemed fitted with . . . [my dialogue]. I said to him, "If you think I'm going to be an item with you in [Hedda] Hopper's column you're crazy." With that he turned to see if she [Hopper] was around and it brought down the [studio audience] house.[28]

Regardless, the small screen's addictive powers were brought home to Dunne by her daughter. In the early 1950s their home was television headquarters for Mary Frances' teenage friends. Irene remembered the company as fun, except once when technical problems made them videoless for two days: "the house was shrouded in gloom. And that's just another of the reasons why television, in my opinion, is really here—and to stay. The youngsters wouldn't stand for letting it go."[29]

Dunne's *Schlitz Playhouse* contract was for $26,000, against ten percent of the profits.[30] But she chose not to renew the arrangement—"People didn't like to see me promoting beer."[31] In the future she would limit herself to the occasional television guest spot. Her most well-reviewed small screen visit was to the first filmed installment (1953) of *The Jack Benny Show* (earlier episodes were done live). The main sketch premise had Benny trying to become Dunne's movie leading man. *Daily Variety* said, "with Irene Dunne, Gregory Ratoff, Vincent Price, and a butler named Rex Evans as co-protagonists, it bagged more laughs than the limit allows . . . with Benny and his polished helpers, it was a classical gem of atomic humor."[32]

Her dramatic television debut occurred the following year (1954). The program was the *Ford Theatre* (1949–1957), another half-hour anthology specializing in both original stories and adaptations of plays and novels. *Ford Theatre* began as a live New York–based show. But in 1952 the program moved to Hollywood and became a filmed series, making it a popular vehicle for screen performers intent on trying this new medium. Dunne's installment seemed tailor-made for her. The strongly Catholic actress, whose frequent charity work often focused on Los Angeles' St. John's Hospital, played Sister Veronica—the compassionate administrator of a big-city hospital, who did *whatever* it took to help people. *Daily Variety* credited her with giving "a sterling performance with all the sympathetic charm of her calling. She is taken through a series of changing emotions, becoming dramatic and capricious by turns."[33]

Fittingly, given Dunne's real-life philanthropic nature, her television work also included charity-related programming. For example, in 1955 she joined other stars in a Jack Benny-hosted *Benefit Show for Retarded Children*. *Variety*'s review of the special singled out Dunne and Art Linkletter as making the most "effective pitches for the retarded kids."[34] Irene also occasionally donated time to television programming for the nonsectarian Christophers movement, founded in 1945 by priest Father James Keller. Dunne's original involvement with the organization was triggered by the Christophers activity of her close Catholic friend and former director, Leo McCarey. The movement was originally formed to fight the spread of Communism, but by the late 1950s it had expanded to a charity-oriented scope.

Though Dunne had retired from the screen and decided not to run for office, she was still very interested in politics and the film industry. Consequently, her periodic television appearances sometimes also embraced these two areas. For instance, on the eve of the 1956 elections, Dunne and Jimmy Stewart cohosted a CBS birthday special for the President—the *Ike Day Surprise Birthday Party*. An impressed *Variety* observed, "With the genuine admiration expressed by the [guest] stars for Ike, along with his modest and gracious acceptance of the situation, this show was easily a bigger vote-getter than a half-dozen speeches."[35] And along film industry–related television appearances, Dunne sometimes surfaced at Oscar time. Thus, in 1955 she joined Humphrey Bogart, Donna Reed, Jack Webb, and Louella Parsons in emceeing an NBC special announcing the Oscar nominations for 1954.

Though Dunne no doubt had fun with her randomly varied television appearances, they represented little more than a diversion for the actress. One has only to go through her private papers (now housed at the University of Southern California's Cinema and Television Library) to get a sense of how she compared her television work with the earlier films.[36] Starting in 1935, Dunne subscribed to a print journalism clipping service for over twenty years. As long as she remained active in the movies, everything was neatly preserved in scores of scrapbooks, though history has not recorded who did all the official pastings. However, as soon as she left film, countless clippings (television-related and other subjects) were allowed to stockpile in envelopes and folders. Nothing in her postscreen career seems worthy of scrapbook status.

With the death of Dunne's husband in 1965, she stopped (with one exception) appearing on television altogether. (This special circumstance involved the 1967 Oscar ceremony, when she presented George Bagnall, president of the Motion Picture Relief Fund, with the Jean Hersholt Humanitarian Award.) Irene's moving away from television did not, however, represent some sort of reclusive mourning of her husband. Naturally, his death was a great loss, or as Rose Kennedy so movingly described it in a letter of condolence to Irene, "He was always so devoted to you and so charming to your friends that I can well understand how poignant must be your sorrow."[37] But with his death the actress rearranged priorities and assumed a more active involvement in the many business investments Frank had made with their capital. Unlike the husbands of many actresses, including Doris Day and Debbie Reynolds, who mismanaged them into bankruptcy, Dr. Griffin had the proverbial "Midas touch." Already a wealthy medical man at the time of their marriage, between his business acumen and her movie star salary (which had reached $200,000 for *Life With Father* alone), the widowed Dunne found herself a multimillionaire.

Irene lived a quarter of a century after the death of her husband, and never seemed to slow down. Besides the many charities (including St. John's Hospital, National Easter Seal Chairwoman, Cancer Society, and various other Catholic outreach organizations), in 1965 she became the first woman to serve on the Board of Directors of the Technicolor Corporation. Chairman Patrick J. Frawley, Jr. said:

> Her knowledge of and her participation in the motion picture field give her an invaluable insight into the business upon which the Tech-

nicolor Corporation is based, and her wide interest in diversified fields also makes her an important and welcome addition to our Board of Directors.[38]

In the 1970s then California governor Ronald Reagan would appoint Dunne to a special state arts commission which would create several innovative developments to showcase the arts, including a first-ever "hands on" approach to sculpture for the blind.

Not surprisingly, family remained a priority, too; no *Mommie Dearest* phenomenon occurred in the Dunne household. Indeed, not only did Irene remain close to her daughter, when her two grandchildren reached college age they both permanently moved in with Grandma! They helped her keep up with current movies and current trends; Irene especially enjoyed learning how to talk like a "Valley Girl."

Dunne also kept her sense of humor. When a contributing editor of *American Classic Screen* managed to wrangle a rare 1977 interview from the nearly eighty-year-old actress, she briefly kept him waiting in her elegant living room. Then suddenly she swept into the room. "Now, how was that for a movie star entrance?" she asked, trying to suppress a laugh. "Oh, I do hate to do that to people, but it's so much fun. Or did you expect them to wheel me in?"[39]

Thankfully, she lived long enough to see her movies rediscovered by several new film fan generations. The formal recognition of her cinema achievements began with a 1975 "Los Angeles Film Exposition" (Filmex) salute, which involved a five-hour retrospective of her career. (This entailed clips from fifteen Dunne films and a showing of the complete *Love Affair*, 1939). After the screenings, the actress appeared for a question-and-answer session hosted by the admiring Roddy McDowall, who had played her young son in *White Cliffs of Dover* (1944). McDowall credited the sampled films with showcasing Dunne's "inner substance and strength." He then added, "She was never wishy-washy. She always brought stamina to her roles, even the ones that didn't have it."[40] And he called their longtime friendship "one of the jewels in my life."

While this "Filmex" tribute was well-done and well-received, it was the Kennedy Center Award (1985) which returned Dunne to a national stage for one final round of applause, before her death in 1990. In the last years of her life she allowed herself to quite literally stop and smell the roses: "My garden . . . [has] the most beautiful roses, they tell me, in town. In the old days I was so busy and I didn't appreciate my home. Now I appreciate it."[41]

Dunne also frequently kidded about formerly not having much regard "for widows who live in large houses." But the actress had come to realize she would never be happy in a small apartment. Plus, a large home enabled her to continue a unique living arrangement with her granddaughter and grandson—both of whom continued to live with her. When they were in their twenties and active, a sage Dunne observed, "I never say, 'Where are you going and what time are you coming home?' That's why they like me. That's one of the great differences between being a mother and being a grandmother."[42]

She continued to entertain for a circle of friends which included Loretta Young, Jimmy and Gloria Stewart, and Bob and Dolores Hope. As in so many of Dunne's films, laughter was always in abundance. And while the actress was no longer active as a performer, she enjoyed keeping up with the arts, such as casting her annual votes for the various Academy Award categories. Dunne also enjoyed occasional tongue-in-cheek speculation about various high-profile period parts, such as one of the nasty matriarchs on the hit 1980s television melodrama, *Falcon Crest*:

> I would play such a role altogether differently. I would be very charming, very sweet, and then put the knife in the back, twisting it a little. A heavy is really very predictable. But a heavy with a veneer of sweetness keeps the other characters—and perhaps the audience—off guard.[43]

Though never reclusive in retirement, like her contemporary Marlene Dietrich, Dunne avoided photo ops as she approached ninety. For example, she gave *Life Magazine*'s entertainment editor, James Watters, her standard explanation of wanting "to be remembered the way I was in the movies." But amused by Watters' persistence, Dunne further fleshed out her refusal with both signature self-deprecating humor and generosity to friends:

> I haven't held up as well as Loretta [Young], who is a marvel, hasn't changed or aged a day since I met her and that was 50 years ago. . . . I suppose you got the gal down the street [neighbor Claudette Colbert] to pose—she takes youth pills.[44]

Dunne died at her Holmby Hills home (Los Angeles) of a heart attack on September 4, 1990. She was ninety-one. Former President

Reagan spoke for Dunne fans everywhere when he said, "Losing her is like losing a member of the family. She's a special lady who will live in our hearts forever."[45] Film critic and professor Andrew Sarris, who introduced the auteur theory to American viewers, said, "Having screened her best movies for my film classes, I can safely say that her womanly charms will endure through the ages."[46] And for many the succinct title of the *New York Times'* editorial page tribute to Dunne said it best—"Class Act."[47] But I remember something her friend and favorite director, Leo McCarey (who preceded her in death), once said about Dunne: "There was nothing she couldn't play, nothing. I was always glad when she wanted me on a picture of hers. It meant I could relax—and still bring in a winner."[48] For students of film, she will always be a "winner."

NOTES

1. Richard Cuskelly, "A Five-Hour Irene Dunne Film Festival," *Los Angeles Herald-Examiner*, March 23, 1979, E-7.

2. Irene Dunne, "The Role I Liked Best . . .," *Saturday Evening Post*, March 9, 1946.

3. Review of *Never a Dull Moment*, *Variety*, November 1, 1950.

4. Otis L. Guernsey, Jr., review of *Never a Dull Moment*, *New York Herald Tribune*, November 22, 1950, 17.

5. Bosley Crowther, review of *Never a Dull Moment*, *New York Times*, November 22, 1950, 20.

6. "King George 'Loves' Night at the Movies," *Los Angeles Times*, November 1, 1950, sec. 1, p. 2.

7. "Irene Dunne's Role as British Queen 'Insult,'" *Los Angeles Examiner*, March 30, 1950.

8. Ibid.

9. Vivien Batchelor, "'Queen Victoria' Is Practicing English," *London Evening Standard*, May 18, 1950, 1.

10. "She Practices English on Her Husband," *London Evening News*, May 18, 1950.

11. Batchelor.

12. Ibid.

13. James Harvey, "Irene Dunne Interviewed by James Harvey," *Film Comment*, January–February, 1980, 28.

14. Review of *The Mudlark*, *Variety*, November 8, 1950.

15. Alton Cook, "A London Urchin Looks at a Queen and Moves an Empire in 'Mudlark,'" *New York World-Telegram*, December 26, 1950, 23.

16. Louella O. Parsons, "'Mudlark' Film of Great Charm," *Los Angeles Examiner*, January 31, 1951, sec. 2, p. 7; Archer Winsten, "'The Mudlark' at the Rivoli," *New York Post*, December 26, 1950, 41.

17. Bosley Crowther, review of *The Mudlark, New York Times*, December 25, 1950, 25.

18. Pauline Kael, *I Lost It at the Movies* (Boston: Little, Brown and Company, 1965), 206.

19. See both "Loretta's First," *Los Angeles Daily News*, January 17, 1951; Wanda Henderson, "Benefit Show Draws Elite," *Hollywood Citizen News*, January 31, 1951.

20. James Bawden, "A Visit with Irene Dunne," *American Classic Screen*, September 10, 1977, 11.

21. Cuskelly, E-7.

22. Camilla Snyder, "The Star Who Still Shines off the Stage," *Los Angeles Herald-Examiner*, October 18, 1970, F-1.

23. Ibid.

24. "Irene Dunne Finds Career in U.N. 'Highlight of My Life,'" *New York Herald Tribune*, October 16, 1957, 3.

25. "Irene Dunne Describes Work as U.N. Delegate," *Los Angeles Times*, February 3, 1958.

26. John Foster Dulles to Irene Dunne, January 6, 1958, in the "Irene Dunne Collection," Box 1, "Correspondence" folder, Cinema and Television Library, University of Southern California, Los Angeles.

27. Bawden, 11.

28. Walter Ames, "TV's Revolving Door Gay Whirl for Irene," *Los Angeles Times*, July 20, 1952, 3.

29. Ibid., 9.

30. *Schlitz Playhouse of Stars* contract (January 23, 1952), in the "Irene Dunne Collection," Box 1, "Television" folder, Cinema and Television Library, University of Southern California, Los Angeles.

31. Bawden, 11.

32. Review of *The Jack Benny Show, Daily Variety*, December 7, 1953.

33. Review of *Ford Theatre, Daily Variety*, April 19, 1954.

34. Review of *Benefit Show for Retarded Children, Variety*, November 16, 1955.

35. Review of *Ike Day Surprise Birthday Party, Variety*, October 17, 1956.

36. "Irene Dunne Collection," 10 boxes of material, Cinema and Television Library, University of Southern California, Los Angeles.

37. Rose Kennedy to Irene Dunne, September 6, 1966, in the "Irene Dunne Collection," Box 1, "Correspondence" folder, Cinema and Television Library, University of Southern California, Los Angeles.

38. "Irene Dunne Named Technicolor Exec," *Hollywood Reporter*, February 16, 1965.

39. Bawden, 8.

40. "Irene Dunne at Filmex Tribute Rates 'Affair,' 'Mama' Her Best," *Variety*, March 25, 1975.

41. George Shea, "Irene Dunne," *Northwest Orient*, December 1985, 35.

42. Ibid.

43. John McDonough, "Screening a Star: A Rare Interview with Irene Dunne," *Chicago Tribune*, May 12, 1985, sec. 13, p. 8.

44. James Watters, "Irene Dunne: No Oscar, Just Love," *New York Times*, September 23, 1990, sec. 2, p. 20.

45. "Good Night, Irene Dunne; Hollywood Loses an Airy and Elegant Gal from Film's Golden Age," *People*, September 17, 1990, 119.

46. Andrew Sarris, "Irene Dunne obituary," *New York Observer*, September 17, 1990, 25.

47. "Class Act," *New York Times*, September 9, 1990, sec. 4, p. 24.

48. "Irene Dunne, Leading Star of '30s and '40s, Dies at 88," *Los Angeles Times*, September 5, 1990, A1, A2.

EPILOGUE

If Irene Dunne isn't the first lady of Hollywood, then she's the last one.[1]

—Director Gregory LaCava

When Dunne received her Kennedy Center Award (1985) she had been retired from the screen over a decade longer than the length of her movie career (1930–1952). But this was no reclusive Norma Desmond-type (*Sunset Boulevard*, 1950) retirement. From United Nations alternate delegate to occasional television work, she in no sense disappeared. Plus, her nonstop charity work had been responsible for countless awards, from honorary doctorates to a special recognition from St. John's Hospital (1985). The latter honor, which occurred several months prior to the Kennedy Center ceremony, involved dedicating a courtyard and fountain to Dunne, as well as unveiling a life-size bronze bust of the actress (on a marble base). A beaming Dunne observed at the time, "I've never been to an unveiling, let alone one of my own."[2]

Still, the Kennedy Center Award is the highest tribute an American performer can receive. And while the recognition for Dunne was long overdue, the actress put it first among her many honors: "This is the one I will cherish."[3] As previously noted, Irene was also pleased to be included in such an august group of Kennedy recipients: comedian Bob Hope, lyricist/playwright Alan Jay Lerner and composer Frederick Loewe, opera soprano Beverly Sills, and dancer/choreographer Merce Cunningham. Though acquainted with everyone but Cunningham, her inclusion with Hope and Sills made it most memorable for Dunne. Not only was Hope her favorite comedian, but his strong ties to both the Republican Party and charity work put him in a special category for the actress. And since Dunne's first performing goal in life was to be an opera singer, she was especially pleased the Kennedy "class of 1985" included the great Sills. As President Ronald Reagan told the honorees as they assembled in the White House's East Room:

> You have enhanced life—you've moved us and made us laugh, made us cheer, and made our souls soar as you soared through the air in dance or filled the air with the sound of your music.[4]

Fittingly for Dunne, with the exception of the dance credit, everything the president said could be applied solely to the actress.

A full appreciation of Dunne's importance must, of course, begin with her amazing film legacy. It was enough to turn the normally unflappable Jimmy Stewart into a nervous wreck prior to narrating the Dunne portion of the Kennedy program. That is, Stewart was so impressed with her movie accomplishments that he was afraid of not doing them justice. His central point, as noted in the prologue, was the actress' versatility. Her five Oscar nominations occurred in almost as many genres—the Western *Cimarron* (1931), two screwball comedies: *Theodora Goes Wild* (1936) and *The Awful Truth* (1937), the romantic comedy *Love Affair* (1939), and the populist *I Remember Mama* (1948).

The character link which connected these roles and her equally celebrated forays into musicals and melodramas was an ability to endure—what film historian David Chierichetti once called her "inner strength." Whether this involved a marriage on the farcical rocks, à la *The Awful Truth*, or *Cimarron*'s excursion into Western melodrama, the viewer had faith that Dunne would carry the day . . . with style and grace and a sense of humor. Comedy was her forte, both on and off the screen. Indeed, Irene often used "funny" to find a character. For example, when the actress religiously worked on her dialect for *I Remember Mama*, she honed it with humor: "The real way to learn an accent is to read jokes. When you're reading a joke you forget that you're trying to learn something, and the dialect comes naturally."[5]

The reason, moreover, she worked so well in the screen world of her pivotal collaborator, Leo McCarey, was that they both looked for that humanizing humor in every film, regardless of the genre. Credit their proud-to-be-Irish connection, or a shared zeitgeist, their cinema sense of survival was grounded in amazingly likeable characters. To view Dunne in a signature film is to want to know her, even to be like her. Consequently, when you find her in a typical comedy mix of bemusement and frustration, one does not know whether to laugh with Irene, or to hug her. Certainly to put audiences so completely under his or her spell, especially one defined by both friendly frankness and a witty warmness, is the ultimate achievement for an actor/actress. Ironically, the fact that comedy was second nature to Dunne led her to undervalue it:

> I never admired a comedienne . . . yet it was very easy for me, very natural. It was no effort for me to do comedy at all. Maybe that's why I wasn't so appreciative of it. I liked the heavier [more dramatic] things. . . . I liked playing Mama in I Remember Mama. [Yet even here there is an undercurrent of comedy.][6]

Interestingly enough, while Dunne did not admire comediennes, arguably the greatest one who ever lived, Lucille Ball, very much admired her. Lucy had appeared in two of Dunne's RKO pictures. First, Ball had an unbilled spot as a model in a fashion show sequence from *Roberta* (1935). But by *Joy of Living* (1938) she had graduated to playing Irene's kid sister. Though originally mentored by Carole Lombard, years later Lucy would tell an American Film Institute seminar that Dunne was *the* RKO actress she studied—crediting her with inspired comic variations on every take. (Ball and then-husband Desi Arnaz would later *buy* RKO, 1957, when they formed Desilu Productions!)

Building upon Lucy's praise of Dunne for comic inventiveness, as well as the aforementioned kudos for Irene's marriage of character versatility and just plain likeableness, one cannot omit her special brand of sexiness. This is no mean accomplishment, given her image as "first lady" of Hollywood. But this is precisely what creates part of her attraction. For example, no less a film critic than Andrew Sarris, one of America's greatest arbiters of cinema study, said:

> Talk about sexy. When she takes off her necklace in the train compartment in Gregory LaCava's "Unfinished Business," and later whispers with post-tryst intensity to Preston Foster, "I love you," well, with censorship and all, that was part of my own rite of passage, and I feel a little sorry for kids today caught up in a kind of slut-worship.[7]

Though this implied screen affair was atypical of Dunne, her characters were sometime sexy based upon the *possibility* of "a good girl deciding thoughtfully to be bad."[8] Though the going "bad" part was not the normal Dunne destination, this possibility was ever so erotic.

Film historian Maria DiBattista best described Dunne's sex appeal component by again returning to the actress' inherent comic nature—she had a "campiness that elevated such games [as the interaction of men and women] out of the realm of childish fun into decidedly adult entertainment."[9] Though DiBattista does not couple the quote with an example, Dunne's comic "campiness" immediately brings to mind, for this author, a brief throwaway bit from *Love Affair*, that also manages to incorporate the actress' love of baseball.

The scene in question finds playboy Charles Boyer reading a telegram on the deck of an ocean liner when a gust of wind blows it through an open porthole. A passing Dunne picks up the communication and starts reading, only to be interrupted by Boyer, requesting its return. But she asks for verification, and he repeats the jest of what is a romantic note—"Remembering a warm beautiful night and . . . you." While an embarrassed Boyer then gets the telegram back, a suddenly attentive Dunne (with an endearing cheekiness) asks, "It was alright, huh?" Abruptly, she disappears from her side of the porthole, only to briefly return with some signature silliness— "Do you think it'll [sex] ever take the place of baseball?"

Her sexiness might also be noted as yet another facet of her effectiveness in playing the screen mother. I am reminded of the references to Paulette Goddard in Charles Chaplin, Jr.'s biography of his father.[10] Goddard was a beautiful screen contemporary of Dunne, as well as Chaplin's third wife. The comedian's son describes her as the most genuinely thoughtful of stepmothers, from playful interactions with Charles (and his brother Sydney), to also meeting the basic demands of motherhood—going that proverbial extra mile to make them happy. But on top of this, young Charles confesses that both he and his brother had major league crushes on this stepmother, who also just happened to be a sexy movie star. Applying this analogy to Dunne, her sensitive matriarchal tendencies in numerous films were still permeated with an inherent aura of sexuality. For male film fans through the years, was this almost erotic mix that different from Charles' crush on a movie star stepmom?

Moving beyond Dunne's amazing movie legacy, one admires her all the more for the stellar person behind the film roles. Unfortunately, pop culture today often feeds upon revisionist biographies that relish finding the unsavory in their subjects. Dishing has become a national pastime. I was reminded anew of this while recently reading a *New York Times* piece by a current biographer of the great Los Angeles Dodger pitcher, Sandy Koufax. Author Jane Leavy was feeling like a failure as a researcher, because all her evidence suggested Koufax was nearly as flawless as the perfect game he once pitched—which was the framing device of her biography. Leavy was embarrassed to confess that she needed a friend to remind her that, "It is a privilege to write about someone you actually like."[11]

Though I never needed such a reminder about Dunne, I did immediately relate to Leavy's position—the irony of modern biography, where it is daring (chancy?) to chronicle niceness. Moreover, I was struck by the fact that Dunne would probably have appreciated the baseball connection. She was a fan, and in later years often spoke in the vernacular of the sport: "My [screen] career was not the longest, but I had a high batting average." What's more, the Los Angeles Dodgers were her hometown team, with Koufax being a special favorite.

There were also all these Dunne-Koufax parallels, beyond the model citizen moniker. Each of them was so intensely private that journalists sometimes labeled them "mysterious," "aloof," and even the Garbo-like "an enigma." Both reached the top of their profession early, and then walked away before age could diminish their accomplishments. And each of them kept his or her equilibrium with humor, turning the focus away from themselves. Even in a thirty-minute phone interview I had with the actress, years before this project, she was most concerned about "the neglected Leo [McCarey]."

The celebration of great accomplishments in the arts, or on the playing field, do not necessitate, nor should they, that we admire the ethics of a particular gifted performer. As a biographer I have frequently experienced what Robert A. Caro once labeled the profession's "dark-side"—the proverbial skeletons in the closet.[12] What has made the experience of doing Dunne's life story most memorable to me is that she is the first subject I have profiled that gave me no "dark side" moments. This is not an easy accomplishment by the actress, given that I pride myself on the intense investigation that once moved Virginia Woolf to liken the craft's extensive research demands to "donkey work."[13] (This probably also explains why Woolf once observed, "Writing lives is the devil.")

This is neither to say my Dunne preparation was infallible, nor that she was perfect. But I am a great believer in the old adage that while a good biographer can never be assured of having found the "absolute truth," a job well done can deliver the "best truth" available.[14] Thus, while I continue to admire Dunne's spirited screen characters, particularly her forays into screwball and romantic comedy, I am now an equal fan of this praiseworthy lady herself. The greatest compliment I can pay her is that while her art deserves an army of biographers, she always conducted herself with the humbleness of someone aware that movies (whether hers or others) are only made possible by the collaboration of countless men and women who will never have biographers. But lest I let Dunne sound too common, to borrow a complimentary use of the word my grandmother gave to important people who retained a modest hat size, let me close with the actress' own affectionate admonishment to an interviewer, late in her life—"Now don't you dare call me normal. I was never a Pollyanna. There was always a lot of Theodora in me."[15]

NOTES

1. Larry Swindell, *Charles Boyer: The Reluctant Lover* (Garden City, New York: Doubleday & Company, Inc., 1983), 141.

2. Untitled coverage of Dunne dedication at St. John's Hospital, *Hollywood Reporter*, May 8, 1985, in the Irene Dunne Files, Margaret Herrick Library, Academy of Motion Picture Arts and Sciences, Beverly Hills, California.

3. Jody Jacobs, "Irene Dunne Cherishes Latest Honor," *Los Angeles Times*, July 18, 1985, sec. 5, p. 4.

4. Barbara Gamarekian, "Six Receive Kennedy Center Honors," *New York Times*, December 9, 1985, C-13.

5. Dick Pitts, "The Cinema," *Charlotte Observer*, July 8, 1947, 8.

6. James Harvey, "Irene Dunne Interviewed by James Harvey," *Film Comment*, January–February, 1980, 30.

7. Andrew Sarris, "Irene Dunne obituary," *New York Observer*, September 17, 1990, 25.

8. Ibid.

9. Maria DiBattista, *Fast-Talking Dames* (New Haven: Yale University Press, 2001), 205.

10. Charles Chaplin, Jr., *My Father, Charlie Chaplin* (New York: Random House, 1960).

11. Jane Leavy, "Tape from 1965 Easier to Find Than Ill Will Toward Koufax," *New York Times* (September 1, 2002): Sports: 6.

12. William Zinsser, ed., *Extraordinary Lives: The Art and Craft of American Biography* (Boston: Houghton Mifflin Company, 1986), 217.

13. Leon Edel, *Writing Lives* (New York: W. W. Norton, 1984), 206.

14. Paul Murray Kendall, *The Art of Biography* (New York: W. W. Norton, 1985), 130.

15. James Bawden, "A Visit With Irene Dunne," *American Classic Screen*, September 10, 1977, 11.

DUNNE FILMOGRAPHY

September 1930   *Leathernecking* (81 minutes) RKO
Director: Edward Cline. Screenplay: Alfred
Jackson and Jane Murfin, from the play
Present Arms by Herbert Fields, Richard Rogers,
and Lorenz Hart. Stars: Irene Dunne, Ken Murray, Louise Fazenda, Ned Sparks, Lilyan Tashman, Eddie Foy, Jr., Benny Rubin.

January 1931   *Cimarron* (124 minutes) RKO
Director: Wesley Ruggles. Screenplay: Howard
Estabrook, from the Edna Ferber novel. Stars:
Richard Dix, Irene Dunne,
Estelle Taylor, Nance O'Neil, William Collier,
Jr., Rosco Ates, George E. Stone, Stanley Fields,
Robert McWade, Edna May Oliver.

May 1931   *Bachelor Apartment* (77 minutes) RKO
Director: Lowell Sherman. Screenplay: J. Walter Ruben, from a John Howard Lawson story.
Stars: Lowell Sherman, Irene Dunne, Mae
Murray, Norman Kerry.

August 1931   *The Great Lover* (79 minutes) MGM
Director: Harry Beaumont. Screenplay: Gene
Markey and Edgar Allan Woolf, from the play

by Leo Ditrichstein, Frederick Hatton, and Fanny Hatton. Stars: Adolphe Menjou, Irene Dunne, Ernest Torrence, Neil Hamilton.

October 1931   *Consolation Marriage* (82 minutes) RKO
Director: Paul Sloane. Screenplay: Humphrey Pearson, from the William Cunningham story. Stars: Irene Dunne, Pat O'Brien, Myrna Loy, John Holiday.

April 1932   *Symphony of Six Million* (94 minutes) RKO
Director: Gregory La Cava. Screenplay: Bernard Schubert, J. Walter Ruben, and James Seymour, from the Fannie Hurst novel. Stars: Irene Dunne, Ricardo Cortez, Gregory Ratoff, Anna Appel.

August 1932   *Back Street* (89 minutes) Universal
Director: John M. Stahl. Screenplay: Gladys Lehman and Lynn Starling, from the Fannie Hurst novel. Stars: Irene Dunne, John Boles, June Clyde, George Meeker, ZaSu Pitts.

October 1932   *Thirteen Women* (73 minutes) RKO
Director: George Archainbaud. Screenplay: Bartlett Cormack and Samuel Ornitz, from the Tiffany Thayer novel. Stars: Ricardo Cortez, Irene Dunne, Myrna Loy, Jill Esmond.

January 1933   *No Other Woman* (58 minutes) RKO
Director: J. Walter Ruben. Screenplay: Wanda Tuchock and Bernard Shubert, from the Eugene Walter play, *Just A Woman*. Stars: Irene Dunne, Charles Bickford, J. Carroll Naish, Eric Linden.

February 1933   *The Secret of Madame Blanche* (83 minutes) MGM
Director: Charles Brabin. Screenplay: Frances Goodrich and Albert Hachett, from the Martin Brown play, *The Lady*. Stars: Irene Dunne, Lionel Atwill, Phillips Holmes, Una Merkel.

May 1933

The Silver Cord (74 minutes) RKO
Director: John Cromwell. Screenplay: Jane
Murfin, from the Sidney Howard play. Stars:
Irene Dunne, Joel McCrea, Frances Dee, Eric
Linden, Laura Hope Crews.

September 1933

Ann Vickers (72 minutes) RKO
Director: John Cromwell. Screenplay: Jane
Murfin, from the Sinclair Lewis novel. Stars:
Irene Dunne, Walter Huston, Conrad Nagel,
Bruce Cabot, Edna May Oliver.

December 1933

If I Were Free (66 minutes) RKO
Director: Elliott Nugent. Screenplay: Dwight
Taylor, from the John Van Druten play, *Behold,
We Live*. Stars: Irene Dunne, Clive Brook, Nils
Asther, Henry Stephenson, Vivian Tobin,
Laura Hope Crews.

April 1934

This Man Is Mine (76 minutes) RKO
Director: John Cromwell. Screenplay: Jane
Murfin, from the Anne Morrison Chapin play,
Love Flies in the Window. Stars: Irene Dunne,
Constance Cummings, Ralph Bellamy, Kay
Johnson, Charles Starrett, Sidney Blackmer,
Vivian Tobin, Louis Mason.

May 1934

Stingaree (76 minutes) RKO
Director: William Wellman. Screenplay: Becky
Gardiner, from the stories of E. W. Hornung.
Stars: Irene Dunne, Richard Dix, Mary Boland,
Conway Tearle, Andy Devine.

September 1934

The Age of Innocence (81 minutes) RKO
Director: Philip Moeller. Screenplay: Sarah Y.
Mason and Victor Heerman, from the Edith
Wharton novel and the Margaret A. Barnes
play. Stars: Irene Dunne, John Boles, Lionel
Atwill, Laura Hope Crews.

January 1935   *Sweet Adeline* (87 minutes) Warner Bros.
                 Director: Mervyn LeRoy. Screenplay: Erwin S.
                 Gelsey, from the play by Jerome Kern, Oscar
                 Hammerstein II, Harry Armstrong, and Dick
                 Gerard. Stars: Irene Dunne, Donald Woods,
                 Ned Sparks, Hugh Herbert.

March 1935   *Roberta* (106 minutes) RKO
                 Director: William A. Seiter. Screenplay: Jane
                 Murfin, Sam Mintz, Glen Tryon, and Alan
                 Scott, from the Alice Duer Miller novel and
                 the Jerome Kern and Otto Harbach play. Stars:
                 Irene Dunne, Fred Astaire, Ginger Rogers,
                 Randolph Scott, Helen Westley.

December 1935   *Magnificent Obsession* (101 minutes) Universal
                 Director: John M. Stahl. Screenplay: George
                 O'Neil, Sarah Y. Mason, and Victor Heerman,
                 from the Lloyd C. Douglas novel. Stars: Irene
                 Dunne, Robert Taylor, Sara Haden, Charles
                 Butterworth, Betty Furness.

May 1936   *Show Boat* (113 minutes) Universal
                 Director: James Whale. Screenplay: Oscar
                 Hammerstein II, from the Edna Ferber novel
                 and the Oscar Hammerstein II and Jerome
                 Kern play. Stars: Irene Dunne, Allan Jones,
                 Charles Winninger, Helen Westley, Paul Robe-
                 son, Helen Morgan, Donald Cook, Sammy
                 White, Queenie Smith.

November 1936   *Theodora Goes Wild* (94 minutes) Columbia
                 Director: Richard Boleslawski. Screenplay: Sid-
                 ney Buchman, from the Mary McCarthy story.
                 Stars: Irene Dunne, Melvyn Douglas, Thomas
                 Mitchell, Thurston Hall, Rosalind Keith, Spring
                 Byington, Elisabeth Risdon, Margaret McWade.

July 1937   *Hide, Wide and Handsome* (112 minutes) Para-
                 mount

Director: Rouben Mamoulian. Screenplay: Oscar Hammerstein II and George O'Neil. Stars: Irene Dunne, Randolph Scott, Dorothy Lamour, Raymond Walburn, Alan Hale, Elizabeth Patterson, Charles Bickford, William Frawley, Akim Tamiroff, Ben Blue.

October 1937   *The Awful Truth* (92 minutes) Columbia
Director: Leo McCarey. Screenplay: Vina Delmar, from the Arthur Richman play, but McCarey largely improvised the film. Stars: Irene Dunne, Cary Grant, Ralph Bellamy, Alexander D'Arcy, Cecil Cunningham, Molly Lamont, Esther Dale, Joyce Compton.

March 1938   *Joy of Living* (90 minutes) RKO
Director: Tay Garnett. Screenplay: Gene Towne, Graham Baker, Allan Scott, Dorothy Fields, and Herbert Fields. Stars: Irene Dunne, Douglas Fairbanks, Jr., Alice Brady, Guy Kibbee, Jean Dixon, Eric Blore, Lucille Ball, Warren Hymer, Billy Gilbert.

March 1939   *Love Affair* (87 minutes) RKO
Director: Leo McCarey. Screenplay: Delmar Daves, Donald Ogden Stewart, Mildred Cram, and Leo McCarey. Stars: Irene Dunne, Charles Boyer, Maria Ouspenskaya, Lee Bowman.

May 1939   *Invitaton to Happiness* (95 minutes) Paramount
Director: Wesley Ruggles. Screenplay: Claude Binyon and Mark Jerome. Stars: Irene Dunne, Fred MacMurray, Charlie Ruggles, Billy Cook, William Collier, Sr.

August 1939   *When Tomorrow Comes* (90 minutes) Universal
Director: John M. Stahl. Screenplay: Dwight Taylor, from a James M. Cain unpublished novel. Stars: Irene Dunne, Charles Boyer, Nydia Westman, Onslow Stevens, Fritz Feld.

May 1940   *My Favorite Wife* (88 minutes) RKO
Director: Garson Kanin and an uncredited Leo
McCarey. Screenplay: Bella and Samuel
Spewack, and McCarey. Stars: Irene Dunne,
Cary Grant, Randolph Scott, Gail Patrick, Ann
Shoemaker, Scotty Beckett, Mary Lou Harring-
ton, Donald MacBride, Hugh O'Connell,
Granville Bates.

January 1941   *Land of Liberty* (137 minutes) MGM
(Under the supervision of Cecil B. DeMille).
A compilation history of the United States, in-
cluding a segment from *Cimarron* (with Irene
Dunne). The film was a Hollywood cooperative
for the war effort.

April 1941   *Penny Serenade* (118 minutes) Columbia
Director: George Stevens. Screenplay: Morrie
Ryskind, from a Martha Cheavens story. Stars:
Irene Dunne, Cary Grant, Beulah Bondi, Edgar
Buchanan, Ann Doran.

August 1941   *Unfinished Business* (96 minutes) Universal
Director: Gregory La Cava. Screenplay: Eugene
Thackrey, but La Cava improvised a great deal.
Stars: Irene Dunne, Robert Montgomery, Eugene
Pallette, Preston Foster.

July 1942   *Lady in a Jam* (78 minutes) Universal
Director: Gregory La Cava. Screenplay: Eugene
Thackrey, Frank Cockrell, and Otho Lovering,
but La Cava improvised a great deal. Stars: Irene
Dunne, Patric Knowles, Ralph Bellamy, Eugene
Pallette, Queenie Vassar, Jane Garland.

December 1943 *A Guy Named Joe* (120 minutes) MGM
Director: Victor Fleming. Screenplay: Dalton
Trumbo, from an unpublished story by Chandler
Sprague, David Boehm, and Frederick H. Bren-
nan. Stars: Spencer Tracy, Irene Dunne, Van

Johnson, Ward Bond, James Gleason, Lionel
Barrymore, Barry Nelson, Don DeFore.

March 1944
The White Cliffs of Dover (126 minutes) MGM
Director: Clarence Brown. Screenplay: Claudine
West, Jan Lustig, and George Froeschel, from
the Alice Duer Miller poem, "The White Cliffs,"
with added verse from Robert Nathan. Stars:
Irene Dunne, Alan Marshall, Frank Morgan,
Roddy McDowall, Van Johnson, C. Aubrey
Smith, Dame May Whitty, Gladys Cooper, Peter
Lawford, John Warburton, Jill Esmond, Brenda
Forbes, Norma Varden, Arthur Shields, Eliza-
beth Taylor, June Lockhart.

March 1944
Follow the Boys (110 minutes) Universal
Director: Eddie Sutherland. Screenplay: Lou
Breslow and Gertrude Purcell. Stars: Univer-
sal's all-star war effort contains USO footage
of Irene Dunne.

November 1944
Together Again (100 minutes) Columbia
Director: Charles Vidor. Screenplay: Virginia
Van Upp, F. Hugh Herbert, Stanley Russell, and
Herbert Biberman. Stars: Irene Dunne, Charles
Boyer, Charles Coburn, Mona Freeman.

July 1945
Over 21 (102 minutes) Columbia
Director: Charles Vidor. Screenplay: Sidney
Buchman, from the Ruth Gordon play. Stars:
Irene Dunne, Alexander Knox, Charles
Coburn, Jeff Donnell.

June 1946
Anna and the King of Siam (128 minutes) 20th
Century-Fox
Director: John Cromwell. Screenplay: Talbot
Jennings and Sally Benson, from the Margaret
Landon biography. Stars: Irene Dunne, Rex
Harrison, Linda Darnell, Lee J. Cobb, Gale
Sondergaard.

August 1947	*Life With Father* (118 minutes) Warner Bros. Director: Michael Curtiz. Screenplay: Donald Ogden Stewart, from the Howard Lindsay and Russell Crouse play, based upon the writings of Clarence Day, Jr. Stars: Irene Dunne, William Powell, Elizabeth Taylor, Edmund Gwenn, ZaSu Pitts, Jimmy Lydon, Emma Dunn.
March 1948	*I Remember Mama* (134 minutes) RKO Director: George Stevens. Screenplay: DeWitt Bodeen, from the John Van Druten play, based upon the Kathryn Forbes novel, *Mama's Bank Account*. Stars: Irene Dunne, Barbara Bel Geddes, Oscar Homolka, Philip Dorn, Sir Cedric Hardwicke, Edgar Bergen, Rudy Vallee, Barbara O'Neil, Florence Bates.
November 1950	*Never a Dull Moment* (89 minutes) RKO Director: George Marshall. Screenplay: Lou Breslow and Doris Anderson, from the Kay Swift novel, *Who Could Ask For Anything More*. Stars: Irene Dunne, Fred MacMurray, William Demarest, Andy Devine, Gigi Perreau, Natalie Wood.
November 1950	*The Mudlark* (99 minutes) Twentieth Century-Fox Director: Jean Negulesco. Screenplay: Nunnally Johnson, from the Theodore Bonnett novel. Stars: Irene Dunne, Alec Guinness, Andrew Ray, Beatrice Campbell.
November 1952	*It Grows On Trees* (84 minutes) Universal Director: Arthur Lubin. Screenplay: Leonard Praskins and Barney Slater. Stars: Irene Dunne, Dean Jagger, Joan Evans, Richard Crenna.

SELECTED BIBLIOGRAPHY

SPECIAL COLLECTIONS

"Charles Davidson Collection of Irene Dunne Letters." Private Collector, Madison, Indiana.

"Gregory La Cava Clipping Files." Performing Arts Library, Billy Rose Special Collection, New York Public Library at Lincoln Center, New York, New York.

"Gregory La Cava Clipping Files." Margaret Herrick Library, Academy of Motion Picture Arts and Sciences, Beverly Hills, California.

Individual clipping files for all 43 (see Filmography) Irene Dunne films. Performing Arts Library, Billy Rose Collection, New York Public Library at Lincoln Center, New York, New York.

"Irene Dunne Clipping Files." Madison Historical Society, Madison, Indiana (Dunne's hometown).

"Irene Dunne Clipping Files." Margaret Herrick Library, Academy of Motion Picture Arts and Sciences, Beverly Hills, California.

"Irene Dunne Clipping Files." Madison Public Library, Madison, Indiana (Dunne's hometown).

"Irene Dunne Clipping Files." Performing Arts Library, Billy Rose Special Collection, New York Public Library at Lincoln Center, New York, New York.

"Irene Dunne Collection." 10 boxes of material (scrapbooks, letters, contracts, loose clippings, and stills). Cinema and Television Library, University of Southern California, Los Angeles.

Irene Dunne–related materials—*extensive* use of the "Tombs" (dead newspapers—microfilm department) at the New York Public Library's Main Branch at Fifth Avenue and 42nd St., New York, New York.

"Leo McCarey Clipping Files." Margaret Herrick Library, Academy of Motion Picture Arts and Sciences, Beverly Hills, California.

"Leo McCarey Clipping Files." Performing Arts Library, Billy Rose Special Collection, New York Public Library at Lincoln Center, New York, New York.

BOOKS AND SCRIPTS

Bellamy, Ralph. *When the Smoke Hit the Fan.* Garden City, New York: Doubleday, 1979.

Bogdanovich, Peter. *Who the Devil Made It: Conversations with Legendary Film Directors.* New York: Ballantine Books, 1997.

Carey, Gary. *Katharine Hepburn: A Hollywood Yankee.* New York: Dell, 1983.

Cavell, Stanley. *Pursuits of Happiness: The Hollywood Comedy of Remarriage.* Cambridge, Massachusetts: Harvard University Press, 1981.

Chaplin, Charles, Jr. *My Father, Charlie Chaplin.* New York: Random House, 1960.

Curtis, James. *James Whale: A New World of Gods and Monsters.* Boston: Faber and Faber, 1998.

DiBattista, Maria. *Fast-Talking Dames.* New Haven: Yale University Press, 2001.

Edel, Leon. *Writing Lives.* New York: W. W. Norton, 1984.

Fenin, George N., and William K. Everson. *The Western: From Silents to the Seventies.* New York: Penguin Books, 1977.

Gehring, Wes D. *Carole Lombard: The Hoosier Tornado.* Indianapolis: Indiana Historical Society, 2003.

Gehring, Wes D. Charlie *Chaplin: A Bio-Bibliography.* Westport, Connecticut: Greenwood Press, 1983.

Gehring, Wes D. *Leo McCarey and the Comic Anti-Hero In American Film.* New York: Arno Press—A *New York Times* Company, 1980.

Gehring, Wes D. *The Marx Brothers: A Bio-Bibliography.* Westport, Connecticut: Greenwood Press, 1987.

Gehring, Wes D. *"Mr. B" or Comforting Thoughts about the Bison: A Critical Biography of Robert Benchley.* Westport, Connecticut: Greenwood Press, 1992.

Gehring, Wes D. Parody as Film Genre: *"Never Give a Saga an Even Break."* Westport, Connecticut: Greenwood Press, 1999.

Gehring, Wes D. *Populism and the Capra Legacy.* Westport, Connecticut: Greenwood Press, 1995.

Gehring, Wes D. *Romantic Versus Screwball Comedy: Charting a Difference.* Lanham, Maryland: Scarecrow Press, 2002.

Gehring, Wes D. *Screwball Comedy: A Genre of Madcap Romance.* Westport, Connecticut: Greenwood Press, 1986.

Gehring, Wes D. *W. C. Fields: A Bio-Bibliography*. Westport, Connecticut: Greenwood Press, 1984.

Gehring, Wes D. *The World of Comedy: Five Takes on Funny*. Davenport, Iowa: Robin Vincent Publishing, 2001.

Guy Named Joe, A, script (January 28, 1943). In the "Irene Dunne Collection." Box 1, Cinema and Television Library. University of Southern California (Los Angeles).

Harvey, James. *Romantic Comedy in Hollywood: From Lubitsch to Sturges*. New York: Da Capo Press, 1998.

Kael, Pauline. *I Lost It At The Movies*. Boston: Little, Brown, 1965.

Kendall, Paul Murray. *The Art of Biography*. New York: W. W. Norton, 1985.

McCarthy, Todd. *Howard Hawks: The Grey Fox of Hollywood*. New York: Grove Press, 1997.

McGilligan, Patrick. *Film Crazy: Interviews with Hollywood Legends*. New York: St. Martin's Press, 2000.

Nelson, Nancy. *Evenings with Cary Grant*. New York: William Morrow, 1991.

Rogers, Betty. *Will Rogers*. Garden City, New York: Garden City Publishing, 1941.

Sarris, Andrew. *The American Cinema: Directors and Directions, 1929–1968*. New York: Dutton, 1968.

Schickel, Richard. *Matinee Idylls: Reflections on the Movies*. Chicago: Ivan R. Dee, 1999.

Schultz, Margie. *Irene Dunne: A Bio-Bibliography*. Westport, Connecticut: Greenwood Press, 1991.

Steinberg, Cobbett. *Reel Facts: The Movie Book of Records*. New York: Vintage Books, 1978.

Swindell, Larry. *Charles Boyer: The Reluctant Lover*. Garden City, New York: Doubleday, 1983.

Taylor, Robert Lewis. *W. C. Fields: His Follies and His Fortunes*. 1949; rpt. New York: Signet Books, 1967.

Wansell, Geoffrey. *Haunted Idol: The Story of the Real Cary Grant*. New York: William Morrow, 1984.

Wiley, Mason, and Damien Bono. *Inside Oscar*. New York: Ballantine Books, 1993.

White Cliffs of Dover, The, script (January 18, 1943). In the "Irene Dunne Collection." Box 1, Cinema and Television Library. University of Southern California (Los Angeles).

Wilson, Robert, ed. *The Film Criticism of Otis Ferguson*. Philadelphia: Temple University Press, 1971.

Zinsser, William, ed. *Extraordinary Lives: The Art and Craft of American Biography*. Boston: Houghton Mifflin, 1986.

SHORTER WORKS

"Actress Prepares to Portray Blind Role." *Times*, November 31, 1935.

"AFI Gets Passionate With Another 100-Best List." *USA Today*, June 12, 2002, 4-D.

Age of Innocence, The, review. *New York Times*, October 19, 1934, 27.

Age of Innocence, The, review. *Variety*, October 23, 1934.

Ames, Walter. "TV's Revolving Door Gay Whirl for Irene." *Los Angeles Times*, July 20, 1952, 3.

Ann Vickers review. *Variety*, October 10, 1933.

Arden, Doris. "'Cliffs of Dover' Touches the Heart." *Chicago Sun Times*, July 2, 1944.

Ardmore, Jane. "Irene Dunne: She'll Always Be Hollywood's Perfect Lady." *Photoplay*, December 1975, 86.

"'Awful Truth' Comedy; Certain of Good Boxoffice." *Hollywood Reporter*, October 6, 1937.

Awful Truth, The, review. *New York Sun*, November 5, 1937.

Awful Truth, The, review. *Time*, November 1, 1937, 45.

Awful Truth, The, review. *Variety*, October 20, 1937, 12.

Bachelor Apartment review. *Variety*, May 20, 1931.

Back Street review. *Variety*, August 30, 1932.

Barnes, Howard. "'Invitation to Happiness'—Paramount." *New York Herald Tribune*, June 8, 1939, 16.

Barnes, Howard. "'Joy of Living'—Radio City Music Hall." *New York Herald Tribune*, May 6, 1938, 19.

Barnes, Howard. "'Lady in a Jam'—State." *New York Herald Tribune*, September 11, 1942, 17.

Barnes, Howard. "'The White Cliffs of Dover'—Music Hall." *New York Herald Tribune*, May 12, 1944, 12.

Barnes, Howard. "'Love Affair'—Music Hall." *New York Herald Tribune*, March 17, 1939, 16.

Barnes, Howard. "'Stingaree'—Music Hall." *New York Herald Tribune*, May 18, 1934, 17.

Barnes, Howard. "'Theodora Goes Wild'—Music Hall." *New York Herald Tribune*, November 13, 1936, 23.

Batchelor, Vivien. "'Queen Victoria' Is Practicing English." *London Evening Standard*, May 18, 1950, 1.

Bawden, James. "A Visit with Irene Dunne." *American Classic Screen* (September 10, 1977): 8–11.

Beatty, Jerome. "Lady Irene." *American Magazine*, November 1944, 28–29, 117–119.

"Beer Parade, The." *New York Post*, February 4, 1933, 5.

Berman, Pandro S. Interview by the author, Hillcrest Country Club, Beverly Hills, California, June 1975. Author's files.

Biery, Ruth. "Irene's Secret Marriage." *Photoplay*, April 1931, 35+.

Birmingham, Stephen. "Irene Dunne." *McCall's*, August 1964, 100+.

Boehnel, William. "Irene Dunne Effective in Film 'Back Street.'" *New York World-Telegram*, August 29, 1932, 10.

Boehnel, William. "'Joy of Living' Offers Sophisticated Farce. *New York World-Telegram*, May 6, 1938, 25.

Boehnel, William. "Love and Thrills in Two Pictures." *New York World-Telegram*, August 17, 1939.

Boehnel, William. "'Love Affair' Seen as Outstanding Film." *New York World-Telegram*, March 17, 1939, 23.

Boehnel, William. "New Film Sparkling Comedy." *New York World-Telegram*, May 31, 1940, 12.

Boehnel, William. "'Roberta' Is a 'Must' if You Like Astaire." *New York World-Telegram*, March 8, 1935, 31.

Boehnel, William. "'Ruggles of Red Gap' Grand and Hilarious." *New York World-Telegram*, March 7, 1935, 21.

Boehnel, William. "'Unfinished Business' A Nifty Comedy Drama." *New York World-Telegram*, September 2, 1941, 12.

Boone, Betty. "Inside the Stars' Homes." *Screenland*, July 1936, 15.

Burden, Janet. "Parted—But Happily Married." *Motion Picture Story Magazine*, July 1932, 26+.

Burdett, Winston. "'Theodora Goes Wild,' with Irene Dunne, Opens at the Music Hall." *Brooklyn Daily Eagle*, November 13, 1936, 23.

Calhoun, Dorothy. "Irene Dunne Leads Two Lives." *Motion Picture Story Magazine*, September 1935, 39+.

Cameron, Kate. "'Age of Innocence' Charmingly Filmed." *New York Daily News*, October 19, 1934, 60.

Cameron, Kate. "Another Love Affair for Dunne and Boyer." *New York Daily News*, August 17, 1939, 44.

Cameron, Kate. "Delightful Romance Reunites Dunne, Dix." *New York Daily News*, May 18, 1934, 62.

Cameron, Kate. "Easter Comes Early to Music Hall Stage." *New York Daily News*, March 12, 1948, 54.

Cameron, Kate. "Exquisite Romance on Music Hall Screen." *New York Daily News*, March 17, 1939, 48.

Cameron, Kate. "Gaiety Is Keynote of Music Hall Film." *New York Daily News*, August 17, 1945, 34.

Cameron, Kate. "A Good Time Is Had by All At Music Hall." *New York Daily News*, November 13, 1936, 64.

Cameron, Kate. "'A Guy Named Joe' an Air Forces Show. *New York Daily News*, December 24, 1943, 15.

Cameron, Kate. "Irene Dunne Gives Real Life to Film." *New York Daily News*, December 31, 1935, 24.

Cameron, Kate. "Irene Dunne Shines As Lewis's Heroine." *New York Daily News*, September 29, 1933, 48.

Cameron, Kate. "Irene Dunn [*sic*] Goes Wild Again in 'Joy of Living.'" *New York Daily News*, May 6, 1938, 50.

Cameron, Kate. "A Lavish 'Show Boat' Sails Into Music Hall." *New York Daily News*, May 15, 1936, 54.

Cameron, Kate. "Music Hall Presents Entertaining Film." *New York Daily News*, November 24, 1944, 40.

Cameron, Kate. "'Penny Serenade' Is Most Affecting Film." *New York Daily News*, May 23, 1941, 46.

Cameron, Kate. "Rivoli Reopens with a Delightful Picture." *New York Daily News*, September 2, 1941, 42.

Cameron, Kate. "'Roberta' Scores a Second Hit as Film." *New York Daily News*, March 8, 1935, 56.

Cameron, Kate. "'The Silver Cord' Faithfully Filmed." *New York Daily News*, May 5, 1933, 58.

Cameron, Kate. "'The White Cliffs of Dover' Tears at the Heartstrings." *New York Daily News*, May 12, 1944, 15-c.

Carmody, Jay. "Irene Dunne Asks for Remake of Cinema's Saddest Story." *Washington Star*, February 7, 1949.

"Cary Grant Paired with Irene Dunne Again in 'Joy of Living.'" *Los Angeles Times*, October 15, 1937, 10.

Champlin, Charles. "Irene Dunne: Always a Lady of the House." *Los Angeles Times*, December 5, 1985.

"CHARLES as Seen by Irene Dunne." *Photoplay,* October 1939, 25, 87.

Churchill, Douglas W. "Latest Scarlet Letter." *New York Times*, December 18, 1938, sec. 9, p. 7.

Cimarron entry. In *Movie & Video Guide: 2001*, edited by Leonard Maltin, 249. New York: Signet Book, 2000.

Cimarron review. *Photoplay*, April 1931.

Cimarron review. *Variety*, January 28, 1931.

"Clark Gable No. 1 In New Film Poll." *New York Times*, January 4, 1937, 21.

Clary, Patricia. "Studio Wanted $50,000 in Time for Irene Dunne." *San Francisco News*, April 24, 1946.

"Coffin Nailers Busy Boxing Axis Rulers." *New York Times,* September 9, 1942, 26.

Cohn, Herbert. Review of *Love Affair*. *Brooklyn Eagle*, March 17, 1939, 11.

"Col's 'Serenade' Emotional Smash For Dunne and Grant." *Hollywood Reporter,* April 17, 1941.

"Columbia 'Together Again' Smash For Van Upp, Vidor." *Hollywood Reporter*, November 3, 1944.

"Conquest and 'Awful Truth.'" *New York Daily Mirror*, November 5, 1937, 39.

Cook, Alton. "A London Urchin Looks at a Queen and Moves an Empire in 'Mudlark.'" *New York World-Telegram*, December 26, 1950, 23.

Creelman, Eileen. "A Bright Farce, 'My Favorite Wife.'" *New York Sun*, May 31, 1940, 22.

Creelman, Eileen. "'A Guy Named Joe,' Drama of the War, with Spencer Tracy and Irene Dunne." *New York Post*, December 24, 1943, 7.

Creelman, Eileen. "Irene Dunne Talks of 'Together Again,' Columbia Comedy Which Opens Thursday." *New York Sun*, November 21, 1944, 21.

Creelman, Eileen. "Leo McCarey Tells of Directing Irene Dunne in a New Comedy, 'The Awful Truth.'" *New York Sun*, November 3, 1937.

Creelman, Eileen. "'Penny Serenade,' with Irene Dunne." *New York Sun*, May 23, 1941, 24.

Creelman, Eileen. Review of *Show Boat*. *New York Sun*, May 15, 1936, 29.

Crewe, Regina. "Mme Ouspenskaya, back from Coast, Offers Helping Hand To Fledgling." *New York Journal*, March 19, 1939.

Crowther, Bosley. Review of *Lady in a Jam*. *New York Times*, September 11, 1942, 25.

Crowther, Bosley. Review of *My Favorite Wife*. *New York Times*, May 31, 1940, 15.

Crowther, Bosley. Review of *The Mudlark*. *New York Times*, December 25, 1950, 25.

Crowther, Bosley. Review of *Never a Dull Moment*. *New York Times*, November 22, 1950, 20.

Crowther, Bosley. Review of *Over 21*. *New York Times*, August 17, 1945, 20.

Crowther, Bosley. Review of *Unfinished Business*. *New York Times*, September 2, 1941, 20.

Crowther, Bosley. Review of *The White Cliffs of Dover*. *New York Times*, May 12, 1944, 15.

Cuskelly, Richard. "A Five-Hour Irene Dunne Film Festival." *Los Angeles Herald-Examiner*, March 23, 1979, E-7.

Delehanty, Thornton. "Charles Laughton and Others in 'Ruggles of Red Gap.'" *New York Post*, March 7, 1935, 14.

Delehanty, Thornton. "Irene Dunne and Richard Dix in 'Stingaree.'" *New York Post*, May 18, 1934, 13.

Delehanty, Thornton. "'Magnificent Obsession' on the Music Hall Screen." *New York Post*, December 31, 1935, 9.

Delehanty, Thornton. Review of *Sweet Adeline*. *New York Post*, January 7, 1935.

Devine, John F. "Irene Goes Wild." *Modern Movies*, April 1937, 34–35.

Dickens, Homer. "Carole Lombard: Her Comic Sense Derived from an Instinctual Realism." *Films In Review*, February 1961, 70–86.

"Dunne." *Detroit Free Press*, October 10, 1936.

Dunne, Irene. "Dignified." *American Magazine*, August 1942, 84–85.

Dunne, Irene. "Tell Me Your Problems." *Silver Screen*, November 1947, 34–35, 70.

Dunne, Irene. "The Role I Liked Best . . ." *Saturday Evening Post*, March 9, 1946.

Dunne, Irene. "The Twin Cities." *Hollywood Reporter* (19th Anniversary Issue), December 1949.

Dunne, Irene. Telephone interview by the author, Los Angeles, June 1975. Author's files.

"'Favorite Wife' at Memoria." *Boston Post,* June 21, 1940.

"Film Star Irene Dunne Exceeds Million Mark in Sale of War Bonds. . . ." *Wilkes-Barre Record*—PA, September 11, 1942, 1.

Fletcher, Adele Whitely. "If You Had One Hour." *Movie Mirror,* November 1936, 54+.

Fletcher, Adele Whitely. "The True and Tender Story of Irene Dunne's Daughter." *Photoplay,* June 1938, 20+.

Ford Theatre review. Daily Variety, April 19, 1954.

Fortune, Dick. "Dunne-Boyer Film Is Full of Laughs." *Pittsburgh Press,* November 24, 1944.

French, William F. "Untold Stories of Love That Have Lasted." *Motion Picture Story Magazine,* January 1935, 59+.

Gamarekian, Barbara. "Six Receive Kennedy Center Honors." *New York Times,* December 9, 1985, C-13.

Garcia, Guy D. "People." *Time,* December 23, 1985, 61.

Gehring, Wes D. "Carole Lombard and Irene Dunne." *The Indianapolis Star Magazine,* October 14, 1979, 54+.

Gehring, Wes D. "'Inside Benchley': The Early Diaries." *Studies in American Humor,* Volume 7 (1989/1992): 85–93.

Gehring, Wes D. "Love and Laughter: [Romantic Comedy]." *USA Today Magazine,* January 2000, 64–71.

Gehring, Wes D. "The Many Faces of Movie Comedy." *USA Today Magazine,* July 1998, 80–89.

Gehring, Wes D. "McCarey vs Capra: A Guide to American Film Comedy of the '30s." *Journal of Popular Film and Television,* Volume 7, no. 1 (1978): 67–84.

Gehring, Wes D. "Screwball Comedy: An Overview." *Journal of Popular Film and Television,* Winter 1986, 178–185.

Gilbert, Douglas. "Song and Sentiment Pageant in 'Show Boat' at Music Hall." *New York World-Telegram,* May 15, 1936, 27.

Graham, Sheilah. "Hollywood Today." *Chicago Daily News,* March 25, 1938.

Great Lover, The, review. Variety, August 25, 1931.

Guernsey, Otis L., Jr. Review of *Never a Dull Moment. New York Herald Tribune,* November 22, 1950, 17.

Guy Named Joe, A, review. *New York Times,* December 24, 1943, 17.

Guy Named Joe, A, review. *Variety,* December 29, 1943.

"'A Guy Named Joe' Fantasy of Beauty, Action and Delight." *Hollywood Reporter,* December 24, 1943.

Guldager, Carl. "'A Guy Named Joe' Fights Fanciful War." *Chicago Daily News,* April 3, 1944.

Haber, Joyce. "The Sweet Smell of Irene Dunne." *Los Angeles Times*, March 16, 1975, Calendar Section, 33.

Haffernan, Harold. Personal Column. *Chicago Daily News*, August 9, 1943.

Hale, Wanda. "'The Awful Truth' Now at Music Hall." *New York Daily News*, November 5, 1937.

Hale, Wanda. "'High, Wide and Handsome' A Real Thriller." *New York Daily News*, July 22, 1937, 44.

Hall, Mordaunt. Review of *Cimarron*. *New York Times*, January 27, 1931, 20.

Hall, Mordaunt. Review of *Consolation Marriage*. *New York Times*, October 30, 1931, 26.

Hall, Mordaunt. Review of *If I Were Free*. *New York Times*, January 5, 1934, 25.

Hall, Mordaunt. Review of *The Secret of Madame Blanche*. *New York Times*, February 4, 1933, 11.

Hamilton, Sara. "This Is Really Irene Dunne." *Photoplay*, April 1936, 26+.

Hartl, John. "Belle of the Screwball." *Chicago Tribune*, September 25, 1990, sec. 5, p. 3.

Harvey, James. "Irene Dunne Interviewed by James Harvey." *Film Comment*, January–February, 1980, 28–32.

Heebner, J. Donald. "The Big Wig Mystery—with Irene Dunne." *Photoplay*, September 1937, 10, 121.

"He Makes Hits Sans Scenarios." *San Francisco Bulletin*, October 25, 1941.

"'High, Wide and Handsome' Colorful Entertainment." *Hollywood Reporter*, July 22, 1937.

"Hilarious Comedy Despite Crusade." *Hollywood Reporter*, July 23, 1945.

Hodel, Emilia. "Engaging War Fantasy: Tracy Dunne Duo Excels." *San Francisco News*, May 26, 1944.

Hoffernan, Harold. "Comedy by LaCava: Off the Cuff." *Chicago News*, March 14, 1941.

Hoffernan, Harold. "The LaCava Technic Hurdles Word Hitch." *Detroit News*, March 13, 1941.

Holland, J. "The Lady Speaks Her Mind." *Silver Screen*, May 1946, 35+.

Hopper, Hedda. "Irene Dunne Becomes Hollywood's Own Good Will Envoy on American Way." *Los Angeles Times*, February 27, 1949, 1.

Hopper, Hedda. "Praise For Picture." *Washington Post*, March 31, 1944.

"How Stars Face the Facts of Flops!" *Screenland*, June 1938, 88+.

Hoyt, Caroline S. "Irene Dunne's True Life Story" (Parts 1 and 2). *Modern Screen*, December 1938 and January 1939.

"Human Touch in 'Serenade' Wins Praise." *Los Angeles Examiner*, April 17, 1941.

Hyams, Joe. "Irene Dunne's Husband: 'Be a Trailer.'" *New York Herald Tribune*, March 20, 1958, sec. 3, p. 12.

If I Were Free review. *Variety*, January 9, 1934.

Ike Day Surprise Party review. *Variety*, October 17, 1956.

Invitation to Happiness review. *Variety*, May 10, 1939.

"'I Remember Mama' Hits Superb Heights on Film: Brilliant Picture Tops Play, Novel." *Hollywood Reporter*, March 9, 1948.

I Remember Mama review. *Cue*, March 13, 1948.

I Remember Mama review. *Variety*, March 10, 1948.

"IRENE As Seen By Charles Boyer." *Photoplay*, October 1939, 24+.

"Irene Dunne at Filmex Tribute Rates 'Affair,' 'Mama' Her Best. *Daily Variety*, March 25, 1975, 17.

"Irene Dunne Describes Work as U.N. Delegate." *Los Angeles Times*, February 3, 1958.

"Irene Dunne Finds Career In U.N. 'Highlight of My Life.'" *New York Herald Tribune*, October 16, 1957, 3.

"Irene Dunne." In *Current Biography 1945*, edited by Anne Rothe, 160–163. New York: H. W. Wilson Company, 1945.

"Irene Dunne Returns From Convention Trip." *Los Angeles Times*, July 11, 1948.

Irene Dunne RKO contract, April 10, 1930. In the "Irene Dunne Collection." Box 1, RKO folder. Cinema and Television Library, University of Southern California, Los Angeles.

Irene Dunne RKO contract—clause five, December 16, 1931. In the "Irene Dunne Collection." Box 1, RKO folder. Cinema and Television Library, University of Southern California, Los Angeles.

Irene Dunne RKO contract, September 1933. In the "Irene Dunne Collection." Box 1, RKO folder. Cinema and Television Library, University of Southern California, Los Angeles.

"Irene Dunne's Role as British Queen 'Insult.'" *Los Angeles Examiner*, March 30, 1950.

"Irene Dunne Talks of 'Penny Serenade,' Which Opens Today at the Music Hall." *New York Sun*, May 22, 1944, 15.

"Irene Dunne to Appear on Local Stage Tonight." *Madison Courier*, June 6, 1933, 1.

Jack Benny Show, The, review. *Daily Variety*, December 7, 1953.

Jacobs, Jody. "Irene Dunne Cherishes Latest Honor." *Los Angeles Times*, July 18, 1985, sec. 5, p. 4.

"'Joy of Living' Heavy on Slapstick, But Full of Fun." *Hollywood Reporter*, March 18, 1938.

Joy of Living review. *Variety*, March 23, 1938.

Kael, Pauline. "The Man from Dream City." *The New Yorker*, July 14, 1975, 40+.

Kennedy, Rose, to Irene Dunne, September 6, 1966. In the "Irene Dunne Collection." Box 1, "Correspondence" folder. Cinema and Television Library, University of Southern California, Los Angeles.

Kerr, Martha. "She's No Lady." *Modern Screen*, October 1939.

"King George 'Loves' Night at the Movies." *Los Angeles Times*, November 1, 1950, sec. 1, p. 2.

LaBelle, Claude. "Irene Dunne Shines at Head of Fine Cast." *San Francisco News*, July 26, 1944.

Lady in a Jam entry. In *Movie & Video Guide: 2003*, edited by Leonard Maltin, 761. New York: Signet Book, 2002.

"'Lady In A Jam' Plenty Silly But Irene Dunne Will Sell." *Hollywood Reporter*, June 26, 1942.

Lady in a Jam review. *The New Yorker*, July 22, 1942.

Lady in a Jam review. *Variety*, July 1, 1942.

Leathernecking review. *Variety*, September 17, 1930.

Leavy, Jane. "Tape From 1965 Easier to Find Than Ill Will toward Koufax." *New York Times*, September 1, 2002, Sports, 6.

Lee, Sonia. "Discovering the Glamour in Irene Dunne." *Motion Picture Story Magazine*, March 1937, 39+.

Livingstone, Beulah. "The Story of Irene Dunne." *Table Talk*, September 21, 1936, 14–15.

"Long Distance Hubby 'Perfect' to Marlene." *New York Daily News*, May 10, 1937, 3.

"Loretta's First." *Los Angeles Daily News*, January 17, 1951.

Los Angeles International Film Exposition "Tribute to Irene Dunne" program. In the Irene Dunne files. Margaret Herrick Library, Academy of Motion Picture Arts and Sciences, Beverly Hills, California.

"'Luckee Girl' Proves a Tuneful Comedy." *New York Times*, September 17, 1928, 28.

Luckee Girl review. *New York Post*, September 19, 1928.

Ludlam, Helen Fay. "Nucleus." *Silver Screen*, July 1935, 20, 62.

"Madam Queen." *Modern Screen*, May 1947, 44+.

"Madison, Ind., Her Birthplace [sic], Still Is Home for Irene Dunne." *Indianapolis News*, June 5, 1933, sec. 2, p. 1.

Magnificent Obsession review. *Variety*, January 8, 1936.

Manners, Dorothy. "'High, Wide and Handsome' Has Premiere at Carthay Circle." *Los Angeles Examiner*, August 13, 1937.

Manners, Dorothy. "Irene Dunne to Play Girl Reporter: 'Front Page' Revised and Retitled." *New York Journal American*, May 23, 1939, 9.

Manners, Dorothy. "LaCava in a Slump Says Critic on 'Jam' Film." *Los Angeles Examiner*, July 17, 1942.

Marsden, Michael T. "Savior in the Saddle: The Sagebrush Testament." In *Focus On The Western*, edited by Jack Nachbar, 93–100. Englewood Cliffs, New Jersey: Prentice-Hall, Inc., 1974.

Maxwell, Elsa. "A Very Special Woman." *Photoplay*, January 1948, 45.

Maxwell, Virginia. "'Don't Live with Your Mother-in-law' says Irene Dunne." *Photoplay*, September 1933, 74+.

McDonough, Jack. "Screening a Star: A Rare Interview with Irene Dunne." *Chicago Tribune*, May 12, 1985, sec. 13, p. 8.

McManus, John T. "Magnolia of the Movies." *New York Times*, May 17, 1936, sec. 9, p. 3.

Mishkin, Leo. "'Love Affair' a Music Hall Winner; Irene Dunne, Charles Boyer Superb." *New York Telegraph*, March 18, 1939, 2.

"Movie of the Week: 'Life with Father.'" *Life*, August 18, 1947, 65.

Mudlark, The, review. *Variety*, November 8, 1950.

"'My Favorite Wife' Is Riot of Laughter." *Los Angeles Examiner*, April 30, 1940.

"My Secret Dream." *Photoplay*, October 1943, 54–55.

Never A Dull Moment review. *Variety*, November 1, 1950.

"New Films on Broadway." *New York Post*, May 5, 1933, 12.

No Other Woman review. *Variety*, January 31, 1933.

Nugent, Frank S. Review of *Invitation to Happiness*. *New York Times*, June 8, 1939, 31.

Nugent, Frank S. Review of *Joy of Living*. *New York Times*, May 6, 1938, 27.

Nugent, Frank S. Review of *Love Affair*. *New York Times*, March 17, 1939, 26.

Nugent, Frank S. Review of *Show Boat*. *New York Times*, May 15, 1936, 29.

Nugent, Frank S. Review of *Theodora Goes Wild*. *New York Times*, November 13, 1936, 27.

Nugent, Frank S. Review of *When Tomorrow Comes*. *New York Times*, August 17, 1939, 16.

Orme, Michael. "The World of the Kinema." *London News*, April 29, 1939, 760.

Ormiston, Roberta. "To Make You Happier." *Photoplay*, April 1944, 107.

Over 21 review. *Variety*, July 25, 1945.

Paramount Press Release, "Biography of Leo McCarey," April 1, 1937. In the Leo McCarey file, Margaret Herrick Library, Academy of Motion Picture Arts and Sciences, Beverly Hills, California.

Parsons, Louella O. "Cary Grant Gets Lead in 'Holiday': Irene is Slated for Top Spot, Too." *Philadelphia Inquirer*, December 24, 1937, 9.

Parsons, Louella O. "In Hollywood with Louella O. Parsons." *New York Journal American*, March 28, 1948.

Parsons, Louella O. "Irene Dunne and Charles Boyer Engaging in Romantic Film, 'When Tomorrow Comes.'" *Los Angeles Examiner*, August 11, 1939.

Parsons, Louella O. "Irene Dunn [*sic*] Chosen to Play Heroine in 'Cimarron.'" *Los Angeles Examiner*, August 19, 1930, sec. 1, p. 9.

Parsons, Louella O. "'Mama' Film Heart Warming." *Los Angeles Examiner*, April 2, 1948.

Parsons, Louella O. "'Mudlark' Film of Great Charm." *Los Angeles Examiner*, January 31, 1951, sec. 2, p. 7.

Patrick, Corbin. "Irene Dunne Comes to Indianapolis." *Indianapolis Star*, June 6, 1933, 5.

Pelswick, Rose. "Dunne, Homolka Star in a Beguiling Film." *New York Journal American*, March 12, 1948, 21.

Pitts, Dick. "The Cinema." *Charlotte Observer*, July 8, 1947, 8.

Porter, James S. "Irene Dunne Play Is Par Even for Her." *Detroit Free Press*, June 17, 1939.

Queen Mary news item. *Screenland*, October 1936, 58.

"Queen Mary Returns to Britain, The." *New York American*, June 6, 1936, 1.

Reynolds, Quentin. "Give Me Real People." *Colliers*, March 26, 1938, 53.

Roberta review. *Variety*, March 13, 1935.

Ruggles of Red Gap movie ad. *New York Daily* News, March 7, 1935, 45.

Saltzman, Barbara. "A Warm Reception for Irene Dunne." *Los Angeles Times*, August 28, 1979.

Sarris, Andrew. "Irene Dunne obituary." *New York Observer*, September 17, 1990, 25.

Schlitz Playhouse of Stars contract, January 23, 1952. In the "Irene Dunne Collection." Box 1, "Television" folder. Cinema and Television Library, University of Southern California, Los Angeles.

Schultz, Maggie. "Hollywood's Great Ladies: Irene Dunne." *Hollywood Studio Magazine*, January 1988.

"Screen 'Mama' Gets Mothers' Award." *Buffalo Evening News*, February 3, 1949.

Secret of Madame Blanche, The, review. *Variety*, February 7, 1933.

Sennwald, Andre. Review of *Roberta*. *New York Times*, March 8, 1935, 25.

Service, Faith. "My Screen Selves and I." *Silver Screen*, August 1944, 22+.

Shea, George. "Irene Dunne." *Northwest Orient*, December 1985, 30.

"She Practices English On Her Husband." *London Evening News*, May 18, 1950.

She's My Baby review. *New York Herald Tribune*, January 3, 1928.

"'Showboat'—And Shows In General." *Screen Play*, July 1936, 22.

Show Boat review. *Chicago Tribune*, October 2, 1929.

Show Boat review. *Cleveland Plain Dealer*, February 11, 1930.

Show Boat review. *Detroit Times*, February 4, 1930.

Show Boat review. *Hollywood Reporter*, April 27, 1936.

"'Show Boat' of 1936." *London Times*, June 11, 1936, 14.

Show Boat review. *Screen Book Magazine*, July 1936.

Show Boat review. *Screenland*, June 1936, 53.

Show Boat review. *St. Louis Daily Globe-Democrat*, January 21, 1930.

Show Boat review. *Variety*, May 20, 1936.

"Side-Lights on a Star." *Modern Screen*, September 1939, 70.

Silver Cord, The, review. *Variety*, May 9, 1933.

Snyder, Camilla. "The Star Who Still Shines off the Stage." *Los Angeles Herald-Examiner*, October 18, 1970, F-1.

Stanley, Fred. "Hollywood Round-Up." *New York Times*, August 20, 1944, sec. 2, p. 1.

Stanley, Kathryn (as told to Sonia Lee). "Irene Dunne as I Know Her." *Movies*, August 1941, 16+.

"Stars on the Gangplank." *London Daily Express*, June 11, 1936, 1.

Sterne, Herb. "Unrehearsed 'Clinches' Irk Great Lover, Boyer." *Atlantic Constitution*, November 26, 1944.

Stingaree review. *New York Times*, May 18, 1934, 27.

Stingaree review. *Variety*, May 22, 1934.

St. Johns, Adela Rogers. "Thank You, Irene Dunne." *Photoplay*, September 1944, 34+.

Surmelian, Leon. "It's the Irish in Her." *Motion Picture Story Magazine*, July 1936, 38+.

Sweet Adeline review. *New York Times*, January 7, 1935, 13.

Sweet Adeline review. *Variety*, January 8, 1935.

Symphony of Six Million review. *Variety*, April 19, 1932.

"'The City Chap' Full of Dances and Fun." *New York Times*, October 27, 1925, 21.

Theodora Goes Wild review. *Motion Picture Herald*, November 14, 1936.

Theodora Goes Wild review. *Variety*, November 18, 1936, 12.

Thirer, Irene. "'Cimarron' In Globe Premiere." *New York Daily News*, January 27, 1931, 32.

Thirer, Irene. "'Madame Blanche' a Tear Jerker at the Capitol." *New York Daily News*, February 4, 1933, 22.

Tinee, Mae. "Tyranny of a Mother's Love Shown in Films." *Chicago Tribune*, June 11, 1933, sec. 10, p. 1.

"'Together Again' Pleases." *New York World-Telegram*, November 24, 1944, 25.

Together Again review. *New York Times*, November 24, 1944, 19.

Together Again review. *Variety*, November 8, 1944.

"Topics for Gossip." *Silver Screen*, July 1941, 21, 69.

Twigger, Beth. "Eighteen Inches from Camera, Well, Let Irene Dunne Tell of It." *New York Herald Tribune*, May 18, 1941, sec. 6, p. 3.

Unfinished Business review. *Time* magazine, September 15, 1941.

Unfinished Business review. *Variety*, August 27, 1941.

"U's 'Magnificent Obsession' Sure-Fire Box-Office Picture." *Hollywood Reporter*, December 31, 1935, 3.

Wales, Clark. Review of Love Affair. *Screen and Radio Weekly*, March 1939, 5.

Wallen, Jim. "Life of Irene Dunne Is Related by Writer." (Part 2). *Madison Courier*, July 26, 1951, 4.

Watters, James. "Irene Dunne: No Oscar, Just Love." *New York Times*, September 23, 1990, sec. 2, p. 20.

Watts, Richard, Jr. "'Ann Vickers'—Radio City Music Hall." *New York Herald Tribune*, September 29, 1933, 14.

Watts, Richard, Jr. "'Back Street'—Mayfair." *New York Herald Tribune*, August 29, 1932, 6.

Watts, Richard, Jr. "'Consolation Marriage'—Mayfair." *New York Herald Tribune*, October 30, 1931, 16.

Watts, Richard, Jr. "'Sweet Adeline'—Paramount." *New York Herald Tribune*, January 7, 1935, 8.

Watts, Richard, Jr. "'The Age of Innocence'—Radio City Music Hall." *New York Herald Tribune*, October 19, 1934, 16.

Watts, Richard, Jr. "'The Secret of Mme Blanche'—Capitol." *New York Herald Tribune*, February 4, 1933, 6.

When Tomorrow Comes review. *Variety*, August 16, 1939.

White Cliffs of Dover review. *Variety*, March 15, 1944.

Wilson, Elizabeth. "Hollywood's Character Reference." *Liberty*, April 1949, 26+.

Wilson, Elizabeth. "Men She'll Remember." *Silver Screen*, April 1941, 22+.

Wilson, Elizabeth. "The First True Story of Irene Dunne's Baby!" *Screenland*, June 1937, 21+.

Winsten, Archer. "'A Guy Named Joe' Flies at the Capitol Theatre." *New York Post*, December 24, 1943, 16.

Winsten, Archer. "'Joy of Living' Opens at Radio City Music Hall." *New York Post*, May 6, 1938, 21.

Winsten, Archer. "'Lady in a Jam' Opens at Loew's State Theatre." *New York Post*, September 11, 1942, 34.

Winsten, Archer. "'Love Affair' Opens at Radio City Music Hall." *New York Post*, August 17, 1939.

Winsten, Archer. "Musical Romance about First Pennsylvania Oil." *New York Post*, July 22, 1937, 15.

Winsten, Archer. "'Over 21' Comes Late to Radio City Music Hall." *New York Post*, August 17, 1945, 12.

Winsten, Archer. "'Penny Serenade' Opens at Radio City Music Hall." *New York Post*, May 23, 1941, 15.

Winsten, Archer. "'The White Cliffs of Dover' Opens at Radio City Music Hall." *New York Post*, May 12, 1944, 27.

Winsten, Archer. "Tragedy of Old Age at New Criterion Theatre." *New York Post*, May 10, 1937, 15.

Winsten, Archer. "'Unfinished Business' Reopens the Rivoli." *New York Post*, September 2, 1941, 9.

Woodward, Kenneth L. "Bing Crosby Had It Right." *Newsweek*, March 4, 2002, 53.

Yours Truly review. *New York Herald Tribune*, January 26, 1927.

Zeftlin, Ida. "The New Side to Irene Dunne." *Motion Picture Story Magazine*, November 1937, 32+.

INDEX

ABOUT THE AUTHOR

Wes D. Gehring is Professor of Film at Ball State University and an Associate Media Editor of *USA Today Magazine*, for which he also writes the column "Reel World." He is the author of nineteen critically acclaimed books, including biographies of Charlie Chaplin, W. C. Fields, the Marx Brothers, Laurel and Hardy, Robert Benchley, Red Skelton, and Carole Lombard. His other books address various genres of American film comedy, including both screwball and romantic comedy—two genres central to a full appreciation of Irene Dunne. He is currently writing a biography of director Leo McCarey, a close friend and collaborator of Irene Dunne. His articles and poems have appeared in numerous journals.

IRENE DUNNE WAS MARRIED AT THE AGE OF 30 AND DR. FRANK GRIFFIN WAS 42, WHEN THEY MARRIED JULY 16, 1928.

IN 1936 THEY ADOPTED A BABY GIRL NAMED MARY FRANCIS. LOST HER MOTHER DEC 17, 1936.

Made in the USA
San Bernardino, CA
25 January 2018